"This is the best complete biography of Martin Luther, the man and the reformer, available to the English reading world. It is historically solid, factually authentic, psychologically sensitive, personally perceptive, socially aware, and, above all, theologically knowledgeable and persuasive. The more than 30 years that have passed since Roland Bainton published his classic *Here I Stand,* which remains a sparkling gem, have seen the publication of a tremendous amount of Luther and Reformation research. The author of this volume has taken this scholarly work into account and has courageously written *the* life of Luther for our times."

—Lewis W. Spitz, *Stanford University*

"Kittelson brings us as close as we are likely to come to an appreciation of how Luther himself understood the dramatic transitions in his own life."

—James D. Tracy, *University of Minnesota*

"A reliable and vividly written account of Luther's life that gives due attention to his later career."

—Scott Hendrix, *The Lutheran Theological Seminary, Philadelphia*

LUTHER THE REFORMER

The Story of the Man and His Career

JAMES M. KITTELSON

AUGSBURG Publishing House • Minneapolis

INTER-VARSITY PRESS
38 De Montfort Street, Leicester LE1 7GP, England

British Library Cataloguing in Publication Data

Kittelson, James M.
  Luther the reformer.
  1. Lutheran churches. Luther, Martin,
  1483–1546—Biographies
  I. Title
  284.1′092′4

  ISBN 0–85110–666–8

Typeset in the United States of America
Printed in Great Britain at the University Printing House, Oxford

Inter-Varsity Press is the book-publishing division of the Universities and Colleges Christian Fellowship (formerly the Inter-Varsity Fellowship), a student movement linking Christian Unions in universities and colleges throughout the United Kingdom and the Republic of Ireland, and a member movement of the International Fellowship of Evangelical Students. For information about local and national activities write to UCCF, 38 De Montfort Street, Leicester LE1 7GP.

To
Berta Moluf Kittelson
and
Lee M. Kittelson
They have kept the faith and passed it on.

Contents

List of Illustrations   9
Preface   13
Acknowledgments   19
Chronological Table   21

Part One: The Formation of the Young Man

  1   The Son of a Peasant   31
  2   A Man of Sorrows   49
  3   A Student of Theology   64

Part Two: The Genesis of the Reformer

  4   The Maturing Professor   83
  5   The Explosion   101
  6   The Lines Drawn   115
  7   The Public Disputant   131

Part Three: An Outlaw's Work

  8   The Outlaw   145
  9   The Exile   162
 10   Return to the Fray   179

Part Four: The True Church

 11   "False Brethren"   195
 12   Pastor and Teacher   213
 13   Damnable Rome   228
 14   To Build the Church   240

Part Five: The Mature Luther

15	Negotiator for the Faith	255
16	Defender of the Faith	269
17	The Last Years	281
18	"We Are All Beggars"	292

Notes	*301*
Introductory Bibliography	*313*
Index of Names	*327*
Index of Subjects	*329*
Index of Luther's Principal Works Cited	*331*
Maps	*333*

List of Illustrations

Page 32   German peasant couple at table. (*Pictorial History of Protestantism: A Panoramic View of Western Europe and the United States* [New York: Philosophical Library, 1957], p. 18.)

Page 33   Hans and Margaretta Luder. (Paintings by Lucas Cranach the Elder, ca. 1527. Photos by Allgemeiner Deutscher Nachrichtendienst—Bereich Zentralbild [hereafter listed as ADN], Berlin.)

Page 36   Punishments were given to servants who gossiped or misbehaved in other ways. (*Pictorial History of Protestantism*, p. 19.)

Page 38   The house, built in the 15th century, where Luther lived as a student in Eisenach. (ADN photo)

Page 42   A procession of clergy in reverse order of their earthly rank, with Christ and little children at the head and the pope at the rear. (*Pictorial History of Protestantism*, p. 19.)

Page 44   Erfurt, the "city of spires" or "little Rome." (Schedel, *Weltchronik*, 1493.)

Page 52   View of the courtyard at the Black Cloister from a monk's cell. (ADN photo.)

Page 59   Rome with its main churches, the destination of pilgrims. (Copperplate engraving from the second half of the 16th century, from *Speculum Romanae Magnificentiae*.)

Page 60   Pope Leo X, a Medici. (Painting by Raffaelo Santi, 1519.)

Page 62   Wittenberg in the year 1550. (*Pictorial History of Protestantism*, p. 29.)

Page 65   Frontispiece woodcut from Gregor Resch, *Margarita Philosophica noua* . . . (Argentorati: Gruningerus, 1515), a compendium of the seven liberal arts.

Page 68   Erasmus of Rotterdam. (Copperplate engraving by Albrecht Dürer, 1526.)

Page 75   Title page from Luther's edition of *A German Theology*, which he attributed to Johannes Tauler.

Page 84   Johann Staupitz, Luther's superior, confessor, and friend. (16th-century painting.)

Page 87   A page from Luther's psalter with the notes he wrote for his lectures.

Page 102   An indulgence, preprinted, with name and date filled in.

Page 102   Johann Tetzel, the indulgence seller. (*Pictorial History of Protestantism*, p. 26.)

Page 105   Cartoon depicting the sale of indulgences with papal banners on the left and right. (Title-page woodcut for several flyers published in Augsburg beginning in 1520.)

Page 105   Archbishop Albert of Mainz in 1519 at the age of 29. (Copperplate engraving by Albrecht Dürer.)

Page 106   The Castle Church in Wittenberg. (ADN photo.)

Page 108   A cartoon depicting how Christ upsets indulgences and indulgence sellers, including the pope. (*Pictorial History of Protestantism*, p. 31.)

Page 122   Georg Burckhardt from Spalt, known as Spalatin. (Painting by Lucas Cranach the Elder [?], 1537.)

Page 123   Cardinal Cajetan in 1521. (*Pictorial History of Protestantism*, p. 32.)

Page 127   *Elector Frederick the Wise of Saxony*. (Copperplate engraving by Albrecht Dürer, 1524.)

Page 135   Johannes Eck. (From an anonymous engraving.)

Page 141   Cartoon depicting Luther and Hus serving both bread and wine to the electors of Saxony at Communion. (16th-century woodcut.)

Page 146   Caricature of Luther's opponents, with Leo X flanked by Emser and Eck. (Woodcut from the 1620s.)

Page 148   Luther the monk in 1520. (Copperplate engraving by Lucas Cranach the Elder, 1520.)

Page 150   Title page of the bull of excommunication with the symbols of both the papacy and the Medici family. (From the original edition printed in Rome.)

Page 151   Title page of *Address to the Christian Nobility*. (From the first printing in Wittenberg in 1520.)

Page 152   Title page of *On the Babylonian Captivity of the Church*. (From the first printing in Wittenberg in 1520.)

Page 155   Title page of *On the Freedom of a Christian*. (From the first printing in Wittenberg in 1520.)

Page 159   Charles V. (Woodcut by Hans Weiditz, 1519.)

Page 159   Jerome Aleander, papal ambassador at the Diet of Worms. (Copperplate engraving, 1536.)

Page 164   The Wartburg. (ADN photo.)

Page 174   Luther as Junker Jörg. (Woodcut by Lucas Cranach the Elder, 1522.)

Page 180   A *Pietà* defaced in religious riots. (Sandstone sculpture from the second half of the 14th century, Münster.)

Page 182   Luther after his return to Wittenberg. (Painting by Lucas Cranach the Elder, ca. 1522–1524.)

Page 185   Philip Melanchthon. (Copperplate engraving by Albrecht Dürer, 1526.)

Page 189   Thomas Müntzer, according to a 17th-century rendering. (Copperplate engraving, 1608, based on a woodcut by Christian von Sichem, ca. 1524.)

Page 192   A peasant being "burned" at the stake. (The execution of Jäklein Korbach of Böckingen, color illustration in Peter Harer, *Beschreibung des Bauernkriegs*, 1551.)

Page 198   Martin Bucer. (Woodcut, 1544.)

Page 198   Johannes Oecolampadius (16th-century woodcut.)

Page 199   Ulrich Zwingli at the age of 48. (Anonymous woodcut, 1539.)

Page 201   Katie's wedding band. (Photo by Walter Danz.)

Page 202   Katharina von Bora Luther. (Painting by Lucas Cranach the Elder, ca. 1526–1529. ADN photo.)

Page 211   Luther's manuscript of his hymn, "A Mighty Fortress Is Our God."

Page 219   Title pages of the *Small Catechism* and the *Large Catechism*.

Page 223   Philip of Hesse. (Woodcut by Hans Brosamer, colored by Hans Guldenmundt, ca. 1546.)

Page 224   The castle at Marburg. (Photo from the archives of Forschungsinstitut für Kunstgeschichte der Phillipps-Universität, Marburg.)

Page 225   The room where the Marburg Colloquy was held. (Photo from the archives of Forschungsinstitut für Kunstgeschichte der Phillipps-Universität, Marburg.)

Page 231   The Coburg, where Luther stayed during the Diet of Augsburg. (Photo by Balthasar Heinlein.)

Page 233   The Diet of Augsburg. (16th-century copperplate engraving.)

Page 250   Luther confronting the Church of Rome with the Scriptures while Melanchthon stands poised with a pen. (Woodcut.)

Page 251   Cartoon contrasting Protestant and Catholic services.

Page 257   Duke George of Saxony. (Painting by Lucas Cranach the Elder, 1534.)

Page 260   The electors of Saxony during Luther's career: Frederick the Wise, John the Steadfast, and John Frederick the Magnanimous. (Painting by Lucas Cranach the Elder.)

Page 262   Torgau, the principal residence of the electors of Saxony. (ADN photo.)

Page 275   Caricature of a monk. (Woodcut by Erhard Schön, ca. 1530.)

Page 275   The seven-headed Luther. (Cartoon, 1529.)

Page 283   The Luther family's main room. (Photo by Keystone View Co., Inc., of New York.)

Page 297   The room in which Luther died. (ADN photo.)

Page 298   Luther's death mask (reconstructed). (ADN photo.)

Page 298   Luther's grave and pulpit. (Author photo.)

Preface

"In most big libraries, books by and about Martin Luther occupy more shelf room than those concerned with any other human being except Jesus of Nazareth."[1] These words appeared in print in 1982, one year before the 500th anniversary of Luther's birth. The year 1983 then brought with it an additional avalanche of exhibitions, commemorations, lectures, festivals, articles, and still more new books. In the self-consciously Marxist state of the German Democratic Republic, the observation of Luther's birth even overwhelmed the 100th anniversary celebration of Karl Marx's death. Such is the enduring importance of Luther the reformer.

This extraordinary interest in an extraordinary man reaches back almost half a millennium. Even in his own time, Luther was a "media personality," the first such in three thousand years of western history. "We have become a spectacle," he once remarked of himself and his colleagues. He and his followers have been termed "obedient rebels." Others called him a seven-headed devil. At least one of his closest colleagues insisted that he was a prophet—perhaps even Elijah—sent by God himself. He was a subject of controversy then just as he is now.

People still find themselves taking sides on the question of Luther. No matter what he himself really said or did, the sheer bulk of his writings (more than 100 quarto volumes in its modern edition) contains plenty of grist for everyone's mill. Consequently a bewildering variety of well-known people have claimed him as their own, ranging from both orthodox and pietist Lutheran theologians of the 16th and 17th centuries to the Wesley brothers, to Francis Bacon, Handel, and Bach, and including both Nazi propagandists such as Josef Goebbels and a martyr under Fascism such as Dietrich Bonhoeffer.

Luther's lasting memorial may in fact be the so-called Luther Renaissance of the 20th century that has crammed books about him into research libraries all over the world. As a result, Luther is so widely known that it is entirely appropriate to ask why there should be yet another biography of the man.

The primary purpose of this book is to tell the story of Martin Luther to readers who are not specialists in the field of Luther studies and who have no desire to become ensnared in the arguments of specialists. It seeks to pluck the fruit of scholarly discussion for the benefit of general readers.

Other biographies of Luther have been written for just such an audience. The most notable among them is Roland Bainton's *Here I Stand*,[2] which has been read and loved for more than 30 years. But that book itself suggests reasons for writing a new biography of Luther.

In the first place, Luther research has advanced greatly during the past several decades. Professor Bainton's insights into the concerns and convictions of the young Luther remain astounding, but when he wrote *Here I Stand*, the volcano of recent work on Luther's early development had scarcely begun to rumble.[3] Now a generation of research makes it possible to go beyond Bainton's brilliant guesses and trace the genesis of Luther the reformer with great precision.

At the same time, historians of the Reformation have been doing far more than simply adding one piece after another to the jigsaw puzzle of the young Luther. Scholars no longer content themselves with studying Luther's formal theology, but also examine the theological and religious traditions in which he was trained, the actual religious practices of his time, and the conditions of daily life in the 16th century. They have even brought the insights of modern psychology to their work. As a result, it is now possible to provide general readers with a much clearer picture of the man and his career.

In addition, the ecumenical movement had scarcely outgrown its infancy as Bainton wrote his biography at the end of the 1940s. Consequently he and most authors of his era were happily partisan in their approach to Luther. They felt obliged to justify his actions as well as to underline his faithful defense of what they took to be the true faith. By contrast, recently John Todd, the English Catholic scholar, wrote a biographical account of Luther's early years and came to much the same conclusions as did the Protestant Bainton. So too has Father Daniel Olivier of Paris in two of his recent works.[4]

Another limitation of previous biographies of Luther is that no single-volume work has treated his entire career. The vast majority, such as those by Bainton and Todd, E. G. Rupp, Martin Brecht, and Heinrich Boehmer (to name but a few),[5] focus with great care and insight on Luther's "road to Reformation," to cite a common subtitle. But in doing so they virtually end the man's career with the dramatic confrontation at Worms in 1521, or with the Peasants' War, the debate with Erasmus, and his marriage in 1525, or with the Diet of Augsburg in 1530.

Some biographers have appended brief vignettes on various aspects of Luther's later public and personal life. But there is such general ignorance regarding his mature years that a few scholars have begun to concentrate on them alone. Even Luther's "middle years" (1521–1531) are so poorly known that the late dean of Luther scholars, Heinrich Bornkamm, devoted an entire volume (posthumously published) just to them. In addition, the fine recent studies of H. G. Haile and Mark U. Edwards seek to lay bare Luther's last decade.[6] But this piecemeal treatment of Luther leaves the unfortunate impression that the reformer lived one short life, or maybe two lives, or perhaps even three distinct lives.

Martin Luther in fact lived one multifaceted life that is remarkable both for its achievements and for the internal logic by which it unfolded. This biography seeks to present this one life to this generation of readers in one volume. In doing so, it attempts to bring the latest scholarship to bear on Luther and to treat all of his life with reasonably equal coverage. Above all, it seeks to draw as faithful a picture as possible of the whole man.

Biography—or any historical writing—is more than the sum of "the facts" about the subject. At the very least, a writer selects and presents this information in order to provide the present with an interpretation of the past. In addition, such interpretation is a much more subtle matter than simply deciding whether Luther wore a white hat or a black hat.

It requires an accurate description of his career, close attention to his character, a clear understanding of the world in which he lived, and the relationships among these various elements.

Failure to be fully sensitive to these matters has led to some curious results in recent times. Most scholars (in particular, many Luther specialists who are theologians by training) treat him almost as if he were a theological mind that floated unconcernedly above the real world in which he lived. The many accounts that virtually end his life in 1521 or 1525 do so in part because they focus almost solely on his theology. They present Luther's life as having been complete by one or another of these dates on the grounds that by that time his theological development was essentially finished. In a few of the purely doctrinal studies, such as those by Gerhard Ebeling or Paul Althaus,[7] Luther appears to have been a disembodied intellect that lived in the realm of pure thought.

At the same time, an influential minority of scholars has employed the insights of psychology, and sometimes even of psychoanalysis, in an effort to penetrate beneath Luther's religious faith and theological thinking to the structure of his personality. The most well-known of these is the work of Erik Erikson, who found in Luther an "identity crisis" of the sort that modern children frequently suffer. The playwright John Osborne followed Erikson and then pictured the Luther of 1525 as a sort of Macbeth who was frozen into a state of indecisive agonizing by a revolution he himself had unleashed.[8] It must be granted that these approaches have helped make Luther understandable to a world that is very different from his own. But left by themselves, they have also tended to trivialize the reformer's actions and concrete concerns into mere products of his psychological state. The historic figure disappears, and Luther becomes no more than a curious psyche.

The work of another group of scholars has come to much the same sort of implied distortion, but by an alternate route. These historians have by and large forsaken the study of individuals to seek out long-range social, economic, demographic, intellectual, theological, and political trends in western history. Some go so far as to suggest that history is governed by natural laws or impersonal processes within which individuals play a largely involuntary role.

Older Marxist scholarship provides the most obvious example of this assumption at work.[9] To them, Luther's significance lies in the fact that he played a pivotal role in preparing the way for the proletarian revolution. Other examples include social historians such as Fernand Braudel and Philippe Ariès. By virtue of its effect on the picture of Luther, the most recent work of historians of dogma such as Jaroslav Pelikan deserves inclusion here as well.[10] Taken together, such studies have the virtue of making it possible as never before to see that Luther was very much subject to the economic, social, religious, political, and theological conditions of the times in which he lived. By the same token, their overriding concern for the forest inclines them to ignore the mighty oak in its midst. Luther is seen as no more than one factor in the general period under investigation. He is viewed as having been overwhelmed by the tides of impersonal historical change.

Each of these three ways of looking at Luther has serious limitations. The first ignores Luther's humanity and turns him into a theological system. The second sidesteps the fact that he was a theologian and pastor and presents him as a bundle of social or psychic impulses. The third loses sight of his significance altogether. None confronts the full reality of the man.

The life of Luther exhibited two characteristics, and a biographer must treat them both. In the first place, this man had a public career that transcended its own time and still draws attention today. Second, Luther was someone who had an accessible personality; he was a human being who lived in a particular place and at a particular time.

In these respects, Luther was the first figure in history about whom a biography can actually be written. On the one hand, much is known about his public career, though it needs clarification from time to time. On the other hand, his personality is also accessible, if only because one of Martin Luther's favorite topics for writing and conversation was Martin Luther. His books, actions, and even his table conversations (as recorded by his students) display a man who was keenly aware both of himself and of his pivotal position in history. With Luther it is therefore possible to look closely at both the man and the career that made him famous. An examination of his whole life in this way reveals that the man and his career explain one another. The point of view of this book is that this towering figure is indeed understandable, and that therefore he should be understood.

Acknowledgments

Any work of this kind is a group effort. First thanks must go to the generations of scholars who have discovered, edited, and mined the sources. Although they are named only in the bibliography, they will find their work reflected in the pages that follow.

Two fellow scholars proved that learning and friendship can go hand-in-hand. Professor Leif Grane of the Institute for Church History at the University of Copenhagen and Professor Lewis W. Spitz, who is William R. Kenan Jr. Professor of History at Stanford University, checked the entire text for errors and made a number of helpful suggestions.

Students also contributed. Most were in my courses and by their questions revealed to me both what was difficult and what was especially interesting in Dr. Luther. Two were of particular help. Robert Barone began the arduous process of checking all the notes, and Ken Schurb helped me complete them with what can only be called ruthless, but always good-natured, care. To Mr. Schurb goes the accolade of Luther himself, that "historians are the most useful people, and they can never be honored, praised, and thanked enough."

Margaret Ann, Elizabeth Ann, and Amy Marie Kittelson took a hand in the work, too. Margaret is my Katie, and like Dr. Luther, "I would not trade her for Venice and all the Kingdom of France, because God has given her to me and me to her." She, too, read the many drafts more than once, and she was often right about still further changes that needed to be made. Beth and Amy's visits downstairs were a real delight to a father who sometimes felt shackled to the word processor.

Thanks also go to the editors at Augsburg Publishing House, who answered my telephone query with one of their own and then encouraged me in a project that I had no intention of undertaking. They labored over my prose and proved to be a treasury of helpful suggestions.

Finally, the Department of History, the Center for Medieval and Renaissance Studies, the Thompson Library, and the College of Humanities at The Ohio State University have been more than generous with their support.

To all of you, my thanks. I do not hold you responsible for any errors or infelicities that may appear in the pages that follow.

Chronological Table

Listed below are the dates of major events in Luther's life and of his major writings. Significant political events are indicated with boldface type.

1483	November 10	Born in Eisleben.
1484		Family moved to Mansfeld; Hans Luder found work in copper mines.
1492		Latin school in Mansfeld.
1497		Latin school in Magdeburg.
1498		School of St. George in Eisenach; met the Schalbe family.
1501		Entered the University of Erfurt.
1502	September	Bachelor of Arts degree.
1505	January	Master of Arts degree.
	May	Began law studies.
	July	Thunderstorm, vow, and entrance into Augustinian cloister in Erfurt.

1507	May	Ordination and first mass.
1508	winter	Lectured one term at Wittenberg on moral philosophy.
1509	March	Became Biblical Baccalaureate and *Sententiarius*.
1510	November	Sent to Rome on business for the Observant Augustinians.
1511	April	Return from Rome, exile to Wittenberg.
1512	October	Promoted to Doctor of Theology at the University of Wittenberg.
1513	fall	Began lectures on the Psalms.
1515	spring	Began lectures on Romans.
1516	fall	Began lectures on Galatians.
1517	fall	Began lectures on Hebrews.
	October 31	Posted *The 95 Theses*.
1518	April 26	Heidelberg Disputation.
	July	Sylvester Prierias's *Dialogus* against *The 95 Theses*.
	August 7	Luther cited to Rome by Pope Leo X.
	August	**Diet of Augsburg with Cardinal Cajetan as papal emissary.**
	August 31	Luther's reply to Prierias.
	October 12-14	Interview with Cardinal Cajetan in Augsburg.
	November 28	Appeal to a general council of the church.
	December 18	Elector Frederick's refusal to send Luther to Rome.

1519	January	**Karl von Miltitz's mission to Elector Frederick the Wise.**
	January 12	**Death of Emperor Maximilian I.**
	June 28	**Election of Charles I of Spain as Emperor Charles V.**
	July 4-14	Leipzig Debate with John Eck of Ingolstadt.
	late summer	Overtures from followers of Jan Hus.
1520	January	Offers of armed assistance from Hutten and Sickingen.
	June 11	*On the Papacy at Rome.*
	June 15	The bull *Exsurge Domine* gave Luther 60 days to submit.
	August	*Address to the Christian Nobility.*
	October	*The Babylonian Captivity of the Church.*
	November	*On the Freedom of a Christian.*
1521	January 27	**Beginning of the Diet of Worms.**
	March 6	Invitation to the Diet of Worms.
	April 16-18	**Luther's appearance and two hearings at the Diet of Worms.**
	early May	Arrival at the Wartburg; *Commentary on the Magnificat.*
	June 1	*On Confession: Whether the Pope Has the Authority to Require It.*
	June 20	*Against Latomus.*
	November	*On the Abolition of Private Masses: On Monastic Vows.*
	December	Began translation of the New Testament.

December 3-4   Visit to Wittenberg.

December 15   *An Admonition to All Christians to Guard Themselves against Insurrection.*

1522-1524   **Diet of Nuremberg; edict of March 6 deferred action on the Edict of Worms.**

1522-1523   **Pontificate of Adrian VI.**

1522 March 6   Return to Wittenberg; the "Invocavit sermons."

March   *Advent Church Postils.*

September   Publication of the New Testament in German.

1523 March   *On Temporal Authority: the Extent to which It Should Be Obeyed.*

September   **Beginning of the pontificate of Clement VII.**

1524 February   *To the Municipalities of Germany . . . on Founding Schools.*

August   Exchanges with Carlstadt on the Lord's Supper.

September   Erasmus's attack on Luther in *On the Freedom of the Will.*

November   *To the Christians in Strasbourg against the Enthusiasts.*

1525 January   *Against the Heavenly Prophets.*

March   ***The 12 Articles of the Swabian Peasants.***

April 19   *Admonition to Peace Concerning the 12 Articles.*

May 5	**Death of Elector Frederick the Wise;** *Against the Murderous and Thieving Hordes of Peasants.*
June 13	Marriage to Katharina von Bora.
December	*On the Bondage of the Will.*
1526 (early in the year)	*German Mass and Order for Public Worship.*
mid-summer	**Diet of Speyer; refusal of princes to enforce the Edict of Worms.**
1527 April	*Whether These Words, "This Is My Body," Still Stand against the Fanatics.*
August	Negotiations with Elector John of Saxony regarding the church visitations; physical illness and mental and spiritual depression; composition of "A Mighty Fortress Is Our God."
March	Publication of the visitation articles; *Great Confession on the Lord's Supper.*
December	Personal service as a church visitor.
1529 January	Decision to write *The Small Catechism* and *The Large Catechism.*
April 19	**Protest of the Evangelical estates at the Diet of Speyer.**
October 1-4	The Marburg Colloquy with opponents in the Sacramentarian Controversy.
1530 April-August	At the Coburg during proceedings of the Diet of Augsburg.
mid-May	*To the Clergy Assembled at Augsburg.*
summer	**Diet of Augsburg.**

June 25 — **Submission of Melanchthon's** *Augsburg Confession* **at the Diet of Augsburg.**

August 15 — *A Sermon on Keeping Children in School.*

October — **Agreement at Torgau to resist if Catholic forces should attack Protestant princes and cities.**

December — **Beginning of meetings at Schmalkalden that led to a defensive alliance against the Catholic estates and the emperor.**

1531 — Students began to copy down Luther's remarks during meals.

March — Complaints of sickness and weakness.

April — *Warning to His Beloved Germans.*

May — *Against the Assassin at Dresden; Great Commentary on Galatians.*

1532 January — *On Infiltrating and Clandestine Preachers.*

May — **Negotiations concerning the conditions under which religious peace could be maintained in the empire.**

July 23 — **Protesting estates agreed to provide aid against the Turks on the basis of religious toleration until the forthcoming council of the church.**

1534 — Publication of the complete German Bible.

1535 November — **Visit of the papal legate, Pier Paolo Vergerio, regarding an invitation to the forthcoming council at Mantua;** meeting with Vergerio.

1536 May — Signing of the Wittenberg Concord with representatives of the south German cities.

1537	February	Meeting at Schmalkalden; the Schmalkald Articles; Luther nearly died.
	April 20	**Council of Mantua prorogued and later cancelled.**
1538	March	*Letter against the Sabbatarians.*
	June 10	**King Ferdinand and several other Catholic princes signed the Nuremberg Treaty to establish a counterweight to the Schmalkald League.**
1539	April 17	**Death of Duke George of Saxony.**
	April 19	**The "Frankfurt Truce" signed between King Ferdinand and the Schmalkald League.**
	December	**Bigamy of Philip of Hesse.**
1540	June/July	**Colloquy of Hagenau.**
	September 27	**Recognition of the Society of Jesus by Pope Paul III.**
	November 25	**Colloquy of Worms.**
1541	March	*Against Hans Wurst.*
	April 5	**Opening of the Diet of Regensburg, with a parallel meeting of Catholic and Protestant theologians.**
1542	June/August	**Philip of Hesse and John Frederick of Saxony attacked and imprisoned Duke Henry of Braunschweig.**
1543	January	*On the Jews and Their Lies.*
1544	June 10	**Emperor Charles V gave more concessions to the Protestant estates at the Diet of Speyer in exchange for support against Francis I of France.**

1545 March   *Against the Papacy at Rome, Founded by the Devil.*

September 24   **Death of Archbishop Albert of Mainz.**

December 13   **Opening of the Council of Trent.**

1546 February 18   **Luther's death.**

1547 April   **Victory of Charles V over the Schmalkald League at the Battle of Mühlberg.**

PART ONE

The Formation of the Young Man

ONE

The Son of a Peasant

When Martin Luther died, the news was reported throughout Latin Christendom. Soon the story was circulating in Rome that those present at his bedside had seen devils flying out of his body. A far more kindly disposed person declared that with him went Elijah and the chariots of Israel.

By contrast, Luther's birth was a matter of such insignificance that he and his friends later debated the exact year.[1] Moreover, he came from peasant stock and frequently referred to himself as a peasant, even when he was an adult. No one expected great deeds from peasants. In the late 15th century, someone of this class in northeastern Germany commonly farmed a small piece of land. Peasants were always ready to rebel against their lords in defense of their rights. But even then, they were so deeply conservative that they would put their demands in terms of a return to what they called the "old law." Their little plots of ground in the here-and-now were all they had, and their horizons seldom went beyond them.

Hans Luder

Martin Luther's father, Hans Luder (as the family name was pronounced in the local dialect), was a peasant, but he did not long remain one. Local inheritance laws specified that family lands passed intact to the youngest son, so Hans was forced to leave Möhra, his home village, before his second son, Martin, was born. Just how he was earning a living in the town of Eisleben when the baby arrived on November 10, 1483, is unknown.

Whatever else might be said of Hans Luder, the young father and husband was a loyal, right-thinking sort of person who could be counted on to do what was best insofar as he understood it. He therefore acted according to the religious dictates of the time. That very morning, probably a cold and rainy one, he took his infant son to the Church of St. Peter's to have him baptized. He was acting most sensibly in an age when infant mortality ran to 60% or more and everyone feared that an unbaptized child who died might forfeit heaven. Hans Luder followed custom in yet another way on that christening day. Because it was the Feast of St. Martin, he named the baby Martin.

German peasant couple at table.

Hans Luder must have been a desperate man in the months that preceded and followed the birth of his second son. The death of his father had left him with little besides a growing family and a choice. He could become a laborer in his brother's fields, or he could leave. He chose to leave, and so set out to make his own way in the world. But fortune did not smile on him in Eisleben, the family's first stop. Before young Martin was a year old, the family gathered its few possessions and moved to the small town of Mansfeld, which was near the hills about 10 miles away. They probably walked and carried everything they owned, either on their backs or on a pull-cart. Hans was looking for work. When they arrived in Mansfeld he took a job as a copper miner.

Life in a copper mine in 15th-century Germany was far worse than working in a modern coal mine. Landslides, cave-ins, and suddenly rising water were constant, life-threatening possibilities. In addition, the miners were utterly dependent on animal power, and in particular the power of human muscle. It is no wonder that the miners had a patron saint; they needed her. Of those who survived physically, many never became more than common laborers. But Hans Luder did. Within seven years he had started his own enterprise in the copper business. Not long after that he became a member of Mansfeld's city council. Less than 25 years after Martin's birth, Hans and his partners owned

Hans and Margaretta Luder (by Cranach).

at least six mine shafts and two copper smelters. Hans Luder was a very determined man.

During the early, lean years, Hans Luder's children learned that every expenditure had to be watched with great care. Luther recalled that his mother had once beat him until his hands bled merely for taking a nut from the kitchen table. He also remembered that she went with the other women from town into the forests to collect fallen wood for the fire. The children were taught that everything the family did was to be both honorable and productive. Once Luther's father caned him so severely for a childish prank that he became deeply resentful. At last, Hans had to come to him for reconciliation. Luther's family was both strict and loving. It was also a family in which the parents were very ambitious for their children. They would be competent. They would do what was right. The family's future would be secure.

Hard times

In the early 16th century, security of any sort was a very elusive thing to come by. Life in Luther's time was tenuous in ways that are nearly impossible for people living in the modern world to appreciate. To be sure, these were the years that historians refer to as the Renaissance, and Luther was a contemporary of truly extraordinary people—Machiavelli, Michelangelo, Raphael, Erasmus, and Thomas More, among many others. Copernicus's revolutionary book on the solar system was published before Luther died. Christopher Columbus set sail when Luther was halfway through grammar school, and Luther was aware of the discovery of the new world. He remarked that if Europeans did not respond to the gospel, they would likely lose it to these new people.

Luther lived in exciting times. Even today, the magnificent achievements of his 16th-century contemporaries and the splendor of life at a Renaissance court excite the imagination. But these images also obscure the realities of everyday life for ordinary people. Luther lived in hard times. For example, in Florence at the height of the Renaissance, 61 percent of the infants were either stillborn or died within six months. At least one of Luther's younger brothers died in this way. Luther's mother, Margaretta, was convinced that the death of her child was the work of the woman next door, who, she was certain, was a witch.

These were the years when the Plague ravaged Europe. The territory of Alsace, to the southwest, illustrates what could happen when sickness stalked the countryside. In the city of Strasbourg, which normally had about 25,000 inhabitants, some 16,000 fell to the scourge in one year. In the region around this large city, 300 villages were left deserted and the total land under cultivation did not climb back to normal levels until two centuries later.

Nor was the Plague the only new and horrifying disease with which Europeans had to contend. During these same years syphilis (which the Germans called the "French disease") arrived on the continent to torment European lovers. All were agreed on the name for another dread disease, the "English Sweats," which featured a high fever that permanently shattered the victims' nervous systems and left them with long lesions on their bodies.

About a century later, the English philosopher Thomas Hobbes aptly depicted life in Luther's time as being "nasty, brutish, and short." Even those tough enough to surmount the hazards of disease commonly struggled just to find enough to eat. Transportation networks were primitive, so each area had to be self-sufficient. When food production failed to meet the local need, territories removed from the major waterways were especially vulnerable. A local drought, a terribly wet spring, or an early frost could force grain prices up as much as 150% over the previous year.

Speculators, whose numbers included the heads of great churches and monasteries, were therefore in a position to make enormous profits. Ordinary people simply suffered. Many who had once been employed were reduced to begging for their food and clothing. They could be seen on every street of every village and city. The sheer number of beggars was so overwhelming that the authorities on the west bank of the Rhine would annually combine forces, round up all the undesirables, and force them over to the east bank. On that side of the river the procession of beggars and homeless, maimed, insane, and mentally retarded people would be met by another group of princes with their armies, who marched them through the Black Forest and into central Germany. But the constant flow of society's outcasts never stopped. A year later the authorities would start the whole process over again.

In one respect, life at the turn of the 16th century must be painted in even darker hues than these. It was not just the times that were hard. The people were hardened by the world in which they lived. Many were also exceedingly violent. German peasants were far from being placid workers of the land. They quickly exercised the right of feud, and they continued to do so for another 150 years. When they had real or imagined grievances, they sought recourse not in the courts but with their fists, knives, or clubs.

While a peace-loving, respectable family such as Luther's might not have engaged in such random violence, they could not entirely escape it. Hans Luder had a younger brother by virtually the same name who must have been a constant source of embarrassment. Young Hans, as he was called, lived in Mansfeld for 14 years. During that time he was charged with assault and battery on 11 separate occasions. But people in Mansfeld were fortunate in that Young Hans was repeatedly brought to justice. In the early 16th century the arms of the law had not yet

Punishments were given to servants who gossiped ("the tongue clipping") or mis-behaved in other ways. (Note that the servant on the right has stabbed his master's leg.)

grown very long, and they were often simply unable to remove crim-inals from the midst of law-abiding citizens. One of Luther's later followers recalled that his own first professor at the University of Freiburg was struck dead on the street by a wandering soldier. There is no record that the murderer ever had to answer for his crime.

A father's ambition

Considering these horrible conditions, Hans Luder's achievements are all the more remarkable. As Luther well remembered, his father was determined that his children would succeed, and he was very strict with them. Yet he was also capable of the unexpected. Rather than put his son to work in the family business, as other fathers commonly did, Hans Luder sent Martin to the town school, which he attended nearly every day for eight years. In 1497 he sent him to Magdeburg, a year later to Eisenach, and from there in 1501 to the University of Erfurt. Later Luther commented that his father certainly "meant heartily by me."[2] Hans Luder was as ambitious for his son as he was for himself.

By contrast with Luther's attitude toward his family, he looked back at his early education with little but disgust. Sixteenth-century schoolmasters by no means saw their task as drawing forth the best and most creative efforts from their charges. Luther was not quite five years old when he entered a school whose sole purpose was to force the students to learn to read and write Latin in preparation for their later studies. The methods used by his teachers were consistently condemned as "barbaric" by great educators such as Erasmus of Rotterdam. Coercion and ridicule were chief among their techniques. Any child caught speaking German was beaten with a rod. The one who had done least well in the morning was required to wear a dunce's cap and was addressed as an ass all afternoon. Demerits were then added up for the week, and each student went home with one more caning to make the accounts balance.

Under these conditions, all that the children knew for certain was that they wanted to avoid the beatings and the dunce's cap. But the curriculum was so dull that students found little incentive to meet even this modest objective. Music was the subject that Luther preferred, and in time he became a skilled performer and composer. But not even music was taught so that children might enjoy it, much less that they might express themselves. They were taught music because they had to sing in the church choirs.

Most of the time was spent on Latin, for which these poor beginners had only a primer and lists of words to memorize. To accomplish this task, they also learned by heart the Lord's Prayer, the Ten Commandments, and the Apostles' Creed. When they had learned enough Latin, they were allowed to proceed to the second class. There they were introduced to the joys of memorizing declensions and conjugations. And the teacher's rod followed them. Luther was caned 15 times in only one morning for not having mastered the tables of Latin grammar.

In 1497, at the age of 13, Luther had learned Latin well enough to be sent away to school. His first stop was probably Magdeburg. There he lived and studied at a foundation operated by the Brethren of the Common Life, an extremely pious lay religious organization. Although the beatings probably stopped, by no means did Luther now live the life of a pampered boy away at prep school. During out-of-class hours he joined his classmates as they roamed the streets in the children's choirs. These were the origin of the modern practice of caroling. But these boys caroled all year long; far from Christmas revelers, they were beggars who became adept at using this accepted means for students to acquire food and drink.

Eisenach

Circumstances changed somewhat when Luther was sent to Eisenach a year later. There he found relatives on his mother's side who could keep an eye on him, but were themselves so poor that they could not even provide shelter. His daily life therefore remained, at least for a time, more or less the same. He continued to sing in the children's choirs and had little, if anything, to spend on frivolities. In this he was indistinguishable from the vast majority of his classmates. At some

The house, built in the 15th century, where Luther lived as a student in Eisenach.

point during his stay, however, Luther apparently very much impressed a well-to-do woman from a family of merchants named Schalbe. The matron of the family arranged for him to stay at the home of one of her relatives and to take his meals with another. He may have been required to tutor their children, but after 1498 life undoubtedly became a bit easier for him.

Luther's three years at Eisenach also saw a change of far greater significance for his future development. He found a teacher who could awaken his imagination while sharpening his mind. In his case the teacher was the headmaster of the school, one John Trebonius, whom Luther later praised as a gifted man. Trebonius certainly must have instilled a very different atmosphere in this school from what prevailed at Mansfeld, for there Luther also struck up a lifelong friendship with a teacher named Wiegand Geldennupf. These men were more than figures of authority, and they had more to teach than rote memorization of Latin vocabulary, declensions, and conjugations. As Luther now neared the end of his studies in Latin school, he could give speeches and write essays and poetry. He could also read some of the ancient authors and thereby enter the world of Aesop, Terence, and Virgil. The great pleasure he derived from these studies showed later in his life as he sat down to translate *Aesop's Fables* into German and insisted that everyone must be a student of the classics and of history.

Trebonius and Geldennupf recognized Luther's ability. It was undoubtedly they who recommended that the young man, then 17 years old, continue his studies at a university. Just what considerations led Hans Luder to decide in favor of this plan cannot be known. It was unusual for a man in his position to send his son to the university. He was, however, very much aware that even for commoners a university education opened up careers in the church, in law, and in medicine. Although his own business was only at the break-even point, he sent his son to study at the University of Erfurt.

Aside from his intelligence and the fact that he had formal education, there was no evident difference between Luther and any other German boy who passed into young adulthood near the turn of the 16th century. There was also nothing in particular that set Luther apart in his religious life. To be sure, his family was diligent in its religious practices. But they also appear to have been perfectly conventional. Indeed, Hans Luder was one of a number of townsmen who sought a special indulgence for St. George's church in Mansfeld in 1497. This act can almost be considered a normal civic, as well as religious, duty for someone of his stature in the town. Young Luther sang in the children's choirs during services, and he sang in the streets as well. But so did the other students. Religion was something that Luther experienced during his early years but there is no evidence that he thought about it overly much or even tried to understand it.

Luther may, however, have been a bit more diligent in the choirs or a better musician than the others, because it was in this way that he first came to the attention of the Schalbe family in Eisenach. The Schalbes were exceptionally pious people, and Luther had close connections with them. The father of the family spent much of his time promoting the work of the Franciscan monastery not far from town, in fact so much time that Luther later judged him the monks' "servant and slave."[3] Without a doubt the Schalbes' boarder also learned to practice his religion diligently and learned a great deal about monasticism. But there was nothing unusual about Christians in the late Middle Ages being especially solicitous of the clergy. Doing so was considered a good work and just the sort of thing one should be about.

The search for spiritual security

The religion practiced by people of the 16th century was much like the world in which they lived. They struggled to gain spiritual security, just as in their daily lives they struggled to achieve material security. Salvation was something to be earned, and so theirs was a religion of work.

It was an age of pilgrimages. People were exhorted to travel in groups to this or that shrine in order to work off the penalties for the sins they had committed. Frequently enough, they temporarily took up the life of apostolic poverty and begged for their sustenance as they traveled.

It was also an age of saints and relics. The faithful were taught that praying to the saints or venerating their relics would atone for individual sins of both omission and commission. To assist them in this work, the major churches and shrines collected pieces of bone and hair that were alleged to have come from the body of one saint or another. Some boasted of drops of milk from the Virgin's breast or splinters from the cross of Christ.

It was an age of death. Painters, sculptors, and wood carvers seized on this theme and the "Dance of Death" became one of the most common motifs in late medieval art. Like the Pied Piper, the skeletal

Grim Reaper with scythe in hand led representatives of every social group twirling off to their own inevitable end.

Above all, it was an age of fire and brimstone. No one could escape knowing that there was a judgment to come. Christ himself was commonly pictured not just on the cross, but seated on his throne. Coming from one side of his head was a lily, symbolizing the resurrection. From the other side came a sword. The burning question was, How can I avoid the sword and earn the lily?

The church had an answer to this question. By the time Luther was born it had been sharpened into one short command: "Do what is in your power!" "Use well your natural capacities and whatever special gifts have been granted you."[4] Then, through the power of the church, God would add his grace and smile. Although they by no means understood (nor were they intended to understand) just how this happened, people like the Schalbes and Luther's parents did what they were told.

Others did far more. Luther never forgot seeing Prince William of Anhalt, who had renounced his noble estate to become a Franciscan monk and to spend his life as a beggar. "He had fasted so often, kept so many vigils, and so mortified his flesh," Luther later wrote, "that he was the picture of death, just skin and bones."[5] Prince William was certainly exceptional, but there were so many people zealously working out their salvation that the city of Marseilles passed a law forbidding religious beggars from passing its walls. Nearly every city sought at least to control them.

Sin, confession, penance

Most people were not so zealous in their efforts to guarantee their salvation. Leaders of the church therefore tried to make sure that everyone at least *thought* about the status of their souls. Chief among their methods was the obligation to confess one's sins to a priest. At least once a year (commonly at the beginning of Lent, but the more often the better), every man, woman, and child admitted to Communion was obligated to go to their priest and confess all the sins they had committed since their previous visit.

It is impossible to know exactly what happened inside the confessional in Luther's day (even as it is impossible to know exactly what happens in it today), but if the confessors followed the manuals that were written for them, it was a very rigorous examination.[6] A priest would begin by asking what sins a penitent wished to confess to almighty God. When the response was insufficiently detailed or when the penitent, now on his or her knees on the stone floor, could not remember any particular sins, the confessor would begin asking questions. "Have you ever become angry with your spouse?" "Do you wish your house were as good as your neighbor's?" For adolescent boys, "Do you ever have 'wet dreams'?" For girls, "Were you dancing with the young men at the town fair?" For those who were married, "Have you had sexual relations with your spouse for any purpose other than having children?" Or, "Did you use any but the standard position?" Or, "The last time you and your husband (or

A procession of clergy in reverse order of their earthly rank, with Christ and little children at the head and the pope at the rear.

wife) had sexual intercourse, did you enjoy it or experience any feelings of pleasure?" The theologians debated whether sexual relations within marriage were serious sins, but all agreed that they were sins, at least in principle. Therefore even this most ordinary human activity had to be confessed before the throne of a righteous and angry God.

The church also made it clear that people had to be purged of all the sins they had failed to confess and work off in the here and now. If they did not do so, they would surely pay the price in purgatory, where they would sweat out every unremitted sin before they could see the gates of heaven. Given this situation, there can be little wonder that one of the first things Gutenberg issued from his newly developed movable-type printing press was what the church at the time called an *indulgence*. This was granted in exchange for a "gift" to the church and released the donor from the fires of purgatory for a specified time. Gutenberg's form was much like a modern legal document. It came complete with a blank space for the purchaser's name and another space for how much time in purgatory they had escaped. Indulgences were very popular.

As it did for everyone else, the cycle of sin, confession, and penance played a prominent role in Luther's spiritual life. Confession was required at least annually for all who wished to attend the Mass, but the thought of dying suddenly with several individual sins unconfessed amounted to an unbearable risk for pious people. Sensitive religious leaders did concern themselves with the possibility that such rigorous confessional practices might lead truly pious people to despair. *Despair*—the horrifying thought that God's mercy is not for me or that I have fallen too far for it to help me—was the one unforgivable sin. It was the sin against the Holy Spirit, and no one who died with it in their heart could escape the fires of hell. Moreover, it was feared that, when faced with death, some might indeed despair at the last moment and be lost. This fear was so great that nearly everyone was familiar with artistic depictions of angels and devils wrestling for the soul of someone who was dying.

So the theologians composed more manuals. These instructed priests on how to hear final confessions and how, as they did so, to fend off despair while ushering the dying into the next life. However, in spite of all their worries and second thoughts, the theologians still concluded that the dangers of an incomplete confession far outweighed the chance that a penitent would fall into despair. After all, people actually enjoyed sinning. If one's conscience were troubled, surely it would be relieved by some act of penance, whether several "Our Fathers," an "Ave Maria," or, in the case of those who really wanted to be sure, a pilgrimage to a shrine or the purchase of an indulgence.

The religion that Martin Luther learned was very much like the world in which he lived. Much as the world sometimes added good fortune to a person's labors, in this realm the church added grace to one's good works so they would be complete and acceptable to God. But in each realm, hard work was still essential.

Erfurt

This, then, was the religion that a young, swarthy man of medium height took with him as he trudged off to the University of Erfurt in May 1501. His steps took him to the southeast, through the town of his birth, out onto a broad plain, over some hills, and finally to Erfurt itself. Erfurt was a city of hills, woods, streams, and the spires of many churches, including a cathedral that rose up out of the tallest hill and presided over all like a brooding citadel. Nothing could convey the awe and majesty of God with such force as did this great, stone presence. Churchgoers had to climb a great pile of stone steps just to reach it from the city below.

Erfurt, the "city of spires" or "little Rome."

The university itself was made up of a few small buildings gathered around a pleasant stream in the city below. But in the late Middle Ages, a university was even less its buildings than a true university is today. The buildings were no more than necessary structures to house the "company of masters and scholars" that made up the university itself. When Luther arrived, he was inscribed in the great matriculation book as "Martinus Ludher de Mansfeld" and, like all students, assigned to a *bursa,* where for the first years he would eat, sleep, and carry on his studies under the supervision of the master of the house.

The *bursa* was nothing like a modern dormitory, but had far more the character of a monastery. All the students dressed alike and lived by the very strict rules of the bursa and the university. They arose at the same time, began every day with worship and prayers, ate their meals together, participated in other prescribed religious services together, and studied the same subjects. Those who broke the rules were disciplined by the master, the student censor (really an internal spy), or any of the university's many proctors. Students were most definitely not left to go their own way.

Erfurt saw Luther's coming of age. He thrived in its atmosphere.
Here it became apparent that he was not just another bright student,
but extraordinarily able and blessed with a keen and penetrating mind.
University statutes required that students be enrolled at least one year
before they presented themselves for the Bachelor of Arts degree.
Luther received his degree in one year. The statutes also required a
minimum length of time before one could take the master's examination. Again Luther met the race against time, and in January 1505
he passed the examination, second in his class of 17.

Students commonly attain such records at the expense of the friend-
ships and enjoyment that are so much a part of university life. Not
Luther. His companions later nicknamed him "the Philosopher" in
recognition of his brilliance at the disputations, or public debates, that
were crucial to teaching and learning at a late medieval university.

If there had been something odd about Luther, some streak of ear-
nestness, melancholy, or rebellion, surely a classmate would later have
recorded it. None did so. The only such assertions came from the pens
of his most violent enemies, such as Johannes Cochlaeus, who fab-
ricated stories about Luther's early years even though they had met
only once, in 1521. The young Luther appears to have been just another
fun-loving and high-spirited student, certainly more brilliant than many
of his classmates, but in other respects much like them.

A professional education

The most important thing to know about the young man Luther
during these years is what he was taught, and therefore how he came
to think as he moved through the university and into adulthood. In
many respects the organization of teaching and learning in a late medieval university such as Erfurt was very different from what students
experience today. In principle, every university of that time was divided
into four faculties, each of which governed its own affairs. The arts
faculty consisted of those who were masters of arts and who did the
preparatory work with candidates for both the B.A. and the M.A.
degrees. Above them were the three professional faculties of law, medicine, and—the queen of the sciences—theology.

Strictly speaking, only those who taught in these three faculties and
who held the title of *doctor* (or teacher) were professors. But Luther's
own teachers were also students in one of these higher faculties. Pre-

decessors of modern university teaching assistants, these teachers shaped the learning of the arts students to fit the demands of the curriculum in the professional faculties. Although Luther was technically a student of the liberal arts, his university education was a professional one in the most strict sense of the term.

The most important subjects for Luther lay in what educators of the time called the *trivium*, which was composed of grammar, rhetoric, and dialectic. This included many of the subjects that today are associated with the liberal arts. To them were added the *quadrivium* or arithmetic, geometry, astronomy, and music. But for Luther the trivium was the more important of the two. Grammar focused on the explication of certain classical texts, in particular the ancient Roman authors. Rhetoric, technically the art of public speaking, also included advanced written composition, poetry, the moral essays of figures such as Seneca, and portions of the Bible. Dialectic, however, ruled over all. It was the dialectical mode of thinking that made scholasticism and "the schoolmen," as they were called, distinctive, for dialectic was the cornerstone of the professional faculties.

If dialectic ruled over the other disciplines in the trivium, then Aristotle ("the father of those that know," as he was called) ruled over dialectic. His books on logic, chiefly the *Prior* and *Posterior Analytics* (as summarized in popular textbooks), were the principal sources for teaching students how to think. In more advanced work, they studied selections from his *Metaphysics* and *Ethics* as topics on which they could demonstrate their skills. Nothing was more important than learning how to think in this logical and orderly way, and nothing was accorded more time in the typical day of students and masters. Every day featured disputations in which teachers assigned students a thesis or set of theses which they were required to defend according to the strict rules of logic.

At special times the professors would appear at what were called quodlibetal disputations, public debates at which experts would argue with all comers on any topic of interest. This event was the intellectuals' equivalent of a medieval tournament, but one fought with words rather than lances. When the professors tired of the melee, or when the major points had been covered, they might beckon to a favored student and invite him to continue the battle. Given his nickname, "the Philosopher," Luther was probably chosen often.

Assumptions about truth

The entire university system rested on assumptions that were crucial to the way Luther and his contemporaries thought. In the first place, it was assumed (as Aristotle taught) that all important truths had two characteristics. First, they were universal. Circumstances of time and place made no difference to the truth of propositions that could be developed by the exercise of right reason. The objective of true learning was to discover these truths and express them in clear propositions.

Second, if the propositions were true, Luther's education assumed that they would be logically consistent with one another. The great disciplines of law, medicine, and theology were thus systems in which one truth could be logically derived from another. Words, therefore, could also be assigned proper meanings that held true irrespective of time and place.

This pair of assumptions was nowhere more evident than in the way teachers and students approached the ancient and modern texts that formed the core of the curriculum. They would comb through these sources for doctrines on the most important philosophical, legal, medical, and theological issues. For example, when they found two apparently contradictory statements about the proper conduct of life, they would then employ Aristotle's logic to resolve the contradiction. The same procedure could be used with respect to contradictory passages drawn from, say, the Old and New Testaments. All that was necessary was to assign a meaning to the words that would allow the student or professor to construct a logically consistent system.

The old story about medieval theologians debating how many angels can sit on the head of a pin illustrates this mode of thinking. Whether they ever actually did debate this seemingly trivial question is beside the point. To them, it would have masked an issue of great importance. The answer given—whether none, one, or an infinite number—carried with it assertions about whether angels did or did not have bodies, and therefore about whether heaven was material or spiritual. If heaven were material, then it had to be located in a place, because this is the nature of material things. If it were located in a place, then, at least in principle, human beings could find it in the here and now. Moreover, it could not be eternal, because it is the nature of things visible to pass away. By extension, the doctrines of the resurrection and of eternal life would suddenly disappear, and of course that could not be. Just how one answered the initial question was therefore very important.

Some students, such as the famous humanist Erasmus of Rotterdam, hated these disputations. Given his nickname, Luther probably enjoyed them. Whatever the case, a university education in the late Middle Ages inclined the serious student to ask questions, to pose them carefully, and to seek answers with tenacity. Given the right circumstances, a brilliant mind such as Luther's could use this training to pose many penetrating questions.

TWO

A Man of Sorrows

Not long after New Year's Day 1505, Martin Luther became Master Martin. It was an experience he never forgot: "How marvelous it was when the masters were promoted and the tapers were presented to them! I contend that there is no temporal or worldly joy to compare with it!"[1]

Being advanced to master of arts was an immense achievement for this son of a one-time peasant. Father Hans was enormously proud of his son and regarded the M.A. degree as just the beginning. Master Martin (as even his father now referred to him) was to become a lawyer.

This decision had undoubtedly been made once it became apparent that young Martin would earn his master's degree and with it the right to study in one of the professional faculties at the university. Then the whole world would open to him, especially if he were to succeed at the study of law. Good careers were available to bright young lawyers. He might aspire to become the trusted counselor of a prince or a bishop. There he could find a patron who could bless him with both wealth and position. In turn, Master Martin (and eventually *Doctor* Martin) would be able to take care of his parents in their old age. Perhaps he could even find positions for his siblings. Hans was so certain of the future that he presented his son with a copy of the *Corpus Juris Civilis*, the principal law text of the time. It was a very costly gift.

"I will become a monk"

Six months later a thunderstorm overtook Master Martin while he was walking back to Erfurt from Mansfeld. A bolt of lightning suddenly struck him to the ground. "Help me, St. Anne!" he shouted. "I will become a monk!"[2]

One moment of triumph. Another of desolation. Now Master Martin had decided to enter a monastery, and father Hans was furious. Luther wrote to his father and declared that the thunderstorm and the vow were the will of God. Hans replied that he wondered whether his son had misinterpreted what had happened. Were the thunderstorm and the vow the work of God or of the devil? Everyone in that devil-filled age knew that one must "test the spirits to see whether they are of God" (1 John 4:1).

Yet there was much more than this behind his father's anguished response, and Luther knew it. What Hans had lost was his insurance policy. With its brightest member now in a monastery, the Luder family's security was gone. Luther responded that he could do more for his family with his prayers than he could as a well-heeled lawyer. Within days, he received a second letter from his father. Hans praised his precocious son for his decision and wished him well in his new vocation.

Second thoughts of both a personal and a spiritual kind had already come to Hans. He was a man who delighted in discussing religion with wayfaring monks and priests. He knew, as deeply as anyone could know, that the salvation of one's soul came first. Had not one of his friends told him that he owed something—even his beloved son—to the church?

Luther's decision to become a monk nonetheless remains puzzling. At the time of the vow he was walking back to the University of Erfurt. He had taken an unexplained, but officially authorized, leave of absence to visit his family. This leave suggests that the decision was not as sudden as the bolt of lightning that knocked him off his feet.

After receiving his master's degree, Luther had three months of relatively free time on his hands before he began lecturing in the arts faculty on April 23, and then another month before he began his studies in law on May 20. What he pondered during this time can only be guessed. Perhaps he just reflected on his achievements as he wandered about the streams, woods, and spires of Erfurt. He was only one month into his law studies when he took his leave.

To undertake a walk of that distance, several days each way, required some serious purpose. Master Martin was a highly motivated and diligent young man. He also lived at a time when most people took their spiritual lives seriously. During these months of relative ease at the age of 21, he very likely began wondering whether the pattern set out so clearly for him was the right one. So he did the natural thing; he went home to discuss it. But he returned no more certain than he had been when he left Erfurt. It is easy to imagine his father's position, his quick dismissal of his son's questions. But then the thunderstorm settled the matter. It was the voice of God himself. It had to be.

Nonetheless, young Martin Luther did not simply disregard his father's disapproval and any doubts that he himself may have had. First he gathered together his friends and colleagues to discuss the matter. Most likely some advised for the path he had chosen and some against. When he had finally made up his own mind, he called them all again for a leave-taking party. He held it in the quarters he had been given as a master of arts and a member of the Faculty of Arts at the University of Erfurt.

By now it was early September. As was the rule, he gave away everything he owned, because no one could enter a monastery with personal property. He did carry with him copies of the works of two classical authors, whom he cherished for life, but he disposed of everything else. He gave away his lute, on which he was proficient, his other books, and his clothing and eating utensils. Even the *Corpus Juris Civilis* that his father had given him had to go. He was no longer to be a lawyer who arranged his own affairs and those of others in the here and now. He was a man of God who would spend all his time seeking the salvation of souls, above all his own.

The Black Cloister

Luther apparently thought very carefully about becoming a monk (technically, a friar) before taking the decisive step. He took equal care in choosing the order he would enter. There were many monasteries in Erfurt, the "city of spires" or "little Rome," as it was called. Without walking an extra pace from his lodgings, he could have become a Benedictine, Dominican, Franciscan, or a member of one of a number of other orders. But he chose the way of the Observant Augustinians, who resided in the Black Cloister on the left bank of the Gera River (as one looks downstream).

The Black Cloister is an imposing collection of buildings. The church itself seats about 300 people and has a long nave with a remote, high altar. Walking from the back of the church one can turn to the right just before reaching the chancel, pass through a door and enter the *Kreuzweg*, the way of the cross. This interior courtyard has an arched and covered portico of about 20 paces on each side. The architecture alone sets a mood of meditation and contemplation. At the end of the *Kreuzweg* and to the left are the common rooms where the brothers took their meals. On the second floor are their cells, about three feet wide and seven feet long, most with a window. The Black Cloister (so named for the clothing the monks wore) was located on the edge of the city-center. It was richly endowed and its members were freed from physical toil to spend all their time on the more important business of earning spiritual benefits for themselves and others. To be an Observant Augustinian was to engage in serious spiritual work.

View of the courtyard at the Black Cloister from a monk's cell.

Not all who knocked on the doors of the Black Cloister were admitted. First the monks wanted to be sure that Luther was not someone who had been momentarily frightened and would in time return to the ways of the world, even if only in spirit. Consequently, young Luther spent more than a month as the monks' guest, so they could assist him in examining his soul and the reasons why he had decided to join them. Only after he had passed this rigorous time of testing was he allowed to take the vows even of a novice. He knew full well that more rigor would follow. But that was why he had chosen to become an Observant Augustinian.

Much later Luther commented, "Along with many others, I myself have experienced how peaceful and quiet Satan is inclined to be during one's early years as a monk."[3] Every minute was closely regulated. Luther and his fellows commonly awoke early in the morning, about 2:00 A.M., for the first worship service of the day. Six more followed. A novice had no time for those dark nights of the soul for which Luther later became famous.

All the monks were technically religious beggars, so it is entirely possible—especially as a novice—that Luther and the others saw some of the outside world as they begged for alms to support themselves. Financially, it was not really necessary for them to do so. The work was, however, good discipline. Still, most of Luther's time was spent in worship, prayer, and meditation. He did not beg alone and he did not work out his spiritual exercises alone. From the very beginning, he was assigned a proctor who would guide, measure, and encourage his spiritual progress. Luther was learning a new and demanding routine. Given the sort of young man he was, he likely learned it quickly and well.

Luther's first mass

Much later Luther insisted, "If anyone could have gained heaven as a monk, then I would indeed have been among them."[4] All the evidence supports his view of himself as a zealous and successful monk. On Cantate Sunday 1507, little more than a year after he entered the monastery, he was allowed to celebrate his first mass. In a very brief time he had therefore passed not only the rigorous testing reserved for a novice, but also much more. He had demonstrated the kind of spirituality and high-minded purpose necessary to become a priest.

It was said of monks that their tonsure (the shaved head) was better protection for the skull than a helmet. Few dared to lay a hostile hand on a monk. But a monk who was also a priest carried a truly awesome aura of sanctity. This man could utter the words, *"hoc est corpus meum"* (this is my body) and *"hoc poculum est novum testamentum sanguinis mei"* (this cup is the new testament of my blood). With these words he could make bread and wine become the body and blood of

Christ. He could make sacrifice to God. He could bring one of the most important means of salvation to ordinary people.

The rite of the Mass was so central to all of late medieval piety that it was considered a good work, meritorious for salvation. Even the church buildings were designed for the purpose of magnifying it. The naves, where the common people stood, were long and narrow. The altars were far away. The combined effect was to prohibit ordinary people from either seeing or hearing exactly what was happening in this most sacred moment. The priests and their assistants then added to this divine magic their own special robes, bells, incense, and candles. The Mass was, as the theologians called it, effective *ex opere operato,* or by virtue of the work having been done. To take part in the Mass was almost the only instant that an ordinary person could ever hope to be pure and undefiled in the sight of God. Here was the sacred in the midst of the commonplace.

There can be little wonder that Luther approached his own first mass, where he himself was the celebrant, with a certain amount of anxiety. Even though the mass would be valid without respect to the status of the celebrant's soul, it was customary for priests to make a special confession prior to the service. Luther undoubtedly did so, but he likely remained highly agitated in the face of this holy moment. He himself told stories about his first mass, just as they were told about others performing the rite for the first time: that he became so nervous that he could hardly continue; that in saying the sacred words, "This is my body," he almost dropped the bread; and that in saying, "This is the new testament of my blood," he almost dropped the cup. He later admitted that he was so terrified by the words of the Eucharistic Prayer that he almost ran away from the altar. At this crucial moment it would have been odd indeed if his emotions had not run high, and it is certainly understandable that he may have been visibly shaken.

The first mass was an important event for the new priest's family, too. The date of Luther's first mass was rescheduled specifically so that Hans and several of his friends could attend. For the special day Luther's father brought a donation to the Black Cloister of 20 gold gulden. Only princes or the very wealthy could have afforded to give more.

A great banquet followed. This occasion was likely the first time that father and son had been together since their talk just before the thunderstorm and the vow. The conversation showed that some wounds had not yet healed. Luther returned to the old issue. He said something to his father like, "Well now, isn't this better for you than my being a lawyer?" Hans's reply was a verbal body-blow that Luther never forgot. "Have you not heard the commandment to honor your father and mother?"[5] Brother Martin had forsaken his family to become a priest.

A rigorous path

Having passed beyond the novitiate, Luther was now free to choose an even more rigorous path. Long periods with neither food nor drink, nights without sleep, bone-chilling cold with neither coat nor blanket to warm him—and self-flagellation—were common and even expected in the lives of serious monks. Almost a decade later, observers commented on Luther's ascetic appearance. He did not simply go through the motions of prayers, fasts, deprivations, and mortifications of the flesh, but pursued them earnestly. He sought to love God with all his heart, all his strength, and all his mind. To do so required rejecting the world, his family, and his very self. It is even possible that the illnesses which troubled him so much in his later years developed as a result of his strict denial of his own bodily needs.

In spite of the fact that Luther later vehemently rejected monasticism, he rarely bemoaned the years that he had spent as a monk. Many of his lifelong friends were monks, and were Augustinians as well. Moreover, he learned so much in the monastery that his life would be incomprehensible without taking these experiences into account.

There was, however, one part of his vocation that Luther came to despise: confession. Confession (and the acts of penance that followed) was absolutely essential to monastic life. It occurred daily or even more frequently. In this sacrament, the "religious," as monks and nuns were called, sought to purge themselves of their sins almost as quickly as they committed them. Doing so was part of their pursuit of holiness.

Despite popular tales about the lascivious lives of monks and nuns, they rarely (and if they were Observant Augustinians, almost never) engaged in obvious, outward sinning. At the very least, their lives were far too closely supervised for them to do so. Consequently, confession was conducted rather differently for them than it was for ordinary Christians who lived outside the cloister walls. Rather than questioning penitents about the particular misdeeds they had done, the confessor sought to uncover motives, emotions, thoughts, and even repressed feelings. These revealed the evil in the heart. And like the body, the heart, too, had to be purged of every impurity.

These rigorous examinations horrified Luther. After the fact, he would suddenly remember a thought or an emotion that contradicted his vocation and stained his heart. He knew that it would rightly bring the wrath of God down on him. These daily and sometimes hourly experiences were so terrifying that he once said, "When it is touched by this passing inundation of the eternal, the soul feels and drinks nothing but eternal punishment. . . ."[6]

Attacks of doubt

Luther's strong feelings about monastic confessional practices can be seen even in his *Address to the Christian Nobility* of 1520. In the midst of discussing reforms that the princes should carry out he declared that the abbot of a monastery "has no authority over secret sins, even if they should be the worst sins that ever are or can be found."[7] In retrospect Luther insisted that such probing into the heart lay too grievous a burden on sinners. In his own case, the awareness of secret sins nearly drove him to despair.

Yet the searching out of every failing was an integral part of monastic life. This process and the feelings that arose from it were so common that monks all over Europe had slang terms for it. They called the feeling of regret being *"in cloaca,"* literally, "in the toilet" or "in the dumps." The temptation to despair was called the *tentatio tristitiae.* Someone who was afflicted with it was said to have the *tentationes,* or a case of the scruples.

Anfechtung was what Luther later called this grinding sense of being utterly lost. By it he intended the idea of swarming attacks of doubt that could convince people that God's love was not for them. Later he considered this sense of being irredeemably evil to be the work of Satan, who sought to make a Christian's sins, doubts, and anxieties too much even for the grace of God. At such moments just the rustling of dried leaves in a forest sounded like the legions of hell coming to seize one's soul.

This tension between trying so hard to be holy and knowing that he was not led Luther's own confessor and spiritual guide to say on one occasion, "God is not angry with you, but you are angry with God." He urged Luther to "look at the cross" for the assurance he so desperately sought.[8] But whenever Luther did so, he could see only the sword coming from one side of Christ's countenance. He could not believe that his own efforts would ever please God or that there was ever enough in him to make the slightest contribution to his own salvation. Living as a monk and expending all his effort on the search for salvation simply made the prize all the more difficult to grasp.

Tensions within the order

Luther's ordination as a priest was nonetheless just the beginning of a very successful career as an Observant Augustinian. "Impeccable" was the word he later used to describe his life as a monk.[9] Apparently those who knew him best, his brothers in the Black Cloister, agreed. They regarded him highly enough to send him on a special mission to Rome. A serious matter needed to be negotiated, and the designated negotiator needed a companion whose character and good sense were above question.

In spite of the emphasis on holiness in 16th-century monasticism, there were worldly rivalries among the various orders. For example, the Augustinians made fun of the name of their most serious competitors, the Dominicans. Although they were named after their founder, St. Dominic, many of Luther's brothers claimed that the name came from the Latin phrase *Domini canes* and meant "the dogs of the Lord," or (more charitably) "the hounds of heaven."

Rivalries also developed within individual orders. The one that sent Luther to Rome was a struggle between the Observant Augustinians and other houses in the order that were less strict. The issues at stake between these two groups were complex. Basically, the Observants claimed to observe the original rule of the order in all its rigor while the nonobservant monasteries did not. The Observants also claimed the right to govern themselves as a separate entity within the larger order.

Organizational questions came quickly to the fore. Were the Observant monasteries to be brought under the authority of the vicar general for Germany, Johann von Staupitz, or were they to retain their relative independence? Both Staupitz and his superior, the general in Rome, were committed to bringing all the Augustinian monasteries under one central administration. They intended gradually to bring the more lax monasteries up to the standards set by the nine Observant ones. But the Observants did not see matters that way. They also suspected that their relatively greater wealth was the motivation behind the drive for unity. When Staupitz ruled that even the Black Cloister in Erfurt was to submit, the brothers decided to resist.

A trip to Rome

Luther was one of those from Erfurt chosen to discuss the matter with representatives of the other dissenting monasteries in a gathering that was probably held at Nuremberg in mid-fall 1510. Despite the clarity of Staupitz's order to them to submit, they decided to exercise their right to appeal the issue to their general in Rome. Luther was one of two monks the group chose to represent them. Approaching his 27th birthday and utterly unfamiliar with the ways of high ecclesiastical politics, he was the negotiator's travel companion. Luther was suddenly thrust into a much larger world.

The journey itself was an arduous undertaking. Food and lodging were not a problem; for these necessities he and his senior colleague could depend on the hospitality of other monasteries, both en route and in Rome itself. But during what proved to be an especially severe winter, they walked all the way to Rome from Nuremberg. There was snow even in Bologna, to say nothing of what must have greeted them as they labored through the Austrian Alps.

Rome in the early 16th century had lost few of its great, ancient monuments, at least by comparison with what it looks like now, after modern depredations and the infamous *sacco da Roma* of 1527, when Emperor Charles V turned his victorious troops loose on it. To be sure, the great buildings, monuments, statues, and the like were even then only reminiscent of the days of Caesar Augustus. Cows grazed on the grass that grew in the Coliseum.

Such things were of little concern to Luther and his companion; they had not come to study antiquities. Their trip was more pilgrimage than tour. To them, Rome was neither the city of the caesars and their legions nor the evocation of a glorious past. It was the home of hope for the present and the future. It was the center of the church, the residence of the bishop of Rome, the pope (or *papa*), the supreme pastor of the entire church, the man who stood on earth as the vicar of Christ himself.

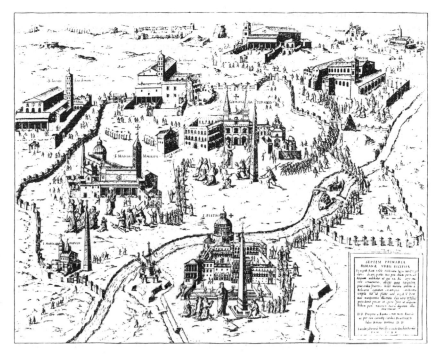

Rome with its main churches, the destination of pilgrims.

There was also the *scala sancta*, the very steps Christ climbed to the palace of Pontius Pilate. There were the bones of St. Peter and St. Paul. There were countless acts of devotion one could do to benefit one's own soul and those of many others, both living and deceased. Just by crawling up the *scala sancta* on his knees, Luther could free one of his loved ones from purgatory. He later said that the first sight of the holy city caused him to "throw myself on the ground and say, 'How blessed are you, Holy Rome!' "

The pope himself was likely not even in the city during the time of Luther's visit, and with good reason. Rome was not a very healthy place to live. The marvelous aqueducts and baths of classical times were now unusable, and there was no provision for public sanitation other than the gutters. It was common practice in the morning for people to throw the contents of their chamber pots out their upper windows and into the street. Pity the traveler who happened to be walking below!

On the other hand, house owners had to endure passersby who commonly relieved themselves against any convenient wall. On account of this practice, Luther insisted that the Romans were no better than dogs.

Europeans who had the means to travel often said that Rome was a "stinking cesspool." But this comment was intended to refer to its public morals as well as its sanitation system. Respectable men would not even allow their wives on the streets unless they were veiled and in the company of an armed guard.

Rome was the center of Latin Christendom. But it also raised spiritual doubts in the minds and souls of more than one pilgrim. And Erasmus of Rotterdam, who did not have much regard for pilgrimages of any kind, wrote (or collaborated with the writing of) a little book called *Julius Exclusus*, a satire that portrayed Pope Julius II as being excluded from heaven on account of his immoral life on earth.

In spite of this, one of the great opportunities for a visiting priest was to say a mass at one of the especially sacred chapels. Saturday after Saturday, Luther tried to do so, but the altars were so jammed with priests saying their own masses that he could not squeeze himself in. When he finally got his turn at the altar, there was an Italian priest behind him muttering, *"Passa, passa!"* "Get going! Move it!" [10] Luther had fasted the entire preceding day just so he could say mass. The irreverence of these admonitions must have been discouraging indeed.

But Luther was so zealous for the holy that he persisted and did all the things that a pilgrim in Rome was expected to do and yearned to do. He later commented that he ran through all the chapels, churches, shrines, catacombs, stairs, and all the rest "like a mad . . . saint." The state of his mind at this time is revealed by yet another comment: "I was so drunk, yes, submerged in the pope's dogmas that I would have been ready to murder all . . . who would take but a syllable from obedience to the pope." [11]

Pope Leo X, a Medici (by Raffaelo Santi).

Luther knew that regardless of the moral or spiritual status of a priest or the proprietors of a shrine, the objective reality of the church and God's grace remained. As mediated through the church, grace changed ordinary human deeds into works that were meritorious for salvation. It really did not matter whether the mass Luther said was hurried and perhaps therefore not sincerely intended. An eight-minute mass was nevertheless a mass, and it still had definable spiritual benefits. So did all of his "mad" running about in the most sacred of cities.

The business of the Observant Augustinians did not, however, work out quite as hoped. In fact, the general of the order, whose policy it had been in the first place to combine the administration of the monasteries, finally refused to hear the case. The man's name was Egidio of Viterbo, and he was learned and upright. A few years later he was also a participant in the abortive Fifth Lateran Council. Called to reform the church "in head and members" (as the common phrase had it), this council closed in 1517 with no more than pious exhortations for all to do better with the affairs of the church. One observer at an earlier council made a comment that could also have applied to this one: "I have not the slightest hope for a general reform of the church either at present or in the near future, for subjects lack good will, and among the prelates reform meets with ill will."[12] Egidio himself sought to reform where he could and what he could, and one of the things he did was to refuse to allow individual Augustinian monasteries, even the Observants in Erfurt, to go their own ways. They were all to be obedient to the church.

Luther and his superior trudged back to Germany. They struggled once more through the snows of the Alps, to Augsburg, to Nuremberg, and from there, after more meetings, to Erfurt. Once the brethren had been informed of the general's decision, they were each faced with their own decision. Would they now submit to Staupitz, or would they continue to resist?

Transfer to Wittenberg

For the first time, Luther found himself in conflict over a public issue. His brothers in the Black Cloister wanted to mount yet another appeal, if only to delay the administrative merger. But he would have

Wittenberg in the year 1550.

nothing to do with it. Luther decided that as a matter of conscience he had to submit to Staupitz, and his good friend, John Lang, agreed. The majority of their brothers in Erfurt were furious. If Luther and Lang were in such agreement with Staupitz, then they could go live with him in the Augustinian house in Wittenberg.

Lang arrived in Wittenberg before mid-August 1511, and after he had settled into the monastery, he entered the small university there. Luther joined him by the end of the summer. Even after a few years had passed, Luther was still defending himself from the slanders of his brothers in Erfurt. He was later forced, as he put it, to "shut the mouths" of more than one monk who was still angry with him for having submitted to the authority of Staupitz.

Wittenberg was by no means a pleasant place to live. Luther had wanted to be a peacemaker and to be loyal to his own house as well as to his superior. But he was forced to choose between the two, and as a consequence he suffered what amounted to exile. Three years earlier he had been sent to Wittenberg temporarily to lecture on Aristotle's *Ethics* while another professor in the university's arts faculty was on leave. Now, as he traveled into exile, he was well aware of the drudgery, indeed the near barbarity that awaited him in this small town in north-central Germany.

In the early 16th century Wittenberg may have had all of 2000 inhabitants, many of whom earned their living by brewing heavy beer, much of which they drank. The surrounding territory was nearly flat and consisted of unproductive, sandy soil with none of the meandering streams and lush vegetation of Erfurt to the southwest. By mid-century the town courtyard would surround an impressive building in which the city council met. But in 1511 it had not yet been built. When Luther arrived, the city church stood at one end of the square and the famous Castle Church was a few blocks away at the other. To this day, neither is much to look at. In Luther's day the monks' residence and church were genuine sinkholes. One had scarcely been built, and the other was propped up with wooden supports. Luther remarked that the worship area looked like the stall where Jesus was born, above all in its "lowliness." When John Lang left the monastery years later, one of the reasons he gave was that it was bad for his health to stay.

No one had anything good to say about the city's inhabitants, either. Many observers remarked that the town market was but a mudhole to accommodate the Wittenbergers' drinking and brawling. But Luther dutifully went to "little Wittenberg," [13] as he called it, and to its version of an Augustinian monastery. Being obedient had earned him an apparently bleak future.

THREE

A Student of Theology

Only occasional shafts of light penetrate the mists that shroud Luther's life from 1505 until his exile to the monastic house in Wittenberg in 1511. Most of even these glimpses are possible solely because years after the fact Luther himself commented on his life as a monk.

Many of these remarks focused on his dark nights of the soul and his deep and painful spiritual struggles. These are the stuff of high drama. But Luther was certainly not the only monk or nun who suffered them. What *did* set Luther apart was his special combination of zeal and intellect, which his superiors soon recognized. While he was still in Erfurt, and with no thought that he would ever go anywhere else, they ordered him to pursue the academic study of theology.

The queen of the sciences

Theology was such a serious and important business in the Middle Ages that it was commonly called "the queen of the sciences." Even pictorial representations of the university showed *theologia* standing at the very top of the tower of learning. Theology was especially important to monks, who had founded their own schools so they could pursue religious knowledge well before there was such a thing as a university. Even in the Dark Ages, the Rule of St. Benedict required every monk to read at least one book a year. As books became more widely available, although still frightfully expensive, monasteries and cathedrals began to designate some of their members as teachers and

Frontispiece from Margarita Philosophica noua . . . , *a compendium of the seven liberal arts.*

to assign them the task of improving the brothers' minds and thereby their souls. Only the most able, diligent, and dependable brothers were called to this work of learning and passing on the very mysteries of the faith.

It was a great honor for Luther to be set on this path. It also had an enormous impact on his development. The spiritual struggles of this devout and conscientious monk suddenly took on an objective character. They were no longer just a personal agony, a matter between himself and his confessor whose resolution lay in various kinds of spiritual exercises. Now the *tentatio tristitiae* or temptation to despair that so wracked Luther became also a puzzle whose resolution could be sought through the disciplined methods of theological investigation, much like the approach taken by a mathematician in solving a difficult equation. Luther gave everything he had to this emotional and intellectual struggle with God. For him the study of theology was not just another obligation. It was a zealous search for the truth.

But at this point the mists swirl in once again, obscuring the view and making it impossible to know exactly what Luther studied and exactly what he thought of it. There were many different paths he could have followed in developing the religious convictions that he would take with him to Wittenberg. It is reasonably certain that he followed one path in particular, and it is essential to examine it in some detail. But he was doubtless aware of many of the others, so they must be understood as well. Only then is it possible to penetrate the mists and discern something of how Luther thought and what he felt during these years.

A modern seminary is something of a cross between a university and the monastery in which Luther actually began his theological studies. The Black Cloister was only a few paces from the rooms of the University of Erfurt, and some of the professors lived within its walls. But as a beginner, Luther was not allowed to go outside the grounds of the cloister to pursue his studies. Rather, he labored first in its spiritual safety and familiar confines, where he and his fellows could be helped and guided in their intellectual and spiritual growth. Here, as in other aspects of their lives, their progress was closely observed, and then decisions were made as to who would study in the world outside.

It was a carefully-planned curriculum, conducted in a monastery that was noted for its learning. The director of studies was himself a professor at the university. Like other beginners, Luther started by reading carefully-selected portions of the Bible under a leader's direction. As was the custom, he probably read not so much for the purpose of understanding the Bible's doctrinal teachings as to provide a point of departure for his own daily prayers and meditation. "What does this mean for me?" he was constantly urged to ask. Having satisfied his mentor, he then moved on to the *Sentences* of Peter Lombard, whose seemingly contradictory statements drawn from the Bible and the teachers of the church constituted the beginning textbook for all students of theology in the Middle Ages. During his studies for the priesthood, he had likely already read Gabriel Biel's *Exposition of the Canon of the Mass*.

Soon Luther became one of those chosen to leave the confines of the cloister to study and attend lectures at the theological faculty of the university. There he encountered the teachings of the more recent theologians, all well-known in the church at large. Biel likely remained the most notable among them. From him and others Luther learned the theological foundations for the religion he practiced as a young man and one rationale for the spiritual life he was leading as a monk. How very enthusiastically he made these ideas his own is evident from a remark he made in 1509 while teaching Aristotle in the arts faculty at Wittenberg. Rather than study philosophy, he declared, he would much rather study theology, for it "penetrates to the kernel of the nut, the germ of the wheat, and the marrow of the bones."[1]

Luther devoured the books of these contemporary doctors of the church so hungrily that he could quote them from memory, even late in life. The texts he was actually studying would appear strange to a modern reader. Except for line drawings, these books looked rather like treatises in geometry; the discussion was put in terms of theses, antitheses, and conclusions, and proceeded according to the strictest rules of logic. Luther's university training had prepared him well for his new studies. He was already thoroughly familiar with Aristotelian logic and with the assumptions and methods that lay at the heart of university life in the Middle Ages. All that differed were the subjects and the sources he probed. He proceeded rapidly.

Via moderna

The edifice of scholastic theology was intellectually and spiritually as immense as Erfurt's cathedral. Erasmus, among others, was inclined to dismiss the whole structure on the grounds that it was unbiblical, contrary to common sense, and obsessed with mere technicalities.

Erasmus of Rotterdam (by Dürer).

Nothing could be further from the truth. The scholastic theologians posed questions of immediate relevance to all Christians. They turned first to the Scriptures and then to the tradition of the church for their answers. And they offered conclusions that were logically consistent with one another.

Luther might have studied in one of several different traditions among the scholastic theologians. But at Erfurt, the *via moderna,* or "modern way" of Occam and Biel held sway. It lay so decisively at the heart of the curriculum that Luther learned all its philosophical presuppositions while he was a student in the Faculty of Arts. Although even these thinkers differed on many points, the theologians who called themselves *moderni* agreed on one central issue. God created this world the way it is, and therefore decided to reveal his will to ordinary mortals within its specific boundaries. Because God was all-powerful, they granted that he could have created any world he wished. As the famous debate question put it, God could have chosen to give souls to asses and not to human beings. But he didn't. Therefore, the important questions were not about the eternal nature of God, the correspondence of human reason with the will of God, or any such philosophical issues. Rather, the critical problem concerned God's purposes in the here and now. As Luther later phrased it, "God must therefore be left to himself in his own majesty, for in this regard we have nothing to do with him, nor has he willed that we have anything to do with him."[2]

Here was the starting point for Luther's teachers, and therefore it was likely Luther's starting point as well. Once this foundation had been agreed to, only one important question remained: What were this awesome God's intentions? What did God plan to do with human beings? In particular, how could a God who was truly righteous be cajoled into being merciful to miserable, weak, and transient human beings who continually violated his laws?

A very important assumption lay beneath this line of reasoning. It made no sense to speculate as to whether God was reasonable, just, or good. God was God, morally right and beyond question. Indeed, God's basic characteristic was to have awesome power, and his righteousness flowed directly from it. Luther's teachers seized on this theme from the Old Testament, and for the most part they disregarded questions about the goodness of God or God's omnipotence. These characteristics were not at issue for them. Whatever God is, is good, they declared, because God is God. God is the law, much as a presiding judge is the law in an earthly courtroom. Human beings must abide by whatever God might decree. Righteousness was therefore just as much a quality or characteristic of God as holding an academic degree is a characteristic of a professor.

This picture of an all-righteous God had another, human, side to it. Just as righteousness was a part of God, sin belonged to human beings. They constantly violated God's laws. Some of them added to this sin by blaming God for having established his laws in the first place. Luther understood this idea perfectly. His teachers were describing his own experience.

Luther's teachers also stated that in addition to being righteous, God was merciful. Therefore, by the side of *iustitia,* or righteousness, God also possessed *misericordia,* or, literally, a grieving heart. Here was the theological position that underlay the artistic depiction of Jesus on the cross with a sword coming from one side of his head and a lily from the other.

To satisfy a righteous God

In this context, one practical theological issue overrode all others in its importance and immediacy. How could this righteous God be begged, cajoled, or propitiated into being merciful to individual sinners? How could this righteous God who tolerated no violation of the law turn his merciful side to me? Then, as now, the theologians looked to the Scriptures for answers.

One answer was offered by Jesus' conversation with the lawyer: "You shall love the Lord your God with all your heart, and with all your soul, and with all your mind. . . . And . . . you shall love your neighbor as yourself" (Matt. 22:37,39). The command was simple enough. Yet rarely, if ever, did anyone love God or their neighbor utterly unselfishly and with complete devotion. Human beings were only capable of partial love, that is, a love that began with love of self. This love was directed only secondarily to the loved one. Even in the family, as Luther well knew, a father's love could be colored by ambition for his son. At its base, all human love was an erotic love that sought to possess rather than, in the first instance, to give. This greatest of human good deeds was therefore sinful, not because it was evil in and of itself, but because the intentions of the doer were impure. The medieval theologians knew that all human motives were mixed. Whatever deeds flowed from these motives could not, therefore, satisfy the demands of a righteous God.

Another possible answer was repentance. Those who recognized the terrible sins in their lives, sins both of omission and commission, could repent of them and be saved. Was this not the preaching of John the Baptist? But again, human beings were capable of only partial repentance and not normally of a complete act of perfect contrition. Once more the problem was the centrality of the self. Anyone who knew that the fires of hell awaited an unrepentant life would be wise to repent. But doing so was not contrition. The repentance of which John and Jesus spoke came from a deep awareness of having offended God and a genuine desire to make amends for God's sake. But human repentance sprang from a desire to avoid punishment, whether in the future or in the here and now. This act, too, was selfish, because it was done not for God's sake but for the sake of oneself. It therefore accomplished nothing for the purposes of salvation.

Then there was the answer of faith. "He who believes and is baptized will be saved," said Jesus (Mark 16:16). Baptism was no problem; in those days everyone, except Jews, was baptized. But a sinner also had to believe. Anyone might grant that God was sovereign, or even assent that Jesus was the Christ and that the Holy Spirit lived and moved in this world. But assenting to these true doctrines of the church was not enough. Jesus referred even to his disciples as "men of little faith" (Matt. 8:26). The faith that was necessary was the faith of Abraham, the one who so trusted God's promises that he would do anything God commanded, even though the command to sacrifice his son Isaac appeared to contradict the promise to establish a new nation through him. This kind of faith was so rare that only the saints themselves exhibited it, and not at all times. Human beings were capable of no more than partial and weak faith, and this faith was not good enough.

The difficult problem that presented itself, then, was that human beings were so weak, partial, and prone to sin and error that they could never offer anything of themselves that might please this righteous God who insisted on absolute obedience. Every good deed that a person could do always fell short of the mark; there was always some element of human selfishness involved. A man complimented his wife or brought her a gift because he wished, in part, that she would love him in return. A child confessed wrongdoing to a parent not solely out of love for the parent but, at least in part, to avoid punishment. These theologians were no ivory tower intellectuals. They knew human nature, both from experience and from the Scriptures.

There was truly no way out, no exit, no relief from the horrors of these observations. Even those who lived "a peaceable and godly life" and earned the honor and respect of their neighbors could never merit the mercy of God. Love of self lay behind almost every human deed. And even though some deeds might, in themselves, be considered good, there were never enough of them. The human balance sheet always showed a deficit.

A spiritual contract

Yet it was at just this point that Luther's teachers offered a way out. In a very modern fashion, they observed that almost all people had a conscience that led them to feel guilt. This sense of having done wrong was a leftover spark of the divine. This spark they called the *synteresis,* and they found it in almost all human actions. By extension, whoever loved self, spouse, and child was nonetheless loving them in spite of human frailty. Granted, this was a partially good deed, but it *was* a good deed. More importantly, there was always the conscience, which convicted people of doing, thinking, or feeling evil, and prompted them to decide to do better next time. Even the most notorious sinners could at least repent for the purpose of saving their own skins, and such repentance was at least a beginning. Anyone of sound mind could assent to the true teachings of the church, if only because the evidence was plain for all to see. Even after the fall, therefore, there remained an ember of the divine fire that could be fanned, partially good behavior that could be encouraged, a decent disposition of the mind that could be enhanced. No one could attain the perfection of God, but people could be improved simply by appealing to the spark of goodness that lay within them.

However, such improvement remained insufficient for the Christian to persevere and find salvation. Late medieval theologians were especially emphatic on this point. They knew very well that St. Paul had insisted that salvation came from grace alone, "lest any man should boast" (Eph. 2:9). They knew that no matter how holy, no matter how "Christian" or "spiritual" one's outward life might be, sin still reigned within. There was no spiritual self-improvement course that would ever impress God.

Yet there remained one more potential source for this missing ingredient. Luther's teachers pointed out that the church mediated the grace of Jesus Christ which, if added to human initiative, could complete the partial work of human beings and make it pleasing to God. More specifically, the church provided the seven sacraments through which human actions were clothed in divine grace. After birth there was Baptism, later there was confirmation, for those who chose it there was marriage, and for all there was confession and penance, the Mass, and, at death, extreme unction. For those who wished to do more and be absolutely certain of their salvation, there were holy orders and the life of self-denial.

The theology that Luther was taught therefore amounted to a contract between God and human beings. God graciously initiated the contract for the sake of Christians, the elect. God did so by creating a world that included the church and human beings who strove for self-preservation. In this way, grace was protected by locating it both in the church and in the makeup of human nature. At the same time, a place was found for human initiative. Individual Christians had active roles to play in their own salvation. All that was necessary was to fulfill the human side of the contract.

This theology made such good sense and was so pervasive in Luther's day that everyone encountered it. It appeared not only in depictions of God's righteousness and mercy, but also in a slogan that at least university students knew by heart: "God will not refuse grace to those who do what is within them." It appeared in sermons for lay people as well. One preacher commonly exhorted his congregation, "Do what is within you! Use well your natural powers and whatever special gifts God has given you!"[3] Salvation would follow. Christians could earn the grace of God simply by doing their best.

People naturally acted on their fear of being lost and condemned, and many pursued holiness through the church as well as through moral self-improvement. They did not do so because some hocus-pocus had been foisted on them by a greedy and power-hungry church. Their actions had a strong theological underpinning that in turn rested on careful observation of human nature, adherence to the teachings of the Scriptures and the traditions of the church, and assiduous exercise of both reason and common sense.

By and large, what the theologians taught, the preachers preached, and what the preachers preached, the people did. For the sake of his own earliest students, Luther once summarized the life of a Christian as consisting of deeds that were "good according to their substance" but "neither qualitatively nor quantitatively" sufficient for salvation.[4] The grace that came from the church completed these incomplete deeds, thoughts, and yearnings. Luther did much more to secure his own salvation than did most others. But even when he engaged in so much self-denial that his health never recovered from it, he was only doing what he was taught to do—what some of the best minds of the age thought to be both prudent and effective.

Other traditions

This theology is what Luther learned as a student. Nonetheless, it existed side-by-side with other traditions which he also encountered later when he was a professor who continued to study. There was an immense variety in the religious thought of the late Middle Ages. There were first the mystics, among them figures such as Thomas à Kempis and Johannes Tauler, who held that salvation was to be achieved by meditations in the quiet places of the soul, and not so much by outward works such as going to mass or confession. There were the humanists, and Erasmus in particular, who insisted that many of the practices of the common people amounted to so much superstition that they did no one any good at all. For him the true Christian knight fought the fight of faith by reading good literature, above all the Bible, and by ignoring both the formalities of ecclesiastical practices and what he called the barbaric quibbling of Luther's own teachers. Finally, there were the heretics, people such as the Spiritual Franciscans and men such as Jan Hus, who declared that the church itself, in particular the papacy, had to return to apostolic poverty and have no dominion or power in this world. Almost everyone, including Luther's teachers, agreed that the church and religious life in general desperately required "reform in head and members." Some, such as Hus and the Spiritual Franciscans, found themselves condemned for their views and actions. Even so, they all agreed with Luther's teachers on one critical point: Christians must do something to persevere and be saved.

Johannes Tauler

Of these "prereformers," so-called because they sought reform well before Luther appeared, two were best-known to him. The first was Tauler, whose *German Theology* Luther later edited for publication and

Eyn deutsch Theologia. das ist

Eyn edles Buchleyn/von rechtem vorstand/was Adam vnd Christus sey/vnd wie Adam yn vns sterben/vnd Christus erstenfall.

Title page from Luther's edition of A German Theology, *which he attributed to Johannes Tauler.*

who was a representative of German mysticism. There can be no question but that Tauler wished the church, or at least its individual members, to be reformed. But the special form of holiness that he sought was thoroughly traditional. For him, the soul had its origins in God. Human beings thus possessed a part of themselves that was truly divine. To be genuinely holy, they therefore needed to find what was truly divine in themselves and so exercise and purify it that they would become ever more like God.

In this sense Tauler and the mystics were not much different from many modern spiritual advisers who urge Christians to take from their days special moments for prayer, meditation, and Bible reading. From this effort, it is said, individuals will reap spiritual benefits. Tauler maintained that all Christians could deny themselves at least a little. Everyone—even if they were not a monk or nun—could engage in special and frequent spiritual exercises. These included confessing one's sins to a priest and going to mass, but also much more, and it was the "much more" that carried genuine spiritual benefits. Rather than go on a pilgrimage, which might bring its own temptations, true pilgrims would reserve special moments of quiet when, removed from the hustle and bustle of the world around them, they could pray, meditate, and contemplate the magnificence and purity of God. In this way their own souls would be elevated from the earthly and the vulgar to God. By thus ignoring the real world around them, even ordinary Christians with work, family, and civil obligations could find and achieve sanctified lives. Having done so, their souls would find at least a partial peace because they were returning to their origin in the one true God. In a humble manner that befitted his understanding of the way to salvation, Tauler always remained true to the church, but was still critical of mere outward observances. He advised that they be supplemented by an interior, personal spirituality. During one period of his life, Luther found this kind of spirituality very attractive because it turned the pilgrim inward and away from externalities.

Desiderius Erasmus of Rotterdam

Erasmus was a rather different spirit. He came from the Low Countries and achieved fame as the most acclaimed scholar of his time. He also bitterly attacked the stupidity of the clergy, the obscurantism of the professors, and the superstition of the common people. One of his methods was satire. To his good friend Thomas More he dedicated his famous book *In Praise of Folly*. There he excoriated the veneration of the saints, including the special honor paid to the Virgin, "as if it is manners these days to place the mother above the son." He declared that there were three concentric circles by which Christendom was governed, each more important than the other. These were the ordinary laity, the princes, and the prelates. One would expect that as one neared the common center of these circles, each circle would be more holy and lead a more exemplary Christian life than the other. Unfortunately, he added, the reverse was the case. It was clear to him that the goddess Folly reigned everywhere. "Perhaps," Erasmus commented, "we have not praised Folly entirely foolishly."[5]

Some of Erasmus's colleagues chided him on the grounds that conditions in the church were so terrible that tears and not laughter were the proper response. But Erasmus was entirely serious, and behind the mocking lay fundamentally the same approach to the Christian life that Luther had found in his scholastic teachers and the church in general. This tendency can be seen in another of Erasmus's books, *The Handbook of a Christian Knight*. Here he couched his view of the Christian's pilgrimage in terms of advice to a knight's wife, who fervently wished that her husband would achieve salvation even though he spent his life as a soldier. Erasmus advised that the knight avail himself of the sacraments of the church. But he said it was far more important for him to see to the inner disposition of his soul and the deeds of love he could do for others. He should certainly attend mass, but above all he should memorize some psalms and recite them daily. Then, by being in direct contact with divine truth, his life would be changed and, ever so gradually, he would become a person whose life pleased God.

Neither Tauler nor Erasmus was a theologian in the strict sense of the term. As Erasmus himself wrote, "I do not mean to condemn modern theologians, but I am merely pointing out that in view of our purpose, namely a more practical piety, they are hardly to be recommended."[6] Both Erasmus and Tauler had grave doubts about whether it was possible or useful to know all the doctrines that Luther was learning from his teachers. Yet neither departed from the fundamental idea that guided Luther's mentors: salvation was a prize that had to be won, at least partially, through efforts here on earth.

Erasmus's choice of a knight as his image of the Christian life is telling. True Christians were warriors against all the forces of death and the devil, and their reward would depend on how well they fought the good fight. Even his choice of a title for his little book is revealing. The word *handbook* is only a handy substitution for the Greek word *enchiridion* used by Erasmus. Literally, *enchiridion* means a short dagger, which prudent Greeks carried with them for self-defense. With this title Erasmus was therefore saying that here was a little book to which the Christian warrior could have quick recourse in time of need. Behind this idea lay the further notion, agreed to by all, that Satan and his minions were constantly roaring about this world, ready to gobble up souls the moment they let down their guard. Moreover, if Christians would but stay at the ready, they would be protected by the grace of God.

Years of silence

Regardless of their particular point of view or method, every authority Luther consulted or could have consulted agreed that the prize of salvation and eternal life required work and constant vigilance. Some, such as his teachers at the monastery and university, placed chief emphasis on the mediation of the church through the seven sacraments. Others, like Tauler, insisted on the primacy of an interior, and essentially private, spiritual life. Still others, such as Erasmus, declared that spiritual growth was basically a moral issue in which the right disposition of the heart, generated by the reading of pious literature, would in turn generate a life of love for one's neighbor. But on the principal question of how one comes to salvation, all were in agreement. In one way or another, salvation came by fanning the spark of goodness that was left even in the most reprobate. If people just did their best, God would be gracious. But they had to do their best.

These were years of silence for Luther, years in which the walls of the monastery and his studies hid him from prying eyes and ears. It is nonetheless clear that he not only studied what was set before him but also that he believed it. In a sermon delivered much later he described his spiritual struggles during this period: "I lost hold of Christ the Savior and comforter and made of him a stock-master and hangman over my poor soul. . . . We have obtained the light. But when I became a doctor I did not know."[7]

His agreement with the dominant theology of his time also shows through in the notes that he put into the margins of some of his books and, later, the notes that he made for his own lectures as a beginning professor. Throughout, it is clear that he lived the life that was expected of him as an Observant Augustinian. And he learned to think about his religion by using the assumptions and methods of the best minds of his day.

Here some straightforward chronology is illuminating. Luther began his theological studies sometime during the spring of 1507. He then went to Wittenberg to lecture in the arts faculty and to study in the theological faculty during the winter of 1508. He stayed until October 1509, when he returned to Erfurt. The journey to Rome consumed the winter of 1510. Prior to that, he continued his studies in Erfurt and gave beginning theological lectures to a small group of monks in the cloister. Beginning in April 1511, he was exiled to the Augustinian house in Wittenberg, where he continued his studies and was finally prevailed on by Staupitz to become a professor of theology. Therefore he was primarily a monk and a student during these years, even though he had been given some teaching duties. Both his spiritual and intellectual progress were monitored very closely.

Luther was educated within a world of rich religious thought. But all its variety amounted to variations on one common theme—everyone had to work at achieving salvation. In addition, there is direct evidence that Luther agreed with at least one of the central theological ideas he was taught, namely the idea of the *synteresis,* the spark of goodness held to exist in everyone. In two early sermons of 1510 and 1512 he insisted that everyone had a double spark of goodness, one of the will and one of the mind. He declared that no one lacked a natural, God-given inclination to seek God and his glory. In addition, he said, everyone had the power to distinguish between good and evil. No one was so reprobate, so utterly lost, that they could not recognize when they had sinned and know what would have been the right thing to do, to think, or to feel. Human beings therefore had within them both a yearning for God and a guide for how to reach God. It was only human weakness that made the task impossible, if unaided. The solution was to be found in confession, penance, and the Mass.

The search for peace

When Luther looked back on these years, he commented, "If anyone could have gained heaven as a monk, I was surely among them."[8] In addition to his studies and monastic life, he was also given administrative chores among the Wittenberg Augustinians. Indeed, he complained that he scarcely had enough time to perform the required daily prayers and meditations. But he still had some 18 months during which, removed from the doings of a large and important house like the one in Erfurt, he could devote himself to improving the status of his soul and mind.

During these years Luther discovered that true religion was far more than just the proper inclination of the heart and earnest attempts to work out his salvation. But every time he tried to fan his own spark of goodness, he found that all he was doing was focusing his attention on himself. From his own teachers he knew that to think of himself was to be in his most sinful state. How then could he "do what was within him" without yielding to the basest of motives, the desire to save his own skin? How could he possibly confess every one of his sins when he knew that he did so only for the purpose of currying the favor of a righteous God who would surely condemn him for them? Every act of confession therefore became yet another sin. The sincerity of the confession and of the acts of penance that followed was always in question. And if he himself questioned his motives, how could they not have been more than dubious in the mind of a God who knew all and was always right?

To all outward appearances, Luther was a highly successful monk. He was promoted to positions of responsibility and directed to become a priest, preacher, and theologian. He was a talented man who did everything expected of him and more. But in the midst of all this success, Luther made the horrifying discovery that the world of late medieval religion—from its theology to its preaching to its monastic life and to the actual practice of ordinary Christians—was not working for him. About to become a professor and a teacher of the church, he had still found no peace.

PART TWO

The Genesis of the Reformer

FOUR

The Maturing Professor

But it will be the death of me!" Thus did Luther respond when his superior, Staupitz (who was by then also his closest confidant), told him that it was time he became a professor of theology at the University of Wittenberg and preacher at the Castle Church. The conversation took place as the two men were sitting under the pear tree in the monastery's courtyard. Staupitz replied, "Are you not aware that our Lord God has much important business to conduct? For these things he needs wise and learned counselors up there too."[1] Luther was to stop taking himself so seriously.

Nonetheless, Staupitz did not easily have his way. The second time he proposed that Luther take his doctorate and the professorship, the 29-year-old monk replied with more than a dozen reasons why such a thing was utterly beyond possibility. Sometime in late September 1511, or about a month after Luther's arrival in Wittenberg, Staupitz became adamant. "My dear fellow," he sputtered, "surely you do not wish to set yourself up as wiser than the whole congregation [of Augustinians] and the Fathers!" Staupitz was exercising his authority and very nearly ordering him to take up this new calling. Luther's own testimony was, "I, Dr. Martin, have been called to this work, and I was compelled to become a doctor without any initiative of my own but out of pure obedience."[2]

An unforgiving conscience

Staupitz probably succeeded in the end not only because he had the right to give Luther orders but also because Luther felt deeply indebted to him. The preceding months had been difficult: "For I hoped I might find peace of conscience with fasts, prayer, and the vigils with which I miserably afflicted my body, but the more I sweated it out like this, the less peace and tranquillity I knew."[3] In this turmoil, Luther came to Staupitz so frequently to confess his doubts, misgivings, sins, and outright hatred of a righteous God that Staupitz once commanded him to go and commit a real sin.

"Pay attention," Staupitz said. "You want to be without sin, but you don't have any real sins anyway. Christ is the forgiveness of awful sins, like the murder of one's

Johann Staupitz, Luther's superior, confessor, and friend.

parents, public vices, blasphemy, adultery, and the like. These are real sins. . . . You must not inflate your halting, artificial sins out of proportion!" But Luther's conscience was an unforgiving monster. "I tried to live according to the rule and I used to be contrite, to confess and enumerate my sins; I often repeated my confession and zealously performed my required penance. And yet my conscience would never give me assurance, but I was always doubting and said, 'You did not perform that correctly. You were not contrite enough. You left that out of your confession.' " The wise counselor probably knew how much his words meant to the troubled young monk. "If it had not been for Dr. Staupitz," Luther once commented, "I would have sunk into hell."[4]

Now it was Luther's turn to be useful to Staupitz, who was himself strained almost to the breaking point. Far too many demands were being placed on his time and he had no hope of fulfilling them all. As vicar-general of the Augustinians he was constantly negotiating with Rome and traveling from monastery to monastery throughout his territory. He was also much in demand as a preacher and teacher, so much so that he was rarely in Wittenberg.

This situation was embarrassing because Staupitz, or someone under his supervision in the Augustinian order, was obligated to Elector Frederick the Wise of Saxony to give the lectures on the Bible in the theological faculty of the elector's brand-new university. With the professorship went also the duty of teaching in the monastery and preaching at the Castle Church. It was all too much for Staupitz. For some time he had failed to complete the required lectures at the university and frequently he was unable even to be present. But here was Luther, both bright and loyal, and one who had completed all the academic requirements that prepared him to receive the doctorate and become a professor. There was little wonder that Staupitz should be so persistent, or that Luther finally agreed, even if he thought it would kill him.

The 16th century was an age that loved ceremony, and Staupitz had already spent an immense sum to celebrate the conferral of four other doctorates on members of the order. As a result, he had nothing left with which to pay for Luther's promotion. So he had to persuade Elector Frederick to provide the necessary funds himself. A year passed before the reluctant elector agreed, and then he did so only under the condition that "for the rest of his life, Martinus will be responsible for the lectureship on the Bible in the theological faculty" at Wittenberg. Frederick was not going to be cheated again.

The doctor's cap

Luther received the special license that made him a candidate for the doctorate on October 4, 1512. Five days later he traveled to Leipzig to collect the fee for his promotion from the elector's representatives. The ceremonies began on the evening of October 18 and continued the next morning at 7:00 A.M. Luther took an oath on the Bible to teach only true doctrine and to report all who promoted falsehood. Then the woolen doctor's cap (in which he was most often pictured) was placed on his head and the silver doctor's ring on his finger. Three days later he was formally received into the Senate of the Faculty of Theology. He began his lectures, perhaps on Genesis, the following Monday, October 25, at 7:00 A.M.

"I could use two secretaries," Luther wrote a friend. "I do almost nothing during the day but write letters. . . . I am a preacher at the monastery, a reader at meals . . . a parish preacher, director of studies, supervisor of eleven monasteries, superintendent of the fish pond at Litzkau, referee of a squabble at Torgau, lecturer on Paul, a collector of materials for a commentary on the Psalms, and then, as I said, I am overwhelmed with letters. I rarely have time for the required daily prayers and for saying mass, not to mention my own temptations with the world, the flesh, and the devil. You see how lazy I am."[5] Later he commented that he was often so tired at the end of a day that he would simply fall into bed and wrap himself in sheets that had not been washed for months.

Yet in the midst of these exhausting responsibilities, Luther worked a revolution in everything he had been taught. "I did not learn my theology all at once," he said, "but had to search deeper for it, where my temptations took me."[6] His life between 1512 and 1517 was full of distractions, but through it all he searched and probed and pressed on until he resolved the issues that were before him. Late in life he urged his readers to "keep in mind that . . . I was all alone and one of those who, as St. Augustine says of himself, have become proficient by writing and teaching. I was not one of those who from nothing suddenly becomes the topmost, though they are nothing and have neither labored nor been tempted nor become experienced, but have with one look at the Scriptures exhausted their entire spirit."[7] In fact, he referred back to Augustine frequently during these years. Like the mature pear tree in the monastery courtyard, Luther the professor also grew slowly to maturity. And he finally bore fruit in a new understanding of how a Christian can stand in the presence of a righteous God.

Luther was assigned a small room above the connecting arch in the monastery where he could prepare for his obligations to his students. His specific task was to lecture on the Bible, particularly on the Old Testament, but in consultation with his colleagues he could choose the book he would treat during any particular term. Once a professor had made this decision, he would usually request that the university printer prepare a special edition of the proposed text. These contained extra-wide margins so that he could conveniently jot down whatever it was he intended to say about each passage. Likewise, his students could make notes on what they heard in the margins of their copies.

These notations of both professor and students are the tracks Luther

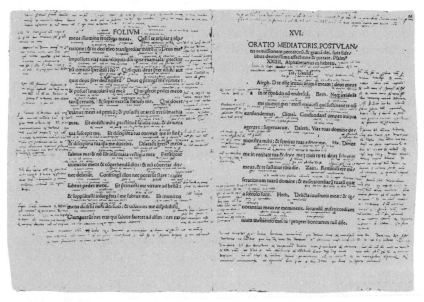

A page from Luther's psalter with the notes he wrote for his lectures.

left as he painstakingly resolved his religious questions. Nothing remains of his presumed lectures on Genesis during his first year as a professor. But then the track becomes clear. There are highly revealing notes for the lectures that followed on the Psalms (1513–1515), Romans (1515–1516), Galatians (1516–1517), Hebrews (1517–1518), and once again on the Psalms (1518–1521). It is possible to see his mind at work throughout. The theology he had been taught was his starting point.

The righteousness of God

Both the lectures and Luther's own reminiscences reveal that he was preoccupied first and foremost with the problem of the righteousness of God. About a year before his death he wrote, "I hated that word [at Rom. 1:17], 'the righteousness of God,' which, according to the custom and the use of all teachers, I had been taught to understand in the philosophical sense with respect to the formal or active righteousness, as they called it, with which God is righteous and punishes the unrighteous sinner." This understanding of the righteousness of God lay at the root of his own search for holiness. "Though I lived as a monk without reproach," he continued, "I felt, with the most disturbed conscience imaginable, that I was a sinner before God. I did not love, indeed I hated the righteous God who punishes sinners and secretly (if not blasphemously and certainly with great grumbling) I was angry with God, and said, 'As if indeed it is not enough that miserable sinners, eternally lost through eternal sin, are crushed by every kind of calamity by the law of the Ten Commandments, without having God add pain to pain by the gospel and also by the gospel's threatening us with his righteousness and wrath!'"[8]

When Luther read Paul's statement that the righteous live by faith, he concluded that he had to be righteous in order to be given faith. He was not agonizing and puzzling over the righteousness of God from a detached, speculative, or philosophical point of view, and he was not primarily concerned with how an unbeliever comes to a righteous God. Luther's sole compulsion was to discover how a Christian could live with a righteous God whom he could never possibly satisfy. Consequently his eyes were drawn in these early years to the word *righteous* and not to the word *faith*. He knew that God was righteous and that he, Martin, was not. How, then, even having heard the gospel, could he possibly "live by faith"?

Luther began his lectures on the Psalms sometime in late 1513 with the same awe that had overcome him at the thought of becoming a professor. "I sense with certainty," he told his students, "the weight upon my neck of this task, which for a long time, all in vain, I was reluctant to undertake and to which I agreed only when compelled to do so on orders. And I confess simply that to this day I cannot understand some of the psalms, and unless, as I hope, the Lord will enlighten me through your talents, I cannot interpret them."[9]

Such a heightened sense of responsibility reduces many beginning professors to mere repetition of what they have been taught. But Luther was different. He responded with great care, reading the most recent commentaries by the best scholars and taking up the study of Greek and Hebrew. As in everything else, he was determined to give the task his best effort. And before he finished, he had come to an utterly new understanding of the righteousness of God and of the Scriptures themselves.

When Luther arrived at Psalm 72, he explained to his students, "this is what is called the judgment of God: like the righteousness or strength or wisdom of God, it is that with which we are wise, just, and humble, or by which we are judged." [10] Something revolutionary was happening. He had told them that the righteousness of God had two different meanings, but he had only been taught the second one: God's righteousness was God's possession and the quality by which he found sinners wanting. But Luther's first and longer explanation was powerfully opposed to this traditional teaching. There he spoke of God's righteousness as a quality *God gave to believers* and by which he made them acceptable in his presence. This was a radically new explanation, but for the moment Luther uttered it in the same breath as the older view that he had been taught as a student.

The pressure of having to prepare these lectures day after day kept Luther thinking and working. Later, probably in 1514, he explained to his students that "whoever wants to understand . . . the Scriptures wisely needs to understand all these things as they apply to the conduct of life: truth, wisdom, salvation, justice, namely the things with which he makes us strong, saved, just, wise. So it is with the works of God and the way of God, all of which things Christ is in the literal sense, and in terms of the conduct of life all these things are faith in him." [11] God judged, but he did so for the purpose of giving miserable human beings his righteousness in Christ.

This change was the beginning of a tide that washed away the central bulwark of late medieval theology and religious practice. Much, if not all, that is popularly associated with Luther's faith logically followed from the resolution of this central problem. If God's righteousness was basically something God gave away, and if the act of giving it away was his mercy, then there was no reason for Christians to try to be righteous in his presence on their own account or even "to do what is in them" as preparation for receiving sacramental grace. Yet even as Luther clearly stated his new understanding of the righteousness of God (which he would later call "passive righteousness"), he continued to hold to the traditional teaching on a number of other points. He had barely begun the process of working out the full implications of his new insight.

The role of humility

One issue that was central to the religion of the late Middle Ages was the idea of humility, that is, the state of utter devastation of the soul that was held to be necessary before the reception of grace. Confession, penance, and other spiritual exercises were means by which the church helped people achieve this psychological condition. In many sections of these first lectures on the Psalms, Luther argued that absolute humility was a necessary precondition to saving grace. It was "judgment of the self," he said, that brought the human mind into harmony with God. At one point he declared, "Humility itself is judgment." Later he said, "and this is judgment . . . that is, to accuse and to judge oneself." However much faith might be necessary to salvation, Luther still put the traditional virtue of humility first. "No one is justified by faith unless first through humility he confesses himself to be unjust." At another point he insisted that "your true righteousness is humility and the confession of sin, the accusation of yourself." He could even write, "Humility alone saves."[12] Christians had to work at being humble.

This understanding of the place of humility in the life of a Christian was fundamental to Luther's life as a monk. He had renounced everything in order to become one of the "meek" who would then be "blessed." There is even a sense in which humility lay at the base of his spiritual struggles. A state of humility had to be genuine and had to be felt by the penitent or else questions could be raised about the worth of the confession. Humility, or the sense of being humble, was either a human work or a gift of God. If a human work, it was always debatable. But if humility came from God and the penitent was at all pleased to feel humble, then pride and self-righteousness soon followed. There could be no comfort in being truly humble.

There may well have been an autobiographical element in Luther's explanation of humility's role in the Christian life, for he himself was crushed again and again by his inability to stand in the presence of a righteous God. He may have only been bravely repeating the views of his teachers when he came to lecture on the subject of the *synteresis* or the spark of goodness that they found in every human being. In spite of the fact that he could not find or be satisfied with his own spark of goodness, he argued that there was in fact such a thing. He insisted that in the conscience, "there is indeed such a natural desire in human nature [for the grace of God], because the synteresis and desire for good is inextinguishable in people, though it is weakened in many." At another place he declared, "there is nobody so bad that he does not feel the murmuring of reason and the synteresis," or later, "For the remnant, that is reason and the synteresis which go on murmuring, always cries to the Lord, even if, forced by sin, the will should sin." Perhaps here was Luther's picture of himself, never righteous enough but always crying out to God. As he once put it, "Living, no, rather dying and being damned make a theologian, not knowing, reading, or speculating." [13]

A pinch of yeast

The fundamental change in Luther's understanding of the righteousness of God, from seeing it as a quality God possessed and with which he judged to understanding it as something God gave sinners, was like a pinch of yeast that gradually worked its way into his thoughts, his being, and his entire life. One of the first of his teachers' ideas that he discarded was the traditional understanding of the spark of goodness. As he moved into 1515 and his lectures on Romans, he still retained this basic organizing principle of scholastic theology. Early on he declared, "For we are not wholly inclined to evil, because a remnant is left to us which is inclined toward good things, as is evident in the synteresis." But he also remarked that human beings can do nothing except love themselves. This, he concluded, was "the sum of all the vices." [14]

Luther was appalled by this human urge to put the self first, last, and always. The more he thought about the idea of a spark of goodness which, if only fanned, would leap into flames of genuine ardor for God and love for the neighbor, the more it struck him as imaginary. Not yet halfway through the fourth chapter of Romans, he summarized the doctrine he had been taught as the idea that "by his own powers a person can love God above all things and can perform the works of the law according to the substance of the act but not according to the intentions of him who gave the command, because he is not in a state of grace." This much was standard fare. But Dr. Luther had already referred to this idea as "plainly insane." Just in case his students had not been paying attention earlier, he added another comment: "Fools! Pig theologians!" [15]

With that the idea of the synteresis was gone. "And this tiny motion toward God which someone can perform by nature, they dream to be an act of loving God above all things. But look! The whole person is full of selfish desires, this tiny movement notwithstanding." To be sure, human beings could yearn for God and wish to be truly good, but even this they did in a self-serving way. Just in case he had not impressed this new idea clearly enough on his students, he repeated himself, using different words: "It is said that human nature has a general notion of knowing and willing what is good, but that it goes wrong in particulars. It would be better to say that it knows what is good in particular things but that in general it neither knows nor wills the good." [16] For Luther, therefore, whenever people hated or behaved badly toward their neighbors, they were not just committing a single sin for which they could seek forgiveness. They were acting in perfect accord with their basically selfish nature.

Now the theological consequences of his initial rereading of the biblical term, "the righteousness of God," truly made themselves felt. Luther's mind was moving quickly. It seized on Paul's insistence that human beings had nothing to offer God. "Where is 'free will' now?" he asked. "Where are those who would have it that from our own natural strength we can perform an act of love to God above all things?" He brushed aside the careful distinction between the nature of the act and the intention of the actor. Everything human beings did was finally selfish in God's eyes because human beings were selfish. It was not just "a lack of light in the intellect and of strength in the memory" that caused people to fall short of the glory of God. The cause was "the loss of all uprightness and the powers of all of our faculties, whether of the body or of the soul, of the whole person both inward and outward." Nor—and here he went far beyond the spiritualizing of mystics like Tauler or even of humanists like Erasmus—did the horrors of the human condition derive from its fleshly existence. "For it is like a sick man whose mortal illness is not only the lack of health in one of his members, but, in addition to having lost the health of all his members, also has such a weakness in all his senses and powers that he finally disdains those things that are healthful and desires things that make him sick." [17] Human beings were so sunk in sin that they could not even recognize their own condition.

Those of Luther's students who had been with him long enough had only to compare what they were hearing now with their notes on the Psalms to become confused. But Luther went even further. What he said next may well have scandalized the more pious among them. "The term 'old Adam' describes what sort of person is born of Adam. . . . The term 'old Adam' is used not only because he performs the works of the flesh but more especially when he acts righteously and practices wisdom and exercises himself in all spiritual works, even to the point of loving and worshiping God himself." By virtue of the old Adam, Luther said, human beings not only "enjoy the gifts of God" but also seek to "use God."[18]

Just when they thought they were being most spiritual, human beings sought themselves and their own advantage. The Scriptures, he declared, "describe man as so turned in on himself that he uses not only physical but even spiritual goods for his own purposes and in all things seeks only himself." Again, "Man, I say, turns all these things to himself, seeks his own good in them all, and horribly makes idols out of them in place of the true God." Finally, human beings "make God into an idol and the truth of God into a lie."[19]

Moreover, according to the Scriptures the old Adam continued to live in Christians. "For the judgment of God is infinitely exact. And nothing is done so minutely that it will not be found gross in his sight, nothing so righteous that it will not be found unrighteous, nothing so truthful that it is not found to be a lie, nothing so pure and holy that it is not polluted and profane in his sight."[20]

Luther's picture of the human condition in the presence of God was bleak indeed. But it was here that he also began to develop a different understanding of humility from that which had filled his lectures on the Psalms. He still saw this state of being utterly drained of self-worth as being necessary for salvation, but now he insisted that it was God himself who graciously taught and provided humility. "The whole task of the apostle and his Lord is to humble the proud and bring them to a realization of this condition, to teach them that they need grace, to destroy their own righteousness, so that in humility they will seek Christ and confess that they are sinners, and thus receive grace and be saved."[21]

Here was what Luther called the "proper" work of the law, which he often described as a hammer or an anvil that smashed down human pride and made room for God's love. Luther loved plays on words and here chose to refer to the law by using the German word *Spiegel*. God's law was a *Spiegel* (which could also mean "mirror") that revealed to human beings what they truly were—in need of grace. Thus, when

God was most terrifying and most righteous, he was in fact most gracious. God's mercy was a loving hand within an iron fist.

Christ alone

By now the old wineskins were leaking badly. Just as God's righteousness and mercy were the same work, so too were a Christian's humility and faith. Both were gifts of God, Luther told his students. Faith therefore was not a matter of believing this or that doctrine on the one hand and having a personal relationship with the divine on the other. "Faith is indivisible," he said. It was also invisible: "The righteousness of God is completely from faith, but in such a way that through its development it does not become visible but a clearer faith. . . by growing more and more." Simply put, faith trusted God's promises. "This understanding . . . is faith itself, a knowledge of things invisible and trustworthy. It is a hidden understanding, for it is one of those things that a man cannot know by his own powers." Indeed, nothing was more humble than faith. "For whenever God gives a new degree of grace, he gives it in such a way that it conflicts with all our thinking and understanding. . . ."[22] Therefore neither humility nor faith were human undertakings; both were gifts of God that came with the righteousness of God.

Without being fully aware that he was doing it, Luther was completely rebuilding the road to salvation. For his teachers, faith had been like the other virtues of hope and love that were supposed to characterize Christians. A small amount of faith remained after the fall, but this faith had to be augmented by the sacraments in order to ensure salvation. For the mystics, faith was to be exercised by an ever greater distancing of the self from this world and an ever more single-minded contemplation of the goodness of God in God's own essence. The focus was on partial, weak, human faith on the one hand and the absolute demands of God on the other. By contrast, Luther made it clear that by "faith alone" he intended "Christ alone." Paul, he noted, inveighed against "those presumptuous persons who think they can come to God apart from Christ, as though it were sufficient for them to have believed and . . . then having once accepted the grace of justification, not needing him. . . ."[23] Salvation and the gift of faith were not one-time events but a never-ending process.

This focus on Christ could give even the most tormented soul absolute assurance. Where was the release from accusations of the conscience or God's law? "Nowhere save from Christ and in Christ. For if some complaint should be registered against a heart that believes in Christ, and testify against it concerning some evil deed, then the heart turns itself away, and turns to Christ, and says, 'But he made satisfaction. He is the righteous one, and this is my defense. He died for me, he made his righteousness mine and made my sin his own; and if he made my sin his own, then I do not have it, and I am free.' "[24]

Here was the answer that Luther now pressed on others when they were assailed by doubts. Two letters he wrote in April 1516 revealed the change that had overcome him. In one he advised, "The cross of Christ is distributed through the whole world; each person is always allotted his portion. Do not therefore cast it aside but rather take it up as a holy relic to be kept not in a golden or a silver case but in a golden, that is, a gentle and loving, heart." For Luther the cross was the objective fact of righteousness, grace, and faith. Human strivings had no part in it. In the other letter he put the matter more bluntly. "Therefore, my sweet brother, learn Christ and him crucified; despairing of yourself, learn to pray to him, saying, 'You, Lord Jesus, are my righteousness, but I am your sin; you have taken on yourself what you were not and have given me what I was not.' Beware of aspiring to such purity that you no longer wish to appear to yourself, or to be, a sinner."[25]

Only in the gospel

Luther had turned late medieval theology and religious practice on its head. He denied that human beings could become humble by any means whatsoever. The monastic life of poverty and asceticism, the personal life of self-denial and abnegation, the mystical life of spiritual exercises and otherworldliness—all of these availed nothing. Only in the gospel, in both the teachings and the life of Christ, could sinners learn that they were sinners. "We must know we are sinners by faith alone, for it is not manifest to us; rather we are more often not conscious of the fact. Thus we must stand under the judgment of God and believe his words with which he has declared us unjust, for he himself cannot lie."[26] Earlier, Luther had found the law within the gospel. Now he realized that the purpose of the law was to drive Christians to Christ alone.

No matter what their emotional or psychological state, a knowledge of their own sin forced Christians to repent and trust God simply because there was nothing else to do. "For because he repents, he becomes just from being unjust. Therefore repentance is a medium between unrighteousness and righteousness. And thus he is in sin as a beginning point and in righteousness as an end point. If therefore we are always repenting, we are always sinners, and yet at the same time we are just and are justified, partly sinners, partly just, that is, nothing more than penitent."

For Luther the entirety of the Christian life was exactly this series of apparent contradictions. In order to explain this tension to his students, he once used the concepts of Aristotle: "Man is always in not being, in becoming, in being, always in privation, in potentiality, in act, always in sin, in justification, in righteousness, that is, always a sinner, always penitent, always righteous."[27]

There was therefore truly no exit from the human condition. There was no way that Christians could attain to divinity or please God in anything they did. "Now, righteousness and unrighteousness are understood in the Scriptures very differently from the way in which the philosophers and the lawyers interpret them," he advised, "for they assert it to be a quality of the soul, but in the Scriptures righteousness depends more on the imputation of God than on the essence of the thing itself. It is not he who possesses a certain quality who possesses righteousness; rather, this one is altogether a sinner and unrighteous; but he has righteousness to whom God mercifully imputes it and wills to regard as righteous before him on account of his confessing his unrighteousness and his imploring of God's righteousness. Thus we are all born and die in iniquity, that is, unrighteousness. We are just solely by what the merciful God imputes to us through faith in his Word."[28]

Pastoral concerns

Here was the deep irony in the Christian life. Here was where Luther found solace. Here was how he could advise his correspondent not to seek to be too holy. Luther found God's grace precisely in the fact and the knowledge of sin. He filled the lectures on Romans with this message: "For God leaves us thus in this sin, in this tinderbox, in self-seeking, so that he may keep us in fear of him and in humility, in order that we may always keep running to his grace, always in fear of sinning, that is, always praying that he not impute it to us and sin begin to dominate." Certainly human beings remained self-seeking even when they thought they were most spiritual, but precisely at this moment God himself was gracious. "For by this alone does sin become trivial and not imputed, because it causes us to groan out of fear that God may damn us for it, that he might leave it on our account, and, seeking his mercy, we implore him to take it away by grace and thus confess ourselves sinners, and hold ourselves to be sinners through weeping, penitence, grieving, and tears." [29] For Luther, the fundamental mystery was this: salvation started from being sinful and knowing it.

During the course of his early lectures Luther resolved the problem of the dark night of the soul by insisting that human beings could never escape being precisely who they were and doing precisely as they did. In those very moments when they were most human, most fragile, and most guilty, God was most gracious. "And so sin is left in the spiritual person for the exercise of grace, for the humiliation of pride, and for the repression of presumption. . . ." God would have sinners only on *his* terms, and this meant not ignoring the fact that they were sinners. Human beings dared not ignore the reality of their own sinfulness even when they were the most spiritual. To do so would be to turn their backs on the grace of God. "For if the confessions of the saints are to be understood as only about past sins and that in the present they show themselves pure, why then do they confess not only their past but also their present sins? Is it not truly that they know that there is sin in them, but that for the sake of Christ it is covered and not imputed to them, so that they may declare that all their good is outside of them in Christ, who yet through faith is also in them?" [30]

Luther's revolutionary understanding of the way to salvation thus spoke primarily to practical pastoral concerns. The most obvious of these was his advice to a fellow monk not to expend himself in seeking to be pure. He could never achieve this goal in any event, and just the intention of doing so turned his mind away from Christ and toward himself. "For this entire life," he told his students, "is a time of willing to be righteous but never achieving it, for this happens only in the future life." Indeed it was absolutely dangerous to become so "good" as to live no longer in fear: "For when this fear and anxiety cease, then very soon smugness takes hold of us, and as soon as this happens God's imputation of sin returns. . . ."[31]

Even the key word *peace* received a new meaning from Luther's rereading of the righteousness of God. No longer was it the tranquillity and passivity of the soul that he had been taught to seek. By contrast, he insisted that "the royal way and the way of peace in the spirit is to know one's sin and to hate it and thus to fall into the fear of God lest he count it and permit it to dominate, and at the same time to pray for his mercy, that he would free us from it and not impute it."[32] For Luther, those who had genuine peace were constantly striving, but they were secure only in the twofold conviction that they would never succeed and that God had already granted them grace.

Both sinful and righteous

Speaking of the Christian, he declared, "at the same time he is both a sinner and righteous, a sinner in fact, but righteous by the sure imputation [of Christ's righteousness] and the promise of God that he will continue to deliver him from sin until he has completely cured him. And thus he is entirely healthy in hope, but is in fact still a sinner; but he has the beginning of righteousness so that he continues more and always to seek it, yet realizes that he is always unrighteous." Being in need of and receiving grace daily was therefore not an excuse to rest in one's present state, but an impetus to try harder. "For we are not called to a life of leisure but to struggle against passions that would carry guilt with them unless the mercy of God did not take account of them. . . . Consequently, let whoever comes to confession not suppose that he is laying down his burdens so he might live quietly, but let him know that with the burden laid down, he fights in God's army and takes on another burden for God against the devil and against his own personal vices."[33]

The end was therefore secure, but the present was only a beginning. "Now notice what I said above," he reminded his students, "that the saints at the same time they are righteous are also sinners; righteous because they believe in Christ whose righteousness covers them and is imputed to them, but sinners because they do not fulfill the law and are not without self-seeking, and are like sick men under the care of a physician; they are sick in fact, but healthy in hope and because they are beginning to be healthy in fact, that is, they are being healed. They are people for whom the worst possible thing is the presumption that they are healthy, because they would suffer a worse relapse."[34]

Perils of the search for holiness

The life of a Christian was thus such that, even for the most spiritual, the very human search for holiness carried with it two great dangers. On the one side lay the peril of repeated failure and then of despair, a peril he knew well from personal experience. But on the other side lay the more common pitfall of apparent success, together with a complacency that bred self-righteousness. Luther was well-aware that this teaching contradicted what he himself had been taught, but he insisted that "inwardly the words of God are as true and just as God himself. But they are not yet like this in us until our wisdom yields to them, and by believing them gives them a place and receives them." Only someone who had given up all attempts to improve his standing in the presence of God and been totally emptied could receive God's grace. When people were proud of their strengths, they not only deceived themselves but also risked their very salvation. "For it cannot be that a soul filled with its own righteousness can be replenished with the righteousness of God, who fills up only those who hunger and are thirsty. Therefore, whoever is full of his own truth and wisdom is not capable of the truth and wisdom of God, which cannot be received save by those who are empty and destitute."[35]

Before he had completed his lectures on Romans, Luther had developed a way of understanding the Christian life that utterly contradicted what he, and everyone else in his day, had been taught. He flatly denied that there was any possibility of becoming genuinely better in the presence of God. As time passed, Christians could hope only to become ever more radically dependent on the righteousness of God in Christ. But to Luther this was a great and sure hope. "The wounds of Jesus are safe enough for us," he counseled. He found solid hope even for those who had become convinced that God had rejected them. "Thus," he advised, "if anyone is too much afraid that he is not one of the elect . . . let him give thanks for such fear, and rejoice to be afraid, knowing with confidence that the God who says, 'the sacrifice of God is a broken, that is a desperate, heart,' cannot lie." No human works, not even the fondest wishes of the most holy, moved God in the slightest. Christ and Christ alone made Christians "perfectly whole in hope."[36]

In posing his questions, Luther followed where his soul-struggles led him. In finding answers, he followed the Scriptures where they led him. He began his lectures on Romans with the following words: "In the presence of God it is not by doing just works that one becomes just, but, having been made just, one does just deeds."[37] For Luther the words of Paul took on monumental significance: "We hold that a man is justified by faith apart from works of law" (Rom. 3:28).

But Luther lived in a world that relied on supposedly good works. And as a professor and teacher of the church, he had taken an oath to promote the truth and to condemn falsehood. All the makings of an explosion were in place.

FIVE

The Explosion

*T*he preaching, selling, and buying of indulgences were a central part of late medieval religious practice, even as revival meetings are a familiar feature of today's religious scene. Indulgences also had a perfectly legitimate standing in the doctrine of the church. Theologians agreed that while Baptism had washed away the penalties for original sin, Christians still had "to do what was in them" in order to be saved. According to this view, death brought believers to purgatory. The stain of sins that remained on their records—particularly those that were unacknowledged and therefore unconfessed—was purged from them there before they were presented to St. Peter and Christ at the gates of heaven. To be "indulged" a sin before death meant simply to have its penalties pardoned by the church and therefore to be released from paying for it in purgatory. As with confession and penance, all that was required was some evidence of a sinner's sincerity.

In purgatory the dead suffered under a severe disability and yet had a distinct advantage over those who were still living. On the one hand they could no longer atone for their sins by going on a pilgrimage, saying several Ave Marias, purchasing an indulgence, or the like. On the other hand, they were also incapable of committing any more sins. The plenary (full) indulgence was therefore especially important for them, because it wiped away all sins committed since Baptism. At least in theory, therefore, if a plenary indulgence were acquired on their behalf by someone whose heart was properly inclined, their accounts with God would be finally and fully squared.

An indulgence, preprinted, with name and date filled in.

Johann Tetzel, the indulgence seller.

The theory and practice of indulgences was thus consistent with other aspects of late medieval theology and spirituality. Even the money that changed hands was seen as just another instance of self-sacrifice—in this case to benefit the work of the church. Strictly speaking, the practice of "selling" indulgences was then nothing more than a special case of the acts of confession, penance, and other spiritual exercises that were commended to all Christians who wished to guarantee their good standing in the presence of God.

Johann Tetzel

Johann Tetzel was a short, dumpy, stump-preacher who was very good at the business of selling indulgences. But the fall of 1517 brought him the biggest opportunity he had ever seen. He was asked to preach a special, plenary indulgence in Germany, the proceeds of which would help build the Sistine Chapel. In addition, the terms of this indulgence had been broadened in such a way that it was not clear that anything beyond the actual purchase (such as having a devout heart) was necessary. Ready cash talked, and Tetzel could exercise his skills to their fullest.

The mission was planned with care. Publicity preceded Tetzel to town after town so people would be expecting him. Several horsemen, drummers, and trumpeters announced the imminent arrival of something important. With Tetzel himself and his armed guard came the symbols of the papacy and Pope Leo X's family coat of arms. A copy of the prized indulgence was attached to a makeshift cross and raised high above onlookers for all to see. Then came Tetzel, who strode to the prepared platform and began to preach.

"Do you not hear the voices of your dead relatives and others, crying out to you and saying, 'Pity us, pity us, for we are in dire punishment and torment from which you can redeem us for a pittance'? And you will not?" Finally there was the appeal: "Will you not then for a quarter of a florin receive these letters of indulgence through which you are able to lead a divine and immortal soul safely and securely into the homeland of paradise?" A money chest, a supply of blank indulgences, a scale to make certain that people's coins were good, and the scribes were all ready and in their places. Then came Tetzel's last exhortation: "Once the coin into the coffer clings, a soul from purgatory heavenward springs!"[1] The transactions were finished quickly. Soon the entourage was on its way to the next town.

Well before Tetzel's appearance in the environs of Wittenberg, Luther had joined many other concerned Europeans in raising an arched eyebrow at the indulgence traffic. Later he called it "The pious defrauding of the faithful,"[2] and others such as Erasmus could hardly have agreed more. In some quarters learned and sensitive uneasiness gave way to anger. "Roman bloodsucking" was what many German princes called this and other money-raising schemes that came from south of the Alps. It was indeed common for someone such as Tetzel to encounter at least mild opposition as he rode into a territory, stayed a few days, and then rode out with its gold and silver in his saddlebags. In fact Frederick the Wise warned Tetzel against even entering Electoral Saxony.

High stakes

This particular indulgence sale was also the outcome of a very carefully negotiated agreement. At the turn of the 16th century, the papacy was in severe financial straits. Pope Leo X's predecessors had figured prominently in the politics of both Italy and Europe as a whole. It was an expensive game, and now Leo was determined to compete directly with the crowned heads of Europe by having Rome outdo all other courts in its magnificence. His contribution would be to complete St. Peter's, a structure that still awes visitors. But stupendous buildings and inspiring works of art were very expensive to come by. And Leo was already deeply in debt.

To the north, in the patchwork of competing principalities, cities, and bishoprics that made up Germany, there was another man who desperately needed money. His name was Albert, and he was a member of the ambitious House of Hohenzollern whose descendants came to rule all of Germany in the late 19th and early 20th centuries. Like other petty princes, the Hohenzollerns were engaged in constant political struggles, and Albert—a soft-skinned, pudgy youngster with scarcely a beard—was doing his part for the family's future. Not legally of age even to hold a bishopric, by 1517 he had already secured both Magdeburg and Halberstadt. Now Mainz was open, and he wanted it as well. To get it would require a substantial dispensation from Leo X, payable in cash.

The situation was ripe for a deal. The biggest bank in Germany, owned by the Fugger family, would advance the money to pay Albert's

Cartoon depicting the sale of indulgences with papal banners on the left
and right. The one on the right shows
the coat of arms of the Medici family.

Archbishop Albert of Mainz in 1519 at
the age of 29 (by Dürer).

fees to Leo X. In return, Leo authorized the preaching of this indulgence
in Albert's territories, both to repay the Fuggers and to help build the
Sistine Chapel. Little wonder that Tetzel should make it sound as if
one could buy salvation! His job was to raise money, and the stakes
were high.

Tetzel's masters planned his mission with great confidence. They
knew there was a good market for his product. Even Luther had at one
time been well-disposed toward indulgences. He had sought them for
his own relatives by saying special masses when he was in Rome in
1510. After returning to Germany he venerated the skeletons of three
famous martyrs that supposedly resided in the cathedral at Cologne.
And both he and his parishioners had another form of indulgences
readily available in Wittenberg itself. Their secular lord, Elector Frederick the Wise, was an assiduous buyer of relics for the Castle Church.
His collection was so extensive that a penitent could earn nearly two
million years' release from purgatory just by venerating them at the
proper times and paying the recommended fees. These indulgences
were also very popular. And Frederick, unlike Leo and Albert, was
pious in his intentions. The scheme that had been concocted in Rome
should have worked.

The 95 Theses

Then came the unexpected. Tetzel was in a town across the river from Wittenberg. On the eve of All Saints' Day, Halloween 1517, a young university professor with too much to do by the name of Martin Luther posted 95 theses against the sale of indulgences.

The Castle Church in Wittenberg. The door on which Luther posted The 95 Theses *is on the other side.*

Tetzel was accustomed to grumbling and critical comments, but this time an explosion followed. The theses themselves, composed in Latin for a learned audience of clergy and professors, were quickly translated into German, and soon popular cartoons showing the love of Christ vastly outweighing an indulgence in the balance of salvation were circulating all over Germany. Luther's protest was so effective that even today the very word *indulgence* has a slightly unsavory smell about it. Tetzel's enthusiastic crowds soon contained substantial numbers of hecklers. His mission was ruined.

The sudden opposition that snared Tetzel differed from the normal complaints of critics in part because Luther was different. Like any pastor concerned for the souls of his parishioners, he could hardly remain silent in the face of a dubious religious practice promoted by an itinerant preacher. By 1517, however, he was more than a watchful pastor who kept a sharp eye on popular religious life. He was also a professor who had taken an oath to teach the truth and to expose error. Just a month earlier, he had presided at a "Disputation against Scholastic Theology" in which he attacked the heavy dependence of theologians on Aristotle. That spring he wrote a friend that at Wittenberg no professor "can expect to have any students if he does not want to teach this theology, that is, lecture on the Bible or St. Augustine or some doctor of real authority in the church."[3] And none of these authorities had said anything about indulgences.

Tetzel was therefore encountering far more opposition than he or his sponsors had anticipated. When Luther condemned his preaching, he acted under the authority of his office as a doctor of the church. His theses were clear to any reader: "All those who consider themselves secure in their salvation through letters of indulgence will be eternally damned, and so will their teachers." Albert of Mainz was one of Luther's ecclesiastical superiors, and Luther sent him a copy of the theses, along with a covering letter. "God on high!" he said. "Is this how souls entrusted to your care are taught?"[4]

Even so, the young professor was surprised at the chain reaction that followed. Later he remarked that he had been led "like a horse with blinders on,"[5] unable to see to the right or the left and unable to predict what would happen next. Luther had not attacked indulgences *as such* in his theses, but only the most blatant forms of them. "The pope does very well when he grants remission to souls in purgatory on account of intercessions made for them," he declared, and added that "the pope justly thunders against those who plot by any means whatsoever against the sale of indulgences."

It is clear that the old theology was jostling with the new for Luther's allegiance, even in the matter of indulgences. *The 95 Theses* did reflect the theology he professed to his students, as when he proposed that indulgences were not "the merits of Christ and the saints, because, even apart from the pope, these merits are always working grace in the inner person and working the cross, death, and hell in the outer." Moreover, "Any true Christian whatsoever, living or dead, participates in all the benefits of Christ and the church; and this participation is granted to him by God without letters of indulgence."

Nonetheless, in this initial encounter with Tetzel, Luther did not apply his faith in a thoroughgoing way to the conduct of daily religious life. Rather, his concerns as stated in the theses remained in a more traditional mode. He feared that the preaching of indulgences would lead Christians away from true repentance and genuine good works. On the other hand, he was concerned that it might erode the authority of the church. In Thesis 81 he warned that "This unbridled preaching of indulgences makes it difficult even for learned men to rescue the reverence which is due the pope from slander or from the shrewd questions of the laity," and he proceeded to list eight such questions. Luther planned no upheaval; he had no idea that anything momentous would happen. Even late in life he commented that if the authorities "had at once quenched Tetzel's fury, the matter would not have come to so great a tumult."[6]

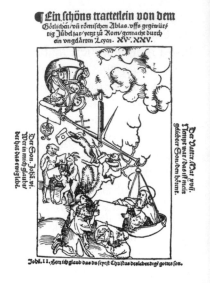

A cartoon depicting how Christ upsets indulgences and indulgence-sellers, including the pope.

From the perspective of distance, Luther could laugh at his own naïveté, but in late 1517 he knew nothing of the agreement that had brought Tetzel practically to his doorstep. Nor did he know that he had set himself against some very determined and influential people for whom doctrinal and spiritual niceties had little meaning. Within months it was arranged for Tetzel to receive his own doctor's degree so he could publish against Luther as a professional equal. At the same time, Archbishop Albert sent Leo X a copy of Luther's theses. Leo appointed a new general of the Augustinians and gave him explicit instructions to silence the Saxon monk and professor.

For his part, Luther now began to explain himself. He embarked on a series of sermons and essays about the proper place of indulgences in the life of a Christian. He remained critical of Tetzel's indulgences by insisting that "He who sincerely contributes to the building of St. Peter's . . . for God's sake acts much more securely and better than he who buys indulgences for it, because there is the danger that he may make a contribution for the sake of the indulgence rather than for God's sake."[7] But even here Luther was concerned only about the spiritual effects of indulgences. Once again, he did not deny them a place in the life of a Christian, although his own theological position and the pressure of scrutiny and criticism from outside Wittenberg could easily have called forth a more radical condemnation.

In the midst of the storm

Oddly enough, while around him all sorts of people talked about the controversy he had started, Luther calmly continued down the theological path that he had begun to walk four years earlier. Ever more insistently he argued that Christ and Christ alone was the sole source of salvation and the only object of hope. During 1517 he completed a series of lectures on Galatians in which he declared that "since faith is an all-encompassing righteousness, it follows that all sin is reduced to unfaithfulness that does not believe in Christ." At the same time he continued to insist that "the Christian life does not consist of being but of becoming, not of victory but the fight, not of righteousness but of justification, not of comprehending but of stretching forward, not of purity but of purification."[8] Regardless of works or the number of indulgences, there was no such thing as genuine, personal holiness in the here and now.

From Galatians Luther moved to Hebrews, where he pressed his vision of the walk of faith even harder. There he charged that "the so-called virtues of the philosophers and indeed of all men . . . may appear to be virtues, but they are really only vices" in the presence of God. Through faith in Christ alone "are we freed from the law; not that it should not exist, but that it should not be feared, and thus we are freed from the devil; not that he should not be, but that we should not be afraid of him, and so from death; not that it should not be, but so that we should not fear it."[9] For Luther, the only comfort worth having was the comfort of Christ, and with this peace all hope for personal righteousness disappeared.

There is no evidence from these lectures that Luther applied this theology—which he would call "the theology of the cross"—to practical issues such as indulgences. Nor did he even mention the indulgence controversy. Rather than being consumed by an issue that was rapidly consuming much of Europe, Luther was bending his energies to ensure that his formal theology would permeate the entire University of Wittenberg. The "Disputation against Scholastic Theology" had been a semipublic step in this direction. Now, in the midst of the public uproar, he worked to bring an able scholar of Greek and Hebrew to Wittenberg so that he and others could readily learn the biblical languages.

There was some irony in the final selection, which was made by Elector Frederick himself. Failing to lure Johannes Reuchlin, Europe's most famous Hebraist, Luther turned to Peter Mosellanus, who was an ornament at the University of Leipzig. But the Wittenbergers finally had no choice except to take Philip Melanchthon, Reuchlin's young nephew. Years later, Reuchlin died as a guest in the home of one of Luther's most staunch opponents. Melanchthon, the epitome of an emaciated scholar (even at the age of 21), whom Luther himself called a "scrawny shrimp," at last took up his post in 1518 and then became Luther's lifelong ally, friend, and spiritual heir.

Winter 1517–1518 therefore found Luther tending to business in Wittenberg with little idea of the stakes involved in the controversy over indulgences. Before the year was over, his sermons, writings, and theses, which had initially been translated into German for the laity, were soon being translated back into Latin so scholars all over Europe could read them. At the same time, a wider public began to make demands on him.

The Heidelberg Disputation

In the spring of 1518 Luther was invited to defend his theology before a large, learned, and public meeting. The triennial gathering of the Augustinians was scheduled for Heidelberg in late April, and Luther would have attended it even without the fame and notoriety that had come with his attack on indulgences. He went not only as a member of the order but also to report on his term of office as district vicar. But not all the time in these meetings was spent on mundane matters such as regular business. One of their common features was a public disputation in which a speaker was selected to defend the theology of Augustine, whom most believed was their founder. This year Luther was the disputant.

The Augustinians assembled at Heidelberg no doubt expected Luther to take up the matter of indulgences, for this question had recently made him the best-known German member of their order. Additionally, recent events gave such a defense a certain urgency. Tetzel was still fulminating, but his place among Luther's critics was rapidly being taken by others of greater stature. John Eck, a theologian from the University of Ingolstadt, was chief among these early opponents. In March, Luther discovered that Eck had composed a treatise against him that had been privately circulated. In this work he accused Luther of heresy, disturbing the good order of the church, discouraging good works, and inciting rebellion among the common people. Indeed, feelings ran so strongly against Luther in some quarters that he was advised not to travel at all, or at least to take extraordinary precautions.

The disputation took place on April 25 in the lecture hall of the Augustinian cloister. Some of those who gathered to watch the fireworks must have been disappointed when they read the 28 theological (and 12 philosophical) theses Luther had prepared for the day's discussion. Not one mentioned indulgences. Instead, Luther took what can only be called the high road and presented his (and what he understood to be Augustine's) theology in the broadest possible terms.

To be sure, Luther had been urged not to engage in petty disputes that might have had only momentary importance and could have exacerbated the situation. On the other hand, the theses show that what he did at Heidelberg was fully in harmony with his own deepest concerns. The very first thesis could easily have been autobiographical: "The law of God, although the soundest doctrine of life, is not able to bring man to righteousness but rather stands in the way." Such had been Luther's own experience. Ten theses followed, detailing how works could not improve anyone's standing in the presence of God. Thesis 11 summarized his position on the law and good works: "It is impossible to avoid presumption; neither can genuine hope exist, unless it is feared that every work brings with it the judgment of condemnation." Human beings could not satisfy God. The more they thought they had done so, the more they were damned.

These beginning theses were rather general, and a casual listener might well have missed their point. But Luther continued and made it clear that this theology broke cleanly with what everyone present had been taught:

13. "Free will" after the fall is nothing but a word, and so long as it does what is within it, it is committing deadly sin.

16. Anyone who thinks he would attain righteousness by doing what is
in him is adding sin to sin, so that he becomes doubly guilty.

Twice Luther publicly declared that the prevailing theology of the day
led to damnation.

Up to this point Luther had emphasized the role of the law to his
listeners. He explained just how powerful this law was by insisting,
"It is certain that a man must completely despair of himself in order
to become fit to obtain the grace of Christ." But then he moved to the
gospel. Near the end of the disputation he declared, "The law says,
'Do this!' and it is never done. Grace says, 'Believe in this man!' and
immediately everything is done." Luther was at his boldest. Of those
who taught differently, he declared, "The theologian of glory calls the
bad good and the good bad. The theologian of the cross says what a
thing is." [10]

The Heidelberg Disputation was a triumph in nearly every imaginable way. Luther had walked to Heidelberg. On the way back, the
delegation from Nuremberg gave him a ride home in their wagon.
Martin Bucer, who later took up what he understood to be Luther's
cause, observed in a letter to his friends, "Luther responds with magnificent grace and listens with insurmountable patience. He presents
an argument with the insight of the apostle Paul. What Erasmus in-
sinuates he speaks openly and freely." [11]

For the first time, Luther had good reason to hope that his theology
would triumph over his scholastic opponents. In the wagon on the way
back he thought about the future. "I am convinced," he wrote to one
of his former professors, "that it will be impossible to reform the church
unless the canon law, the decretals, scholastic theology, philosophy,
and logic, as they now exist, are absolutely eradicated and other studies
instituted." [12] Through his work as a university professor, he had come
to a new understanding of the life of a Christian. Now he made bold
to prescribe this way for all teachers of the church.

Luther had also acquired many new friends, some of whom were
influential. When he arrived in Heidelberg, he and his companion were
even invited to dinner by the Count Palatine and Georg Simler, one of
Germany's most famous educators. On the other hand, many did not
know what to make of Luther's ideas. He had a long conversation with
another former teacher, but was forced to admit that he had simply left
the old man "puzzled and dazed."

Explaining the theses

It was late April 1518, and so far Luther had made no connection between the day-to-day practice of ordinary Christians and the theology he had been developing while lecturing to his students. Now, in the aftermath of the Heidelberg Disputation and with Eck and his other critics very much on his mind, he at last began to see that his distaste for indulgences grew out of more than ordinary pastoral concerns. The fruit of this effort took form in a book with the title, *Resolutions Concerning the 95 Theses*. It was finished in May 1518, or shortly after he returned from the Heidelberg Disputation. But due to printing delays, it did not finally appear until August. There he sought to do what he might have accomplished if the disputation over *The 95 Theses* had ever occurred, that is, to explain what he intended on each point. In so doing, he set forth a much more extensive critique of popular piety than ever before.

As he wrote this book, Luther rethought the entire matter. When he had finished, he added a prefatory letter to Staupitz. There he stated his position in its most trenchant form yet. He began by remembering how very important Staupitz had been to him during his dark nights of the soul. In particular he recalled that in confession Staupitz had always emphasized the inclination of the heart rather than particular sins or particular good works as a determinant of the status of the soul. Luther pointed out that by working with Erasmus's edition of the Greek New Testament, he had discovered that Staupitz had been right and that common confessional practices had no basis in the Scriptures. The Latin translation of Jesus' command at Matthew 4:17 read, "Do penance, for the kingdom of heaven is at hand." But the Greek said, "Be penitent. . . ." Therefore God demanded not outward deeds but a changed heart and mind. "Doing" had literally nothing to do with salvation, particularly with regard to indulgences. "To repent" and "to do penance" were two different things.[13]

From indulgences Luther moved to a general critique of confession, penance, and outward works of any kind. In particular, he focused on the absolution that came from a priest after confession. He concluded that a priest could declare forgiveness in Christ, but had no authority to absolve. "Christ did not intend [by the power of the keys] to put the salvation of people into the hands or at the discretion of an individual." Instead, everything depended on "believing only in the truth of Christ's promise." [14]

In these words a sharp-eyed reader could see an end not only to indulgences, but also to pilgrimages, special masses for the dead, shrines, images, relics, special spiritual exercises, and much that was central to the practice of late medieval religion. Luther had undercut the very foundations of these practices. Still, he did not waver. Just as he followed the Scriptures and his soul-struggles where they led him, so now he followed his faith. In particular, he assaulted the idea that the church possessed a treasury of merits from which, under the proper conditions, Christians could make withdrawals. He insisted that no saint had been saintly enough to make any deposits in this treasury. Only Christ had left behind a positive legacy. He offered it freely, directly, and to all. If the pope had any authority in this area, it extended only to penalties that he himself had established for violations of church law.

One of those who had listened to Luther at the Heidelberg Disputation a month earlier had told him, "If the peasants heard you say that [even good deeds can be sins], they would stone you." Yet in the *Resolutions* Luther pressed on. "The church needs a reformation," he declared, but it "is not an affair of one man, namely the pope, or of many men, namely the cardinals, both of which have been demonstrated by the most recent council. On the contrary, it is the business of the entire Christian world, yes, the business of God alone." Precisely when this reformation would occur, Luther confessed he did not know. That day was known "only by the one who created the seasons." [15]

These were bold, even menacing, words to many. Yet Luther was still not aware of how very far he had come. He dedicated the *Resolutions* to Pope Leo X, and there is no reason to doubt his sincerity in doing so. He insisted that he would "set forth nothing except what is found and can be found in the Holy Scriptures in the first place but also in the church Fathers as received by the Church of Rome and in the papal canons and decretals" of church law. He would even heed earlier theologians to the extent that their views were in harmony with these sources. And in the dedication he declared to Leo, "I put myself at the feet of Your Holiness with everything that I am and have . . . . I will regard your voice as the voice of Christ, who speaks through you." [16]

SIX

The Lines Drawn

Others saw what was happening, even if Luther did not. One of his colleagues at Wittenberg, Andreas Carlstadt, also had a work published in August 1518. It was a collection of theses in which he insisted that only the Scriptures—not the church Fathers, not the papal canons, and not the decretals—were authoritative in matters of faith. By contrast, in the *Resolutions* Luther pictured himself as the very model of loyalty to the genuine traditions of the church. During the following months his reactions were those of a man who could not comprehend what was happening to him.

By the summer of 1518, Luther had provoked powerful opponents who were determined to show him as the danger that he was. Tetzel himself had one last shot to fire; he aimed it at Luther's *Sermon on Indulgences and Grace.* His work was of so little weight that Luther dismissed it with the remark that it treated the Scriptures "like a sow pushes about a sack of grain."[1]

Nonetheless, Tetzel was acute enough to seize upon an argument that would be used over and over again by Luther's opponents. Tetzel insisted on the absolute authority of the pope and declared that anyone (like Luther) who questioned papal pronouncements was a heretic.

Eck took exactly this position in the treatise that he had earlier circulated privately. But he argued it more carefully than Tetzel had done and stated the issues as if he were the teacher and Luther the pupil. To Luther this attack was doubly painful. It was not just that one more person had ignored his appeals to the Scriptures, the practices of the early church, and to what was spiritually beneficial for the average Christian; Eck was not just another opponent. Like Luther, he was a professor of theology. The previous year the two men had been put into contact with one another by a mutual friend, Christoph Scheurl, who was the chief attorney for the free city of Nuremberg. At first Luther thought he would just quietly "swallow this dose of hell" from Eck. But friends insisted that he reply. This he did, but in a private treatise intended only for Eck. Luther thanked him for his friendship and for not having published the attack for all to see. But he would not budge. "I fear God, not you," he concluded. "After this there will be no sin in me if I decide to defend myself publicly." [2]

Meanwhile forces were gathering that required Luther to obtain help in defending himself. In July he learned from Count Albrecht of Mansfeld that several important people had sworn "to seize me and either hang or drown me." Luther believed it, and he knew how easily and suddenly such violence could erupt. To his friend Wenceslaus Linck, a fellow Augustinian who was then serving as a preacher in Nuremberg, he wrote, "The more they threaten, the more confident I become." By this he did not mean to picture himself as having no fear. Rather, he saw such threats as further evidence that he was pursuing the right path. "I know," he added, "that whoever wants to bring the Word of Christ into the world must, like the apostles, leave behind and renounce everything, and expect death at any moment. If any other situation prevailed, it would not be the Word of Christ." [3]

Proceedings in Rome

Local knights, soldiers of fortune, and ruffians were one thing. Rome was quite another. Given the will to do so, people such as Elector Frederick could keep Luther safe. But by now the authorities in Rome had decided that Luther had to be taken seriously, and the elector was one of their targets.

Precisely what started the proceedings against Luther in Rome is not known. There can be no doubt, however, that the Dominicans were involved. Tetzel himself was a Dominican. Just about the time Luther's order was gathering in Heidelberg, the Dominicans were holding their general chapter meeting in Rome. It was attended by the provincial of the order in Saxony, one Herman Rab of Bamberg. It was he who made certain that Tetzel was included among the recipients of 12 special doctor's degrees that had been authorized by the pope. This act meant that the Dominicans were lining up solidly behind Tetzel in the Indulgence Controversy.

Rab also used his presence in Rome to press the case against Luther with papal officials. He worked first through friends of the Dominicans who were in the service of the pope, men who daily walked by the unfinished St. Peter's. By this means he first reached one of the highest papal courts and then finally Sylvester Prierias, the order's watchdog on doctrinal matters. An older man with an already distinguished theological career, Prierias, who was also a Dominican, quickly examined *The 95 Theses* and found Luther in error. The linchpin in Prierias's argument was that the pope was equally as infallible as the church as a whole. In objecting to indulgences, Luther was therefore working against nothing less than the will of the Holy Spirit.

Prierias had his *Dialogus,* as he called it, published in June. It then went back to the papal lawyers, who in turn drew up a formal order citing Luther to Rome. This order was passed on to Cardinal Cajetan, the head of the Dominicans who was also papal legate to the upcoming Imperial Diet (a meeting of the empire) in Augsburg. It finally reached Luther, together with a copy of the *Dialogus,* on August 7.

Luther was stunned. Prierias was not the problem, for this was by no means the first time that Luther had encountered rejection, complete with attendant name-calling. But this was different. The author was neither a Tetzel nor even an Eck. He had official standing in Rome, and his condemnation was accompanied by a citation to appear in Rome to answer charges of heresy. The next day Luther wrote his old friend, Spalatin, who was Elector Frederick's secretary and personal chaplain. He begged Spalatin to work through the elector and the emperor himself to get the case transferred to Germany, for he knew what could happen in Rome. Matters had suddenly moved far beyond Luther's request for a learned debate. "So you see," he wrote, "just how subtly and maliciously those preachers are working for my swift death!"[4]

Arrangements for a hearing

In the meantime, a papal letter did lift from Luther the obligation to travel to Rome on his own. Instead, he was to retract his errors in the presence of Cardinal Cajetan, who was then in Augsburg for the Diet. If Luther did not recant, the cardinal was authorized to put "the notorious heretic" in chains and take him to Rome (or so rumor had it). Frederick the Wise also received a letter. There Luther was called a "son of iniquity" who would bring everlasting shame on the elector if he failed to cooperate with Cajetan's mission.

From little Wittenberg the situation looked desperate. But Luther and his friends were not well-informed about the exact situation in Augsburg. Elector Frederick was there too, and so was everyone else who had political business to conduct in Germany—all the princes, bishops, representatives of the cities, and the emperor himself. What Luther did not know was that Frederick and the other politicians were in a particularly ugly frame of mind when it came to responding to demands from Rome. Frederick had in fact been leading a movement to state the "grievances" (among them, papal fund-raising) of the German nation against the papacy in the most uncompromising way to date. The game was by no means finished.

In addition, Elector Frederick was little inclined just to hand over his prize theologian when no one had proven him to be in error. Moreover, he and his counselors understood the political facts of the situation. He knew that he had to appear to be cooperative without actually cooperating. Near the end of September he therefore ordered Luther to come to Augsburg.

Luther was devastated. To be sure, Frederick had extracted a promise from Cajetan not to seize him. But Luther did not know about this arrangement. What he did know was that a century earlier Jan Hus had traveled to a council of the church on a promise of safe conduct from the emperor himself, and he had been burned at the stake. Yet there was no choice except to obey, as soon as travel arrangements could be made.

Popes and councils could err

The negotiations that preceded Elector Frederick's decision nonetheless left time for a response to Prierias's *Dialogus*. As a theologian, Luther had nothing but scorn for Prierias; he even called his own reply "a most trifling work done off the top of my head." Luther said that he dashed it off with the thought that "it does not appear worthwhile for me to wrack my brains for his sake." Perhaps because he did write so quickly, the reply was another milestone in Luther's development. In it he flatly denied Prierias's insistence that the authority of Christ resided in the pope, who in his office was therefore the essence of the church. "For me," he replied, "the church is virtually present in Christ alone, and it is represented only in a general council."[5]

Perhaps Luther had been listening to his colleagues and friends such as Carlstadt. Whatever the case, here for the first time he directly confronted the repeated assertion that, in criticizing Tetzel's indulgences, he was detracting from the authority of the church. No longer did he pledge allegiance to the Fathers, the canons, and the decretals of the church. But even so he had not yet come to the point of saying that the church of Rome and the pope were in error. He argued only that in principle both pope and councils *could* err, as judged by the standard of the Scriptures. In fact, Luther still declared that the church of Rome "has never contradicted the true faith by any of its decrees." Rather, it retained "the authority of the Bible and of the ancient church Fathers, even if there are many people in Rome who neither believe in the Bible nor pay much attention to it."[6]

Luther had been warned against just the sort of unnecessary bombast that he included in the last phrase. It undoubtedly infuriated his opponents as much as he was infuriated by them. Still, there was nothing truly revolutionary in his approach to the problem of church authority. Medieval church lawyers often debated the question of whether a pope or council could in principle be heretical, and Luther simply aligned himself on one side of the issue. What was happening was that his opponents consistently refused to answer Luther's argument that indulgences were wrong. But at the same time they accused him of violating the authority of the pope and therefore of the church. For his part, during this first year Luther consistently held out for a true debate on the disputed issue and insisted that the authority of the church was not in question. In the reply to Prierias he even went so far as to declare that he would be a heretic if it could be proved that he opposed "the doctrine of the faith and of the church."[7] He could not believe that a fair-minded decision would contradict either *The 95 Theses* or the *Resolutions*.

Faith and hope

The question of authority in the church was yet another issue on which Luther had ventured much farther than he realized. To be sure, he never treated the question of papal authority directly during the series of lectures he gave between 1513 and 1517. Yet at the same time that he moved from a new understanding of the righteousness of God and to an altered appreciation of the role of works in the life of a Christian, he also touched on one more critical and related issue. In doing so, he changed his understanding of the nature of a Christian and therefore of the nature of the church itself.

Late medieval theologians had defined a true Christian as someone who, besides having faith, was in some sense becoming better. As they put it, this was someone whose faith had been "formed by love" and, in particular, by love for God. They were describing a process of sanctification that occurred within the church through the infusion of grace by the sacraments, chiefly the Mass, confession, and penance. Doing spiritual works as prescribed by the church was thus an essential mark that one was a true member of the church. The church certainly continued to have both the good and the bad within it; these were the wheat and the weeds of which Jesus spoke (Matt. 13:24-30). But the truly faithful could still be recognized, because they made zealous use of the sacraments within the church.

Luther's new understanding of a Christian as being both righteous and sinful at the same time worked a revolution. Christians lived in faith and hope. Those who were truly faithful were always beginning the walk of faith and had never reached its goal. Good deeds (in particular, acts of love for one's neighbor) were part of this life, but neither they nor special spiritual exercises added anything to faith, which was created and constantly refreshed by the Word. Consequently, those who were truly faithful were not in a state of loving God, but rather of being loved *by* God. All they required was the Word.

While the scholastic theologians spoke of the true Christian as "obedient," Luther preferred the words of 1 Corinthians 2:15: ". . . judges all things . . . judged by no one." As early as 1514 in his lectures on the Psalms, he declared that those who sat in the seats of authority did so only by virtue of Christ. "But," Luther added, addressing them directly, "when he will occupy your seat, you will give way and yourselves be one with the people . . . on account of Christ who sits in you and subjects them to you."[8] Christ, and not human beings, was the authority in the church.

When he said these words, Luther had little idea that he was saying anything contrary to the common opinion of all teachers of the church.

In the "Disputation against Scholastic Theology" of 1517 he had declared, "We believe we have said nothing that is not in agreement with the catholic church and the teachers of the church."[9] He was simply unaware of how far he had come. It is no wonder that he was mystified and angered by his critics' charges.

Summoned to Augsburg

Luther received the order to come to Augsburg at the end of September 1518. By now, Elector Frederick was the only person who had the power to defend him. But he, too, appeared to be casting him aside. Later, Luther remembered saying as he set out: "Now you must die. . . . Oh, what a shame I have become to my parents!"[10]

Luther was not so much desperate as he was filled with foreboding. Still convinced that he was right, he did everything he could to avoid what he thought was inevitable. He paused in Weimar and Nuremberg to seek the advice of friends. From Nuremberg, Wenceslaus Linck agreed to accompany him as legal counsel. Others, such as Staupitz, learned of his plight as well. As Luther traveled, he wrote his colleagues in Wittenberg, "Live well and hold firm, because it is necessary to be rejected either by men or by God."[11] Yet the aid of friends and the internal resolve that came from his convictions were not enough. When he entered Augsburg on October 7, his stomach was so upset and his bowels ran so freely that he could no longer walk. Thanks to arrangements made by a former student, he stayed in the Carmelite monastery.

"I recovered," Luther wrote Spalatin on October 10. Indeed he had. As would happen so often later in his life, the company of good friends eventually worked its magic and raised his spirits. Two nights earlier the famous scholar Conrad Peutinger had invited him and his party to dinner. "I know now what will happen," Luther continued. "Although the cardinal legate from Rome promises to forbear everything, friends nevertheless do not want me to confide in him innocently. Indeed, they are taking care of matters prudently and diligently."[12]

At that point his friends were arranging a safe conduct for his travel within the city, so that if Luther actually ventured out to see Cajetan, there was some assurance that he would return. The day before he had been visited by a representative of the cardinal who urged him simply to recant and let everything be forgotten. "Do you want to turn this into a tournament?'' he repeatedly asked Luther. ''He is an Italian and will remain an Italian,'' was Luther's comment. ''Now it is certain that I will appeal to a future council if the lord legate of Rome should decide to proceed more with force than with careful judgment.''[13]

Interviews with Cajetan

Cajetan did indeed take Luther seriously. He had not only read many of Luther's works but had also composed thoughtful replies to his views. He was well-prepared to respond specifically, should occa-

Georg Burckhardt from Spalt, known as Spalatin.

sion demand it. Cajetan was probably the finest intellect Luther had yet encountered. He was a man of integrity who was acknowledged as one of the Dominicans' foremost theologians—far better than Prierias. Nonetheless, he had already concluded that three issues were at stake, and that Luther was wrong on all three: the treasury of merits; the necessity of faith for justification and sacramental grace; and the sufficiency of papal authority for the preaching of indulgences.

The cardinal-prince and vicar-general of the Dominicans was also a loyal son of the church, and he had his orders. Chief among them was the stipulation that he was not to debate with Luther but to secure from him one simple word, *revoco* (I recant). Cajetan's attempts to get Luther to say this one word took place in the house of the Fugger family, whose money had been part of the Indulgence Controversy from the very beginning.

In the late Middle Ages, confrontations of this kind included more than just the two antagonists. Luther brought with him both Linck and Staupitz. Cajetan had his rooms at the Fugger house filled with an entourage of aides from Italy. By now Luther's friends had taught him how to behave in front of someone so eminent. First he prostrated himself at the cardinal's feet. When addressed, he rose, but only to his knees. He stood when beckoned to do so. Cajetan was courteous.

He was also clear about his expectations: "First, repent your errors and recant them. Second, promise not to teach them again. Third, refrain from doing anything that might disturb the peace of the church."

Luther asked Cajetan to specify his errors, and here the cardinal's intelligence overstepped the good sense of his instructions. He replied. First he pointed to the decree *Unigenitus*, which did not have the standing of official doctrine but which did employ the doctrine of the treasury of merits as the grounds for indulgences. Second, he declared Luther's insistence that faith (rather than the sacraments) justified sinners to be "a false innovation." Luther replied that he could not withdraw this point. Cajetan became blunt: "You must recant this today, no matter what you wish. Otherwise, on the strength of this one sentence I will condemn everything else you may say." With this his entourage broke out into laughter and jeers.

The exchanges continued, but the discussion finally came to the fundamental issue: the authority of the pope versus the authority of the Scriptures or a council of the church. The two men met again the next day, and again the question of authority was central. This time Cajetan insisted that Luther bow to *Unigenitus* and therefore to the right of the pope to authorize indulgences, even in principle those Tetzel preached. Finally Luther asked if he could reply in writing. At first Cajetan demurred, but Staupitz intervened. The cardinal then turned to Luther and said, "I will be pleased to hear what you have to say and then, in a fatherly rather than a judicial way, to settle everything."

Cardinal Cajetan.

When Luther appeared for the third time, he did so with two lawyers from the court of Elector Frederick the Wise. He also brought with him a document that was several pages long. In it he insisted that a council was above the pope on

matters of doctrine, that faith was necessary before the sacraments
could be effective, and that the Scriptures were finally authoritative in
matters of doctrine because all human beings could err. Therefore
Luther would not agree that indulgences had solid doctrinal standing.
The cardinal accepted Luther's document and promised to forward
it to Rome. Then he told Luther, "Now it is time to recant." With that
the third interview turned into a verbal brawl. Cajetan insisted that
papal authority required Luther to submit to *Unigenitus* and therefore
to indulgences. Luther replied that the decree was contrary to the Scriptures, that indulgences were no more than a scheme to raise money,
and that in any event they were not the same thing as the merits of
Christ. This was too much. Cajetan threatened to shackle Luther and
take him to Rome and at the same time to excommunicate his friends
and everyone who had anything to do with him wherever he went.
"Go now," he thundered, "and do not appear before me again until
you are ready to recant!"[14]

Luther was elated. He returned to his quarters and sat down to write
both Spalatin and Carlstadt. With that last explosion, he said, the
cardinal's "confidence was shattered." The blood was still in Luther's
cheeks. He reported that Cajetan was trying to work through Staupitz
to get a retraction that he could forward to Rome. "This much I know,"
he wrote Carlstadt. "I would be the most accommodating and beloved
person if I were to say the simple word *revoco,* that is, 'I recant.' But
I will not become a heretic by denying the understanding through which
I have been made a Christian."[15]

Appeal to Rome

This determination lasted a few more days. On the advice of Elector
Frederick's counselors, Luther appealed "from the pope badly informed
to the pope better informed," and had the appeal notarized and sent to
Rome. At Staupitz's request he also wrote Cardinal Cajetan a final
accounting of his position. He was polite, even deferential, but insisted
that he was under no obligation to recant his views on debatable questions such as indulgences. He had therefore appealed his case to Rome.
A day later, on October 18, he wrote again and reported that he had
consulted further with his friends, the very ones Cajetan had contacted
and urged to influence him. Luther's words dashed the cardinal's last
hope of rescuing his mission. His friends had told him that recanting

all he had been teaching would amount to creating new articles of faith. "For me," Luther reported, "their voice is this insurmountable consideration: What will you recant?" Luther could not recant.[16]

The reality of the situation—and its real danger—at last crashed in on Luther. So that he would not be hindered if he were forced to flee for his life, Staupitz secretly released him from his vows of obedience as an Augustinian monk. Then Staupitz and Linck quietly stole out of the city by night.

Luther was literally abandoned by his closest friends. All that remained were the counselors of Elector Frederick the Wise. They, too, thought the situation grave. They advised Luther to take the precaution of formally appealing his case from Cajetan to Pope Leo X. Having already appealed from Rome to Germany, he was now told to appeal from Germany to Rome.

Just a few months earlier he had left Heidelberg in triumph. Now he left Augsburg a fugitive. On the night of October 20, 1518, Luther ran. Without the dagger every prudent man carried for protection against robbers, without any means of defense, without spurs, and having left his undergarments behind, he was snuck through a hole in the city walls, mounted on an old nag, and carried miles out of the city. When he finally dismounted, he could hardly walk.

The young monk reached Wittenberg on October 31, one year after he had posted *The 95 Theses*. In that year he had denied the authority of a cardinal-legate, been driven to appeal "from the pope badly informed to the pope better informed," and pledged, if necessary, to appeal to a council of the entire church. All these maneuvers meant that, for Luther, church law had no force if it contradicted his understanding of the Scriptures.

There is no way to know Luther's exact state of mind once he was back in Wittenberg and at least temporarily safe. He wrote to Spalatin and briefly reported what had transpired in Augsburg. Of himself he said only that "my cause is such that I will fear and hope." The bulk of his letter related what was happening at the university. A young man was due to be promoted to doctor and the elector had to provide yet more funds. Greek studies were flourishing under Melanchthon, but the new instructor in Hebrew was trying to teach his students to speak the language rather than just to read it. He himself needed a new robe.[17] The letter seemed little more than a quick note from someone who had

just returned from a particularly strenuous trip and now had to attend
to the business that had collected in his absence.

A dangerous situation

There can be no doubt, however, that Luther's actions in Augsburg
were very serious indeed. Cajetan certainly thought so. On October
25 he wrote Elector Frederick an account of the confrontation and
reminded Luther's temporal lord of his spiritual obligations. His letter
was much longer than Luther's note to Spalatin, and within its calm
and evenhanded words there was a menacing tone. Cajetan even referred to Luther as a *fraterculus,* a "monk of no account." Out of
respect for the elector's wishes, no evil had been done Luther. The
elector ought nonetheless to know "how gravely and pestilently this
business will linger on afterwards, for they will prosecute the matter
at Rome, however much I have washed my hands of it." In a postscript
he commented that he was certain Frederick did not wish to "put a
spot on his glory." He concluded, "I speak the absolute truth and I
will be a slave to the rule of Christ according to which 'you shall know
them by their fruits.' "[18] Frederick was either to send Luther to Rome
or at the very least to eject him from his territories. At the same time
Cajetan forwarded to Rome a copy of Luther's written rejection of the
decretal *Unigenitus.*

Soon Prierias published a new attack on Luther, and then on November 9 a new papal decree on indulgences was drawn up in Rome.
In so many words it declared that the pope's authority included the
right to issue indulgences. In case there might still be any ambiguity
(but without naming Luther or taking any notice of his arguments), it
condemned the views of all "monks and preachers" who declared the
contrary. With the publication of this decree on December 13, Luther's
room for maneuvering was gone. As of that moment, he could no
longer argue that indulgences were a debatable subject. Cajetan was
victorious. Rome had ruled.

Suddenly Elector Frederick was in a tight situation as well. The
collision between Luther and the cardinal left even the prince few
choices. Frederick the Wise was a master at the politician's most powerful weapon—delay. But now he had to make a decision. What was
to be done with Luther?

Working once again through the very useful Spalatin, he sent Luther

Elector Frederick the Wise of Saxony (by Dürer).

a copy of Cajetan's letter and asked for his response. By doing so, he bought himself a little time. However, he also left Luther with the clear impression that he was about to be abandoned by the only person who could protect him. In the days that followed Luther began to think that he would be forced even to leave the seedy little town of Wittenberg that had become his home. To Spalatin he wrote that he was ready to go, "like Abraham I know not where, nay, most certainly where, because God is everywhere." A sense of isolation weighed heavily on him. He recalled that one of Cajetan's emissaries had asked him where he would go if the elector withdrew his protection. "Under the heavens," had been his response.[19] Now he conveyed the same hopeless determination in a letter of thanks to his host in Augsburg.

Presenting his case

In spite of his desolation, Luther wrote Frederick his account of what had happened at Augsburg in a spirited, vigorous, and even amusing fashion. Receiving the copy of Cajetan's letter "gladdened" him, he replied, because "I see now presented the most beautiful occasion to expound my entire cause." Playing with Cajetan's own epithet for him, *fraterculus,* he conveyed his hope that the elector would tolerate "the babblings of this shabby little monk." In any event, he added, the very first meeting with one of Cajetan's representatives convinced him that it was much better to depend on the judgment of Germans than of Italians.

Luther's reply did include a day-by-day recitation of each exchange with Cajetan, one that corresponds with all other accounts—even Cajetan's—of their confrontation. Repeatedly Cajetan insisted that he recant and repeatedly Luther demanded to be shown where he was in error. But Cajetan "was not able to produce even a syllable from the Scriptures against me." Luther insisted that it was he who sought the truth throughout. "Truly, excellent Prince," he wrote, "I protest in the presence of God and of his angels. . . . Concerning my response [to Cajetan], let whatever will be, be; if it is false . . . if it is damnable or to be recanted, then I will do all this if it should be so."

Luther thus presented his case consistently. He was willing to abide with fair and considered judgment. Nonetheless the story he told made one simple point: the representatives of Rome were not addressing the matter fairly; they consistently refused to hear him out. His own position was clear: "To my dying day I will nonetheless confess this point," that "either the merits of Christ are the treasury from which indulgences come . . . or they are not." He was convinced that they were not, "for it is the most certain thing of all that the merits of Christ cannot be dispensed by men." Therefore, he added, indulgences were "not that common custom of the church that [Cajetan] tosses about but corruption and abuse warring against the truth of the Scriptures."

All this and more, Luther wrote, he was ready to debate. But Cajetan would not allow a debate, even though he knew that the exact extent of papal authority had been under dispute for some time. In the recent

past many universities had exercised the right to appeal against papal
authority (and Luther was a university professor). These included Basel, Freiburg, Louvain, "and that father of studies, Paris." Now his
opponents accused him of being contentious and assertive. But while
they denied him the opportunity to debate in the ordinary way, Prierias
was free to launch another written attack against him. Luther advised
Frederick that, like Pilate with Christ before him, he must ask, "What
did that shabby little monk do?" The only answer Cajetan could give
amounted to a version of what the Pharisees and Sadducees had said:
"Believe me, most illustrious Prince, Your Lordship, I speak truthfully,
from certain knowledge, not from opinions." Luther then added, "I
will respond for the prince; make it so *I* can have this certain
knowledge."

Despite his spirited defense, Luther concluded that he was ready to
"leave your territories" before he would harm Elector Frederick or his
good name. What Luther did not know then, or even for some weeks
later, was that his letter convinced Frederick that he was doing the
right thing by protecting Luther—at least for the present. Therefore on
December 7 the elector wrote Cajetan that by delivering Luther to the
cardinal at Augsburg, "we have fulfilled our promise to you." He
added, "There are now many learned people in our principalities and
lands, both in the universities and elsewhere, but in fact to this very
moment we are unable to become firmly and unquestionably any more
certain that the learning of Martin is impious and not Christian but
heretical. . . ." Frederick concluded by saying that he would not send
Luther to Rome or evict him from his territories until he was "convicted
of heresy."[20]

"Pray for me"

But Luther did not know the elector's decision until December 20.
On November 25 he wrote his old superior, Staupitz, that only Spalatin's urgings had kept him from leaving Wittenberg for France. The
same day he wrote Spalatin that he expected the condemnation from
Rome at any moment. "Pray for me," he asked. On December 2 he
wrote Spalatin again: "I am in the hands of God and my friends." He
knew his colleagues and students at Wittenberg stood with him, but
he complained, "In truth the suspicion cast on the prince will force
me to withdraw, if there is anything to be withdrawn." A week later

he reported, "It is untrue that I have bid farewell to the people in Wittenberg. But I did say something like this [to them]: 'As you have learned, I am a somewhat unreliable preacher—how suddenly and without farewell have I left you in the past! If this ever happens again, I want to say good-bye in case I do not return.' " Others, too, thought the situation hopeless. In a letter that did not arrive until Luther knew his fate, Staupitz urged him to "leave Wittenberg at the right moment and come to me [here in Salzburg] so that we may live and die together."[21]

At last the tension was released. "Good God," Luther wrote Spalatin, "with what joy I read and reread" the letter that announced the elector's decision. Of the elector himself he declared, "He is the sort of man whose grasp extends to politics and learning at the same time."[22]

SEVEN

The Public Disputant

During the month from late November to Christmas 1518 Luther could live only from day to day. He nonetheless plunged ahead as if time had no end. Knowing how delicate the situation was, Spalatin had ordered him to publish nothing while the elector deliberated. With the excuse that he had sent the book off to the press the very day that Spalatin's letter arrived, Luther saw to the publication of his account of what had transpired at Augsburg. He wanted everyone to know that his opponents had refused to debate. During this month of uncertainty, he also changed his tactics once more. Having already appealed from Rome to Germany and then to the pope in Rome, he now made good on his promise at Augsburg and appealed to a council of the whole church. On Melanchthon's advice he made overtures of friendship to Reuchlin, who himself had just beaten off an attack from the Dominicans. "Now," he informed Reuchlin, "the teeth of that Behemoth are attacking me."[1]

Luther was doing his best during this month to shore up his position in his own way, regardless of what the elector might decide. But he also paid close attention to the university, almost as if nothing else were at stake. He and the rector agreed to put an end to all lectures that followed the teachings of Thomas Aquinas, whose disciples included Cajetan and most Dominicans. Now, Luther declared, students would be able to "drink in from their sources pure philosophy and theology and all the sciences"[2] without the pollution of the Dominicans' favored theologian. He also launched a new series of lectures on the Psalms that would continue until 1521. Finally, he completed negotiations with Eck for a debate at Leipzig on the question of authority. Although Luther was anxious for his future, he did not let his anxiety interfere with his work.

The mission of Miltitz

In January 1519, the elector commanded Luther to come to his residence to meet with a special emissary of the pope. Karl von Miltitz was the ambassador's name, and his mission was a disaster virtually from the beginning.

Miltitz came from a German family of some pretentions but modest means. He was one of those many people in the late Middle Ages who, as a younger son, embarked on a career in the church because there was no room for him in the family's ambitions. He had worked himself into some favor at the papal court, and in September 1518 he secured a commission to present Elector Frederick with the Golden Rose, a sign of special papal favor. Rome intended that Cajetan would press Frederick hard with respect to Luther, while Miltitz would bear the positive incentive for Frederick to fulfill the pope's wishes. By ejecting Luther from his territories or, better yet, binding him and sending him to Rome, the elector would not only avoid disfavor but actually earn a great reward.

The mission was to be coordinated with Cajetan. But when Miltitz arrived at Augsburg, Cajetan and the emperor had already left the city. Miltitz was an ambitious man, so he set out to meet with Frederick on his own. He told the elector that he had been sent specially to resolve the dispute with Luther on terms that would be acceptable to all parties. Ever the shrewd politician, Frederick saw one more opportunity to muddy the waters. After all, Miltitz did not know that he had already rejected Cajetan's demands.

Without knowing the elector's game, Luther came to negotiate with Miltitz. During their first meeting he agreed to four points: in order that the controversy might die of its own accord, he would be silent if his opponents would be silent; he would confess to the pope that he had expressed himself too sharply, but with no thought of damaging the church; he would urge all to obedience, and confess publicly that he had argued too vehemently against indulgences; finally, he would submit the case to the archbishop of Salzburg with the understanding that he could still appeal to a council of the church at a later date.

The next day Miltitz discovered that neither Luther's letter to the pope nor his public letter included a recantation. So the two agreed simply that Luther would be silent if his opponents would also be silent. For his part Miltitz would persuade the pope to appoint "a learned bishop" to render a judgment on the controversy. But Miltitz could not deliver. All he accomplished in these negotiations was to help Elector Frederick confuse matters and to allow Luther to prove that he would in fact "do anything" he could to end the public strife. In mid-January he wrote Frederick, "I would very much like to recant if only I could hear why I am wrong or they are right."[3] Thanks to Miltitz, his words had the ring of truth.

Political maneuvering

The very same month both Luther and his prince were suddenly provided some room to breathe. Emperor Maximilian died. Pope Leo X quickly put the Luther affair to one side and began exerting all his energies to avoid the election of Maximilian's grandson, Charles I of Spain, as Maximilian's successor. Frederick the Wise was one of the most prominent of the seven electors of the Holy Roman Empire, and they would be the ones to make the decision. It would not do for the pope to incur Frederick's disfavor. So Leo made it known that he would support the candidacy of Elector Frederick himself, if only he would agree. At the same time, he suggested that if Frederick had a favorite cleric in his territories, Leo could grant this person both a cardinal's hat and a wealthy archbishopric. Luther might have become a prince of the church! But like Miltitz's mission, the pope's plan was ludicrous. Each gave the elector good reason to doubt Rome's seriousness. And the political maneuvering gave Luther still more time.

Winter 1518–1519 was therefore a fruitful time for Luther. He began to embellish his letters with long lines of the Greek he was learning from Melanchthon, and he frequently signed them, "Eleutherius" ("the liberator" or "the liberated one"). At the same time he was studying Hebrew, and he put this new language to good use as well. Later he referred to the ancient languages as "the sheath in which we carry the sword of the Spirit, the casket in which we hold this jewel."[4] In his new series of lectures on the Psalms he departed entirely from the medieval way of explaining the Scriptures. Rather than using individual passages as proofs, he sought to understand the whole in its context, and in the language of its own time. He had matured as a biblical scholar, and he quickly left his teachers behind.

Justification by faith

In those months of relative calm Luther also made a very important discovery. He learned just how far he had come, both as a theologian and in his personal faith:

> Meanwhile already during that year [late 1518 or early 1519], I had returned to interpret the Psalter anew. I was confident that I was a better scholar than I had been before lecturing at the university on St. Paul's letters to the Romans, to the Galatians, and the one to the Hebrews. I was seized with the conviction that I must understand his letter to the Romans. I did not have a heart of stone, but to that moment one phrase in chapter 1 [:17] stood in my way. I hated the idea, "in it the righteousness of God is revealed," for I had been taught to understand the term, "the righteousness of God," in the formal or active sense, as the philosophers called it, according to which God is righteous and punishes the unrighteous sinner.
>
> I lived without reproach as a monk, but my conscience was disturbed to its very depths and all I knew about myself was that I was a sinner. I could not believe that anything that I thought or did or prayed satisfied God. I did not love, nay, I hated the righteous God who punishes sinners. Certainly, and with intense grumbling (perhaps even blasphemy), I was angry with God and said, "As if it were indeed not enough that miserable sinners who are eternally lost through original sin and are crushed again by every kind of calamity through the Ten Commandments, God himself adds pain to pain in the gospel by threatening us with his righteousness and wrath!"
>
> At last, meditating day and night and by the mercy of God, I gave heed to the context of the words, "In it the righteousness of God is revealed, as it is written, 'He who through faith is righteous shall live.' Then I began to understand that the righteousness of God is that through which the righteous live by a gift of God, namely by faith. . . . Here I felt as if I were entirely born again and had entered paradise itself through gates that had been flung open. An entirely new side of the Scriptures opened itself to me . . . and I extolled my sweetest word with a love as great as the loathing with which before I had hated the term, "the righteousness of God." Thus, that verse in Paul was for me truly the gate of paradise.

In a moment, perhaps in the twinkling of an eye, Luther suddenly realized that what he had been teaching for four years all fit together. As he put it, "This is the meaning: the righteousness of God is revealed by the gospel, namely, the passive righteousness with which the merciful God justifies us by faith, as it is written, 'He who through faith is righteous shall live.' "

Here was the conviction by which Luther lived the remainder of his life. His conscious realization of it came in a rush during the relative calm that followed Miltitz's mission and the death of the emperor. But Luther was well aware that it had been building for years.[5] In fact, his opponents themselves had provided the impetus for his central theological insight to come to conscious fruition. They did so simply by forcing him to think about the implications of what he was already teaching.

Strong support.

Lengthy negotiations and maneuverings on both sides preceded the Leipzig Debate with Eck. It did not begin until late June 1519. During these six months and more, Luther slowly took one more step toward a complete breach with the medieval church. Already in December he wrote his friend Linck, who had been at his side in Augsburg, "I think I can demonstrate that today Rome is worse than the Turk."[6] The pressure of opposition was again performing its function in Luther's development.

Yet this condemnation of Pope Leo X and his Rome merely echoed the denunciations of this or that pope by theologians and lay leaders of Christendom who predated Luther by a century and more. There were many in the church who could understand Luther's condemnation of an individual pope.

Johannes Eck.

Therefore it was at just this time that Luther attracted strong support from all over the empire. Many prominent and thoughtful people agreed with what they took to be his critique of the corruptions of the Renaissance papacy and prevailing religious life. For the most part these were the humanists, men in the mold of Erasmus who were convinced that the only way to reform the church was to return to the culture of classical and Christian antiquity. They were sharply critical of Luther's teachers, whose books and disputations they dismissed as "two times a thousand nonsensical chatterings." In their place, and in the place of Aquinas, they would put the Bible, the church Fathers, and even figures such as Plato and Cicero, whose moral teachings could provide lessons for the present. Luther had appeared on the scene as someone who based his teachings on the Scriptures and who boldly attacked indulgences and all who sold and defended them. The humanists seized on him as one of their own. They likened him to Reuchlin, who was being unjustly attacked by foes they bluntly labeled "barbarians." To them the entire controversy was just another example of the Dominicans being up to their old tricks.

Many of these defenders of Reuchlin and Luther were well-placed and influential. In Nuremberg, Luther's old friend Linck served just such a group from his post as the city's most prominent preacher. These men included Albrecht Dürer the artist, Lazarus Spengler the city secretary, Willibald Pirckheimer, a patrician member of the government, and Christoph Scheurl, the city attorney. This same group was probably behind the original translation of *The 95 Theses* into German.

Men such as these were located in city after city. Conrad Peutinger provided hospitality and protection while Luther was in Augsburg. The group in Basel that included Erasmus himself and many younger followers saw to translating his German works into Latin and even made bold to advise him. One of their number, Wolfgang Capito, was their conduit for the latest news from Wittenberg. Regarding one of Luther's replies to Prierias, Capito wrote, "You should studiously avoid offending the pope; you should turn aside everything invidious. . . . Believe me, you will succeed through small, repeated strokes, where you would be able to accomplish nothing through a violent outburst." In mid-1520 this man became a principal adviser to the archbishop of Mainz himself! In doing so, he announced, "I have decided to enter the arena." [7]

Yet not one of these people—nor even Luther himself—knew that the pressure of preparing for Leipzig was leading Luther to reconsider the entire issue of authority in the church. Carlstadt's theses of a few months earlier had provided the specific occasion for the planned debate, but it was understood that Luther was the real disputant. At the very end of 1518, Eck published 12 theses of his own that he proposed as the agenda. He defended confession, the treasury of merits, purgatory, and indulgences on the grounds that they had been established by the church. From the very beginning of Christianity, he argued, the church of Rome, headed by the pope, had the divine right to make authoritative pronouncements on the life of faith.

For Luther, this was too much. In mid-January, before even seeing Eck's theses, he had been asked to comment on the new papal decree regarding indulgences. There he said that it "does not allege a single word from the Scriptures, neither of the teachers [of the church] nor of [church] law nor of reason" as support; therefore it was "just empty words" that "I am unable to acknowledge as proper and sufficient teaching of the holy church. I must hold to the commands of God." To Eck's theses he replied two weeks later: "Against them stand the recognized history of the past 1100 years, the text of the Scriptures, and the decrees of the Council of Nicea."[8]

Luther had still not come to his revolutionary insistence that only the Scriptures were authoritative in matters of faith. Yet what he had already said and written had prompted some of his friends, including Spalatin, to urge moderation. "I beg you, my Spalatin," Luther replied, "do not fear anything and do not let your heart be torn to pieces by human considerations. You know that if Christ were not leading me and my cause, I would have been lost long ago. . . ." To Pirckheimer in Nuremberg he wrote, "I will serve and acknowledge the authority and majesty of the pope, but I will not become a corrupter of the Scriptures."[9]

Luther's mind was in motion once again. The authority of the papacy and the history of the institutional church and its laws still had a powerful hold on his loyalties. But everything that he had been teaching his students was coming to the fore. With Melanchthon's help, he began to rework his lectures on Galatians for publication as a commentary. The emphasis on justification by grace through faith remained. But he added the argument that through church law "consciences are only tormented or money is fished for, and in addition trust in Christ is completely destroyed while the church is filled with hypocrites and idols." To Spalatin he remarked at the end of February, "I count papal authority among those things that are neutral, such as health, wealth, and other temporal things." Then he declared that the pope and his representatives were putting forth "an utterly perverse interpretation of the Word of God and conclusions that are contrary to it." [10]

By late February Luther's old loyalties were rapidly disappearing. He had concluded that the papacy was not a divinely-created institution. About two weeks later he wrote Spalatin again: "I am studying the decrees of the popes in preparation for my disputation. And (I whisper this in your ear) I do not know whether the pope is the Antichrist himself or his apostle, so wretchedly in his decrees does he corrupt and crucify Christ, that is, the truth." [11]

Luther had very nearly taken the last step. He was quickly moving away from his criticism of one particular pope and the single issue of whether the papacy had the authority to issue indulgences. By June his study of church law and history led him to publish a *Resolution Concerning the Authority of the Pope*. There he sought to be as clear and evenhanded as possible. The institution of the papacy, he declared, existed by the will of God. But the Scriptures granted it no specifically sacred status, not even in the pastoral office of the keys as given to Peter. The preeminence of the pope was a human creation and the pope was neither infallible nor the sole and final authority in the interpretation of the Scriptures. The issue, then, was no longer *what* was being said about a particular issue (such as indulgences) but the authority that lay behind the statement. Luther had reduced the pope to, at most, the first among equals in the church here on earth.

The Leipzig Debate

The stage was set. The Wittenbergers left for Leipzig and the debate a little over two weeks after Luther sent his book to the printer. The six of them made quite a procession. Carlstadt was alone in the first wagon with his many books that he had brought to help him through the debate. Luther, Melanchthon, the rector of the university, and two others followed in the second wagon. Trailing behind were some 200 students carrying pikes and staves. There was serious business to do in Leipzig.

The debate did not start immediately. First the bishop of Merseburg tried to stop it, but Duke George of Saxony, who was the sponsor along with his own University of Leipzig, insisted that it had to go on. Then the two parties fell into a disagreement regarding the rules. Luther thought he had a promise from Eck that each side would have two notaries to keep an accurate record of what was said. But now Eck wanted the University of Erfurt to judge the exchanges between himself and Carlstadt, and he proposed that the theological faculties of Erfurt and Paris determine whether he or Luther was the winner. Neither side was to publish the transcripts before these universities had made their determinations. Luther resisted these changes to the last moment, but finally friends forced him to agree. "You see," he wrote Spalatin after it was over, "how deviously they stole away the freedom [to debate] that we had agreed on." Now there were to be judges, "And we know full well that the universities and the Roman pontiff will either say nothing or declare against us."

The debate itself was nonetheless a grand affair. It opened on June 27 with a high mass and a great banquet. On the debate's first day Pope Leo lost one battle. Charles I of Spain was unanimously elected Holy Roman Emperor. But for those gathered in Leipzig, the main event was occurring in the central hall of Castle Pleissenburg. Sixty-five armed men from Leipzig stood watch to make certain that no one disturbed the debaters. The 200 students from Wittenberg were somewhere in the town, although they left when they ran out of money. Additional supporters had come to Luther's side from Erfurt and Zwickau, and the whole theological faculty from Leipzig was present to support Eck. A Leipzig humanist, Peter Mosellanus, formally opened the proceedings with an oration of several hours. The debate lasted for 10 days.

Carlstadt and Eck began with the freedom of the will and the necessity of grace as a presupposition for the doing of good works. Luther reported that "Carlstadt was drawing from his books and setting forth the arguments and resolutions . . . in a rich and distinguished manner. . . when Eck objected that he would not debate against a library. To this Andreas replied that he was referring to it so he could adduce the sayings of the Scriptures and the Fathers correctly and not mangle them so violently as Eck was." There had already been an armed confrontation between the students from Wittenberg and the Leipzigers. "But this," Luther wrote, "was the source of another uproar."

By academic custom, Carlstadt was ordered to lay his books aside.

He began to flounder, so Luther set aside the small bouquet of flowers with which he had been toying and took over. Eck immediately confronted him with the traditional argument for papal authority, the passage from Matthew 16:18 according to which Christ said, "You are Peter, and on this rock I will build my church." Eck was outlining the common understanding that the pope, as Peter's successor, held the power of the keys and with it divine authority over the church on earth. Shrewdly, he then said that anyone who denied this authority agreed with Jan Hus, the Bohemian reformer who had been burned at the stake for heresy by the Council of Constance about a century earlier.

"The Saxon Hus"

The issue that had plagued Luther ever since he posted *The 95 Theses* was now clearly and publicly drawn. As he had written in the *Resolution Concerning the Authority of the Pope,* Luther replied that the Greek church had existed for more than a thousand years before this insistence on papal supremacy, and that it continued to exist without acknowledging the authority of Rome. But Eck had laid his trap carefully. With respect to Hus, he said, he was not talking about a pope. It was a council of the church that had condemned Hus.

Luther vividly remembered this part of the debate. To Spalatin he wrote, "At length there was even a debate over the authority of a council. I openly confessed that [councils] have faithlessly damned some articles that have been taught by Paul, Augustine, and even Christ himself in so many words. This truly enraged the snake, and it exaggerated my crime. . . . Nevertheless, I proved from the very words of the Council [of Constance] itself that not all the condemned articles were heretical and in error. . . . And here the matter rests." [12]

Near the end of his letter to Spalatin, Luther wrote, "And so now you have the whole tragedy." Eck had succeeded in pushing Luther beyond every pretense of loyalty to the church as it then existed. Pope-baiting was one thing. Few devout Christians had much good to say about the papacy or the curia at Rome in that time, although many recalled the horrors of a divided church during the Western Schism and therefore bent their knees to the papacy. Many also privately thought that a council might have authority over a pope who could be proven to be a heretic (even though this very notion had been condemned in the harshest language only 50 years earlier in the bull *Ex-*

ecrabilis). But now Luther had denied not only the authority of the pope but also that of councils of the church. He insisted that only Christ was the head of the church, even here on earth.

Luther's understanding of the church did in fact have a distinctly Hussite smell, though he did not realize it. He soon received a letter from two Czech theologians who were still avowed followers of Hus.

Cartoon depicting Luther and Hus serving both bread and wine to the electors of Saxony at Communion.

They applauded him and included a gift of several quality knives, plus a copy of a little book, *Concerning the Church*,. which spelled out Hus's views on the subject. In their letter they freely called Luther "the Saxon Hus." Luther was cautious. He replied by sending copies of his own works, but he had Melanchthon dictate a cover letter to the courier so it could not be positively traced back to him. It would do no good to have real Hussites publicly calling him a Hussite. But later he read the little book. "We are all Hussites without knowing it!"[13] he exclaimed.

His astonished realization had nothing to do with Hus's understanding of faith, grace, works, and righteousness before God, subjects about which Hus had little to say. Nor did it have anything to do with the connection between Luther's insistence that salvation came solely by the grace of Christ and his new understanding of the nature of the church. Rather, his amazement came from the sudden realization that someone who had been publicly hated for more than a century also taught that only Christ was the head of the church, although he reached this conclusion for different reasons. Anyone who did not acknowledge Christ and him alone was the Antichrist, that is, someone who put himself in the place of Christ. This was what Luther now meant when he called the pope the Antichrist. The papacy had put itself in the place of Christ.

Like the interview with Cajetan in Augsburg, the Leipzig Debate was a watershed for Luther. In August he received from Elector Frederick a copy of a letter from Eck in which Eck accused him of being an archheretic. "I give St. Peter the highest honor," Luther replied, "but not the greatest power. For he does not have the power either to create, to send forth, to govern, or to ordain the Apostles." By now Luther was outraged. Eck's entire letter, he said, sounded as if it came from "Minerva's pig." In reply to one of Eck's supporters he wrote, "Away with you, you senseless, bloodthirsty murderer!" To Spalatin he declared that Eck was a man "whom we can judge and accuse without sinning." Henceforth, Luther regarded Eck as "shameless."[14]

PART THREE

An Outlaw's Work

EIGHT

The Outlaw

*A*s a result of the Leipzig debate, Luther made more enemies for himself. He also lost some friends. One famous jurist wrote the group of humanists in Basel, "Tell Luther that I dissent most powerfully when he denies the words, 'You are Peter.' "[1] In Nuremberg, Scheurl agreed. For his part, Eck soon traveled to Rome to assist in preparing a definitive case against Luther.

But Luther had also acquired more friends. Leipzig had made him as well-known as anyone in Europe. Mosellanus, the orator who had opened the debate, soon published an account of the event in which he offered a description of the two disputants (a description that could not have pleased Eck).

> Martin is of medium size with a body made so thin by cares and studies that you can almost count his bones through the skin. He has a manly appearance and is in the prime of life with a high, clear voice. . . . In his manner and bearing, he is very polite and friendly and has nothing of stoic severity or crabbiness about him; he comports himself well at all times. People chide him about only one failing, that in rebuttal he is somewhat more intense and biting than is appropriate for someone who wants to open new paths in theology and be regarded as taught by God. . . . By contrast, Eck is large and tall with a strong, broad body and a big and properly German voice. . . . Yet he lacks the intellectual power to see deeply into matters and to render sharp judgments.[2]

And Mosellanus was a Leipziger!

Many others had similar sentiments. Spengler, the Nuremberg city secretary, published a book in which he openly supported Luther. Melanchthon eruditely sneered at Eck's position, and Johannes Oecolampadius, one of the Baslers, published an anonymous pamphlet in which he bluntly called Eck a fool. From as far away as Italy, one Crotus Rubeanus wrote Luther, "You are the first to have dared to free the people of the Lord from harmful opinions to true piety."[3] As early as February of the same year, the famous publisher Johann Froben of Basel wrote that he had never published an author whose books sold so well as Luther's. At the same time, the number of students at Wittenberg grew so rapidly that the city could not contain them. People all over Germany had good reason to be taking sides.

Caricature of Luther's opponents, with Leo X flanked by Emser and Eck.

Application to life

Through the remainder of 1519 and on into 1520, Luther began to apply his faith to the practicalities of the Christian life. He started this work in earnest in late August or early September, when he heard that Elector Frederick was ill, and wrote *Fourteen Consolations for Those Who Suffer*. There he pressed an image he borrowed from Carlstadt according to which Christ, and Christ alone, was the vessel in whom believers were borne to heaven. He also responded to one of Eck's charges by declaring that there "is no work of the church so much in need of reforming as confession and penance. For it is here that rage all the laws, profits, power, tyranny, error, danger, and innumerable evils for all souls and the entire church." Thereby, he charged, people were led to depend on the power of their confession and its validation by the church rather than on Christ. He then summarized his teaching in a published sermon for lay people. "For whoever believes, everything is beneficial and nothing harmful. For those who do not believe, everything is harmful and nothing beneficial."[4]

Once again Luther's mind was moving as he pressed ever more deeply into the practices of the church. In November he turned to Baptism and the Eucharist. He insisted that the unmerited grace of Christ was the core of each. Of Baptism he said that it was the beginning of the Christian life, the first step of justification before a righteous God, and the source of all true repentance. There was no need to add to Baptism through indulgences; what was needful was remembering the graciousness of a God who through Christ accepted even helpless children. So too with the Mass. It was a sign that pointed to Christ and that strengthened faith. Christ, the suffering Christ, came to believers in these sacraments. Nothing else was necessary. In the last of these essays Luther even threw a bouquet to some of Hus's followers. He added that the common practice of withholding the cup from the laity lest they spill it was misleading, because simple people might conclude that priests were somehow closer to God.

This comment caused an uproar. Duke George of Saxony called it "full of heresy and scandal." Luther characterized such complaints as being rather like "the trumpeting of a sterile pig."[5] Yet he *had* openly identified himself with the hated Hussites. He was also giving his opponents—and Eck in particular—good reason to pursue their case against him in Rome. The sacraments, especially the Mass, were the central piece in the piety of the late medieval church. Through them the church transmitted the grace of God to sinners and turned their partial confessions, partial good works, and partial faith into deeds that were truly pleasing to God.

For just this reason, in mid-December Spalatin asked Luther to spell out his views on all the sacraments and not just those he had treated in his series of published sermons. Luther replied that in his view there were only three sacraments rather than seven. These three—Baptism, confession, and the Lord's Supper—carried a promise with them. "For me," he continued, "the others are not sacraments, because a sacrament does not exist unless there is given with it an explicit divine promise

AETHERNA IPSE SVAE MENTIS SIMVLACHRA LVTHERV'
EXPRIMIT·AT VVLTVS CERA LVCAE OCCIDVOS'

M·D·X·X·

Luther the monk in 1520 (by Cranach).

that promotes faith, because without the Word of promise and without trusting that something has been received, there is no work with God that benefits us."[6] Although this was a private letter, Luther was once again reducing everything in the life of a Christian to the promises of God that called forth trust in his goodwill. In this way he denied the church any power over the life of the individual Christian. God was the constant giver and Christians could do nothing to earn his favor. Not even partaking of the sacraments pleased God.

The threat of excommunication

Every step Luther took drew attention. In early February 1520, Cajetan cochaired a commission in Rome that was called together specifically to examine Luther's writings for heresy. In March he was condemned by the universities of Louvain and Cologne. He commented, "We will pay no more attention to their condemnation than to the silly ravings of a drunken woman." About the same time Luther received an offer of armed assistance from two German noblemen, one of them the well-known humanist Ulrich von Hutten. Hutten wrote, "We seek to defend the common freedom; we seek to free the long-downtrodden fatherland."[7] This letter came in late May or early June. In mid-June another warrior pledged 100 knights to defend Luther, come what may, go where he would. The same month Eck joined the commission in Rome to examine Luther's teachings. Pressure was put on his old friend and mentor, Staupitz, to disavow him so the Augustinians might not be tainted with heresy. Finally, on June 24, 1520, the bull *Exsurge Domine* (Arise, Lord) was published in Rome. It gave Luther 60 days to recant or be excommunicated along with all his followers.

The reformer was in no mood to compromise. In May he had received from Frederick the Wise a copy of a letter from Rome that once again urged the elector to distance himself from Luther. Luther's reply was blunt: "The Romans can overcome us only on the grounds of reason and the Scriptures. With force and the ban they will make of Germany a second Bohemia," in rebellion from Rome. Later the same month he gave this reply theological teeth. He published a small book entitled *On the Papacy at Rome*, in which he declared that there were two churches in the world. One was external and visible and had the hierarchy and the pope at its head. The other "we call a spiritual, inner Christendom" that acknowledged only Christ. He told Frederick that the time appeared to be coming when Germany "must either become a desert or free itself."[8]

The time for decisions was indeed at hand. Even before he learned for certain that he had been excommunicated, Luther wrote Spalatin that he planned to "release a public appeal to the emperor and the nobility in all of Germany against the tyranny and vileness of the Roman curia." Also in June, Eck and a new papal ambassador, Jerome Aleander, were commissioned to publish *Exsurge Domine* throughout the empire. In the 16th century such acts commonly included a public burning of the heretic's books, and so it was with Luther. "If they damn my books and burn them," he announced, "I will burn the entire canon law."[9] In December he did just that.

Title page of the bull of excommunication with the symbols of both the papacy and the Medici family.

Address to the Christian Nobility

The breach with Rome had already become politically irreparable unless Luther were simply to give in and retract everything he had said. During the second half of 1520 many, including Erasmus, Frederick the Wise, and the emperor, desperately hoped to avoid this last step. Many others, including most of the group at Basel and those at Nuremberg, still could not believe that Luther's opponents would press the matter to its bitter end. In the midst of it all, Luther published three works that put an absolute finish to all such hopes.

First, in August he made good on his plan to change the arena for the controversy once again. In his *Address to the Christian Nobility of the German Nation* he called on the secular authorities to legislate the reforms that popes, cardinals, bishops, and the like refused to undertake. Taken together, his 27 proposals struck at each of the ways the church maintained its power in civil affairs. The 4000 copies in the first press run (an enormous number for that time) sold out in two weeks.

The book was a sensation, but there was far more to it than a demand for wide-ranging, specific reforms. Today, Luther's *Address* is remembered and debated for its theological content rather than for the practical impact it had in the 16th century. In that work he put forth his famous doctrine of the priesthood of all believers. With it he destroyed the idea of a special class of priests who, because they held in their hands the means of grace, also held special authority over the spiritual (and sometimes secular) lives of Christians. Rather, every Christian was a "little Christ" in service to the neighbor, and those called "priests" were first and finally servants to the entire community. They had no authority over anyone other than that of the gospel.

There is a strong sense in which Luther's situation forced him to write this book. He conceived it in June when Frederick the Wise was the only prince who stood with him against the official authorities of the church. And Luther unabashedly used the book to recruit more such supporters. He wrote it in German and played skillfully to the strong, anti-Roman sentiments of German rulers. "Here and now, the German nation, its bishops and princes, should regard themselves as Christians. They should govern and defend in their physical and spiritual goods the people who have been commended to them and they

Title page of Address to the Christian Nobility.

should protect them from these ravening wolves who come dressed in sheep's clothing as if they were shepherds and rulers." Luther pulled no punches. "If 99 percent of the papal court were abolished and only one percent were left, it would still be large enough to provide answers to questions of faith." As matters stood, papal officials were a "crawling mass of reptiles" who told everyone, "We are Christ's agents and the shepherds of Christ's sheep, and the senseless, drunken Germans must put up with it." [10] There can be no doubt that the *Address* was a political document.

However, the book was also faithful to Luther's own interior theological development. At least five years earlier, in his first lectures on the Psalms, he had told his students that only Christ properly ruled the church and that everyone, even prelates and cardinals, had to bow to his authority. Now, in late summer 1520, circumstances worked to turn this theological position into a powerful, revolutionary appeal. At Frederick the Wise's suggestion he even dedicated a summary to Emperor Charles V.

Babylonian Captivity of the Church

In October, Luther met Spalatin's request for a public treatment of all the sacraments. But this book, *On the Babylonian Captivity of the Church,* although written in Latin, was by no means the dispassionate, scholarly treatment of the subject Spalatin might have wished. The captivity of which Luther complained was the priests' hold on the sacraments and the insistence that Christians must perform good works in order to gain salvation. He added this charge "against the pope and all the Romanists. . . . If they do not abrogate all their laws and traditions, restore proper liberty to the churches of Christ, and cause that liberty to be taught, then they are guilty of all the souls that perish in this miserable servitude, and that the papacy is identical with the kingdom of Babylon and the Antichrist itself."

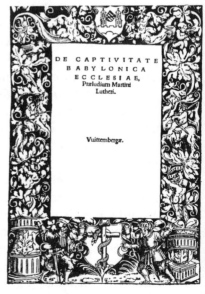

Title page of On the Babylonian Captivity of the Church.

Luther's situation made such language understandable. But once again, there was far more to his position than the rage and frustration that came from his opponents' constant threats and refusal to debate. Here, too, his earlier work as a theologian laid the foundation for his understanding of the sacraments. In the first place, he repeated his private rejection of confirmation, marriage, holy orders, and extreme unction on the grounds that they had no basis in the Scriptures. This reduction left Baptism, the Lord's Supper, and confession, but by now Luther had doubts about confession as well. His works were being published so quickly that the printer's assistant snatched the paper from his desk before the ink was dry and before he had the opportunity to revise them. By the end of the treatise he had reduced confession to a useful practice but no longer a sacrament. Personally, Luther continued daily to confess his own sins, but where there had been seven sacraments there were now only two.

In both Baptism and the Lord's Supper Luther found Christ alone, the fulfilled promise of God. Of Baptism he declared, "The first point is the divine promise," and, "Our entire salvation depends on this. . . ." As an act, Baptism was thus evidence of God's grace. By remembering their baptisms, Christians found their faith "constantly aroused and cultivated. Once the divine promise has been accepted by us, its truth lasts until death." The whole purpose of Baptism was to strengthen faith. "Finally, [the Christian] has a solace in every temptation from the unique truth he utters when he says, 'God is faithful in his promises, and I received his sign when I was baptized. If God is for me, who can be against me?' " As God's work and not the work of human beings, Baptism was "the one ship that remains, solid and indestructible, and its timbers will never be broken to pieces." People could and did abandon ship in times of torment and trouble. But the ship was always there, ever reminding them of God's graciousness in Christ. No spiritual exercises could add anything to it.

"All the sacraments were instituted to feed our faith," Luther wrote. It was just here that he also found the most terrible abuses in the celebration of the Mass. Withholding the cup from lay people divided Christians and suggested that God granted grace only with conditions. The doctrine of transubstantiation (the idea that in the Mass the priest turned bread and wine into Christ's body and blood) made the priest, rather than Christ, the actor. Describing the sacrament as effective *ex opere operato*, a completed work that the priest performed by making sacrifice, denied that grace was a free gift directly from God. Rather, Luther suggested, the Mass should more properly be called an *opus operans*, a work that God was doing and by which he was feeding his people. As practiced, the Mass was therefore blasphemy and idolatry in the most basic sense, because it stood in the place of Christ. "This abuse," he wrote, "has then brought with it countless other abuses to the point that the faith of this sacrament is entirely obliterated and people turn the divine sacraments over to market days, shopkeepers, and tax collectors."

For Luther the central point of the Eucharist was the same as the entirety of the Christian faith. God, he wrote, "does not first accept our works and then save us. The Word of God comes before everything else. Faith follows, and then after faith comes love, and love finally yields every good work." Once again Luther placed the emphasis exclusively on God's work and God's promise. "Thus," he insisted, "it comes down to the most perfect promise, that of the new testament" in Christ's body and blood. "Faith believes Christ to be truthful in these words and does not doubt that these immense blessings have been bestowed on it." Any addition of human works or merit simply had the effect of denying Christ.

This book struck directly at the sacramental foundations of late medieval piety. "It is a gift of no small moment to know what has been given to us . . . and with what understanding the gifts are to be used," Luther wrote.[11] A gulf had opened between his religion and the religion his world had inherited.

Events were moving quickly as this book appeared in early October. On the 12th Luther met again with Miltitz; he agreed to write the pope a defense of his actions in which he would say that he had never attacked Leo X personally and that the entire uproar was the fault of Eck. In early November, Luther received another offer of armed assistance from the knight Franz von Sickingen. At the same time, the papal nuncio Aleander was meeting with Elector Frederick and urging him to burn Luther's books, seize him, and send him to Rome. But Frederick conferred with Erasmus, who said that while Luther was too sharp in his criticisms, his only crimes were to have knocked off the pope's crown and to have kicked the monks in their bellies. Frederick held to his original decision. He would not proceed against Luther until Luther received a hearing before unbiased judges.

For his part, Luther fulfilled his pledge to Miltitz. He wrote Leo X in what would be his last attempt at reconciliation. "I have never," he protested, "removed myself from Your Blessedness, to such an extent that I should not with all my heart wish you and your see every blessing, for which I have begged God with earnest prayers to the best of my ability." Leo was being led astray by the "raging of your godless flatterers," with the consequence that Luther had no choice but to appeal to a council.

Luther was trying to put the best construction on recent actions from Rome. But finally he could not contain himself. "I have truly despised your see, the Roman curia," he confessed; "neither you nor anyone else can deny that it is more corrupt than any Babylon or Sodom ever was. As far as I can see, it is marked by a completely depraved, hopeless, and notorious godlessness." Eck in his vainglory was responsible for the way things had gone. "I detest contentions. I will challenge no one. But I do not want others to challenge me. If they do, as Christ is my teacher, I will not be speechless." [12]

The Freedom of a Christian

Leo could scarcely have taken much comfort from this letter, which was quickly forgotten by all sides. What was remembered was the little book to which it was attached, Luther's *On the Freedom of a Christian.* Here he briefly summarized the practical consequences of his theology for the conduct of the Christian life.

Luther began with "the following two propositions concerning the freedom and the bondage of the spirit:

"A Christian is a perfectly free lord of all, subject to none.

"A Christian is a perfectly dutiful servant of all, subject to all."

He granted that "These two theses seem to contradict each other," but insisted that they simply described two aspects of every Christian,

Title page of On the Freedom of a Christian.

which he said were like "two men in the same man contradicting each other." The one was inner and spiritual, the other was outward, "the old man."

First, he maintained, it was obvious that nothing outward "has any influence in producing Christian righteousness or freedom, or in producing unrighteousness or servitude." Individuals could do what they would, but "even contemplation, meditation, and all that the soul can do, does not help" in making someone righteous before God and therefore free. The other side of the coin was that living within the world and partaking fully of its joys and sorrows could do the soul no harm. "One thing and only one thing is necessary for Christian life, righteousness, and freedom. That one thing is the most holy Word of God, the gospel of Christ."

This gospel created faith. "To preach Christ means to feed the soul, make it righteous, set it free, and save it, provided it believes the preaching." Moreover, "the moment you begin to have faith you learn that all things in you are altogether blameworthy, sinful, and damnable." A Christian was therefore to be constantly penitent. "On the other hand, only ungodliness and unbelief of the heart, and no outer work, make him guilty and a damnable servant of sin," no matter what else the person did or did not do.

Works of love for the neighbor followed naturally. "So the Christian who is consecrated by his faith does good works, but the works do not make him holier or more Christian, for that is the work of faith alone. And if someone were not first a believer and a Christian, then all his works would amount to nothing and would be truly wicked and damnable sins." He concluded that therefore "we are not freed from works through faith in Christ but from false opinions concerning works, that is, from the foolish presumption that justification comes by works." Here, Luther insisted, was the true mystery and freedom of the Christian life. "Thus what we do, live, and are in works and ceremonies, we do because of the necessities of this life and of the effort to rule our body. Nevertheless, we are justified not in these but in the faith of the Son of God." A Christian was both free from the obligation to do good works in order to please God and still bound to do them.

This book contained few references to the critique of ceremonies and outward works of piety that had made Luther such a lightning rod. Rather, Luther presented his most insistent explanation of the heart of the Christian life as he understood it. At this critical moment in his career, when nothing was certain, he expressed himself first and foremost as a pastor. The book was written to this end, he added, so "that the Lord may give us and make us *theodidacti*, that is, those taught by God."[13]

Political complications

Even as the theological issues became clear, the political situation was becoming highly complex. Charles I of Spain had become Emperor Charles V on June 28, 1519. But everyone knew that being elected emperor and actually exercising imperial authority over German princes, cities, and prelates were two different things. Charles was therefore forced to come to Germany and deal with the local political leaders personally and then in a formal diet, or meeting, of the Holy Roman Empire of the German Nation. So he met during late 1520 with several German politicians, including Frederick the Wise. Then he scheduled a diet to meet at the city of Worms, in southwestern Germany, early in 1521.

Charles V's reign was blessed with the luck of a marriage that brought him many territories, but it was plagued with problems from its very beginning. On one side, he himself was a young, slight man who was utterly unfamiliar with Germany and spoke no German. A loyal Catholic and a man who would eventually abdicate his throne to spend his last years in a monastery, he also knew that Pope Leo X had opposed his election. He was of no mind simply to do the bidding of Rome. Then there were the German princes, a notoriously factious lot who were unified in little more than defending their princely liberties. Above all, there were the Turks, pressing inexorably up the Danube and into Charles's Austrian crown lands. Charles knew he had to have help in beating them back. This was his objective for the Diet of Worms.

In addition, the emperor now faced the unwelcome problem of Luther. By tradition and the law of the church, he ought simply to have ratified *Exsurge Domine*, declared him an outlaw, and cajoled the princes into enforcing the decree. But there was also the influential Elector Frederick the Wise, who had refused to let the pope pressure him into being a candidate for emperor and thereby (at least) had saved Charles a great deal of trouble. So on November 28, in reply to Frederick's request, Charles wrote that Luther was to appear at the Diet of Worms for a hearing, but on the condition that he would publish nothing more against Rome.

Luther would get his hearing. Or would he? On December 17, Aleander appeared before Charles. He eloquently pointed to Rome's doctrinal objections, reported that Luther's books had already been burned in Cologne and Mainz, and noted that even now the monk stood under excommunication. Charles had to do his duty and declare him an outlaw. The emperor withdrew his invitation.

For a time it looked as if the game was over. Frederick the Wise arrived in Worms on January 5, 1521. The actual bull of excommunication, *Decet Romanum Pontificem*, which also named Pirckheimer, Spengler, and Hutten, had been published in Rome two days earlier. It was sent to Charles V on January 18, with instructions to announce it to the Diet and to declare that any territory, city, or church that protected Luther would also be under the ban. The Diet officially opened on January 28. Two weeks later Aleander persuaded Charles to let him draw up an imperial edict against Luther. On February 15 it was presented to the princes, prelates, and the representatives of the free imperial cities. Only the electors of Saxony and the Palatinate objected.

At just this moment, Aleander's careful plans fell apart like a house constructed with toothpicks but no glue. The general populace was taking a hand in events. Aleander reported to Rome, "At the present all of Germany is in a decided uproar. Nine-tenths put up the battle cry, 'Luther!' and the other tenth, 'Death to the Roman curia!' "[14] Aleander was not above exaggerating the difficulties of his mission in order to ingratiate himself with his superiors. But on February 19, the assembled princes replied to Charles V that condemning Luther without a hearing could well lead to riot and revolution. They did not suggest holding a public disputation with him, but said that he ought to be called to discuss other matters. The princes assured Charles that they would support an edict against Luther if he did not then recant.

Luther would therefore have a hearing of sorts. He had little idea of what was transpiring. In late February he wrote, "I am completely overwhelmed with work. I preach twice daily; I am working on the Psalms, I have a collection of scriptural meditations for the day in progress, and I am answering my enemies." He himself had doubts

about the public uproar into which the whole affair seemed to be de-
generating. Of Hutten's latest book he wrote Spalatin, "I would not
have it that people fight on the side of the gospel with force and killing.
. . . The world is to be won over with the Word." Two weeks later
he wrote Elector Frederick that he was willing to come to Worms so
long as he had a guaranteed safe conduct there and back. In February
he wrote Staupitz and declared, "This is not the time to be timid but
to raise the voice loudly."[15]

*Charles V, with his full title detailed
below (by Hans Weiditz).*

*Jerome Aleander, papal ambassador at
the Diet of Worms.*

The Diet of Worms

It took Luther and his small party two weeks to travel by wagon
from Wittenberg to Worms far to the west. In Erfurt the humanist
scholars Crotus Rubeanus and Eobanus Hessus received him with fan-
fare. On April 7 he preached in the church of his old monastery to
crowds that spilled into the courtyards. Having left behind a lecture
hall whose students had swelled to 400 in number, he now preached
also in Gotha and Eisenach. When he finally arrived in Worms on April

16, trumpeters announced him, the imperial herald led the procession, and "all the people poured into the streets to see the monk, Martin Luther." [16] Some 2000 sought to escort him through the city gates. Once settled into his quarters, he was visited by the princes Philip of Hesse, William of Henneberg, and William of Braunschweig. He was gaining supporters even among the politicians.

Shortly before leaving Wittenberg, Luther told Spalatin that he was not going to travel all the way to Worms just to be asked to recant. He still wanted a debate, and he still remembered Augsburg. But now he was more determined than ever. "This will be my recantation at Worms: 'Before I said the pope is the vicar of Christ. Now I declare that the pope is the opponent of Christ and the apostle of the devil.' " He knew that this would be a high moment and he met it with none of the fears that had tormented him as he prepared to face Cajetan in 1518. "Unless I am restrained by force or the emperor rescinds his invitation, I will enter Worms under the banner of Christ against the gates of hell." But he also had no doubts as to what might happen. "I have had my Palm Sunday. Is all this pomp merely a temptation or is it also a sign of the passion to come?" [17]

On April 17 he was ushered into the Diet at about 4:00 P.M. He was visibly awed by what he saw. There was Emperor Charles V himself, heir to a 1000-year-old empire. Near him on the raised dais were his advisers and the representatives of Rome. All around were Spanish troops decked out in their parade best. The rest of the hall was filled with the politically powerful of Germany—the seven electors, the bishops and princes of the church, the territorial princes, and representatives of the great cities. In the midst of this impressive assembly there was a table, piled high with books.

The chancellor of the archbishop of Trier gestured toward the pile and announced to Luther that he had been called to the Diet to answer two questions: Had he written these books? Was there a part of them he would now choose to recant?

The monk and professor from little Wittenberg was plainly taken aback. There would be no debate, nor even a judicial hearing. His judges had already made their decision. He could scarcely be heard as he said, "The books are all mine, and I have written more." What would he say to the second question? "This touches God and his Word. This affects the salvation of souls. . . . I beg you, give me time." He was given one day, and back in his quarters he wrote, "So long as Christ is merciful, I will not recant a single jot or tittle."[18]

And he did not. The next day's business at the Diet delayed Luther's return until nightfall. So candlelight added a sense of sanctity to the crowd of dignitaries jammed into the episcopal hall next to the great Romanesque cathedral. Now that Luther knew what game his opponents were playing, he rose to the occasion. The same questions were put to him: "Will you defend these books all together, or do you wish to recant some of what you have said?" Luther replied in a short speech, which he then repeated in Latin.

There were three kinds of books in the stack, he declared. There were some "in which I have taught about the Christian faith and good works in such a proper, clear, and Christian manner" that even his opponents thought well of them. He certainly could not retract these. There were others in which he had "attacked the papacy and papist teaching." To retract them would be to encourage tyranny. Finally, there were some in which he had attacked individuals. Perhaps he had done so too harshly, but he still could not retract them, because these people defended papal tyranny.

Luther was trying to snare his examiner in a debate, but the man would have nothing of it. He countered that Luther had not spoken to the point. Surely a single individual could not call into doubt the tradition of the entire church. Now, the examiner declared, "you must give a simple, clear, and proper answer to the question, Will you recant or not?"

Luther did answer, and it was an answer that, in his words, was without "horns or teeth":

Unless I can be instructed and convinced with evidence from the Holy Scriptures or with open, clear, and distinct grounds and reasoning—and my conscience is captive to the Word of God—then I cannot and will not recant, because it is neither safe nor wise to act against conscience.

He then added: "Here I stand. I can do no other. God help me! Amen."[19]

NINE

The Exile

L uther's dramatic appearance at the Diet of Worms was not, as one might have expected, the end of his dealings with those assembled there. His declaration that he could not and would not recant was followed by several days of meetings and negotiations. Within this collection of Germany's most powerful politicians, many hoped to avoid the consequences of the confrontation. Above all, they were frightened by the sudden appearance all over Worms of placards bearing the sign of the *Bundschuh* (a peasant's boot), the dreaded symbol of peasant revolution. So Luther spent another three days talking first with this person and then with that. Finally it became apparent to all that he would not budge. When he returned to his quarters after the last session, he shouted, "I am through! I am through!"

He could not, however, simply collect his companions and leave. First he had to receive formal permission from Emperor Charles V, who had a speech of his own to give. "Our predecessors, who were also Christian princes . . . have been loyal to the Church of Rome," he declared; "we cannot honorably depart from the example of our forefathers in defending the old faith and coming to the aid of the Holy See of Rome." Luther was to be condemned. Charles would abide by the safe conduct he had granted, but he instructed his messenger to remind Luther that it was good for but 21 days, that he was to return directly to Wittenberg, and was neither to preach nor to write anything on the way.[1] Luther did as he was told—almost.

Unnoticed, he and his party finally left Worms on April 26. They traveled in a northerly direction and reached Friedberg in Hesse two days later. There Luther released his escort, which included the imperial herald and a small troop. They returned with letters to Spalatin and to the emperor in which Luther defended his actions at Worms. On April 29 the abbot of the monastery in Hersfeld met him outside that town, escorted him through its walls, and persuaded him to preach to the assembled monks. Luther and his now reduced party reached Eisenach on May 1, and again he was pressured into preaching, this time to a large crowd of citizens. On May 3 he followed the suggestion that he visit his relatives in Möhra, the village his father had left just before Luther was born. Once more he preached, but this time to a group of peasants in the open air, since Möhra did not have a church.

That evening Luther stayed with his uncle and his family. Together with some friends, they escorted him on his way the next afternoon. They parted company in the vicinity of Castle Altenstein. Soon Luther and his two companions were alone in their wagon on an empty road that led through the woods. Abruptly, four or five armed horsemen plunged out of the forest and demanded to know if Luther was one of the travelers. The driver panicked and pointed to him. They snatched Luther from the wagon and dragged him, half running and half stumbling, up the road and around the bend.

The plot was so carefully wrought and perfectly executed that many thought they had heard the last of Luther. There was, however, nothing to fear. Once they were safely out of sight, Luther's new companions paused, gave him a chance to catch up, mounted him on a horse and then, covering their tracks, turned in a northerly direction. Shortly before midnight they clattered across the drawbridge of Elector Frederick's castle, the Wartburg. It was all so well done that even the elector could honestly report that he did not know Luther's whereabouts.

The Wartburg

Luther was warmly welcomed and well-treated at the Wartburg. The castle itself towers over the valley that leads to Eisenach and from there to Erfurt. "My Patmos," he called it, in reference to the island in the Aegean where John wrote the book of Revelation. "The kingdom of the birds" or "the realm of the air" were other favored ways he found of telling friends approximately where he was. He was to obey only one rule. It was essential that he not be recognized. He was given a room with a retractable stairway, so that none save the most trusted could even see him until his hair and beard had grown out. His monk's habit was taken from him and he was dressed as a knight. Luther was now "Junker Jörg," Sir George. He remained so for 10 months.

The Wartburg.

Luther had known what was likely to happen after he left Worms, and he did not like the plan at all. To Lucas Cranach, the Wittenberg artist, he wrote on April 28, "I am letting myself be put away and hidden (even I do not know where), and, although I would much rather suffer death from the tyrants, especially by the hands of mad Duke George of Saxony, I am obliged not to ignore the advice of good people, at least for the present." At Worms all they had said was, "Are these books yours? 'Yes.' Will you retract them? 'No.' Then get out of here!" Luther was still ready for a fight. "Oh, how blind we Germans are," he added, "and how childishly we act to let the Romanists mock and make fools of us in such a miserable way!"[2]

At the Wartburg, Luther was not going to get his fight. Suddenly and forcibly withdrawn from the fray, he occasionally became depressed. Fed rich food to which his body was unaccustomed, he also had an extended attack of severe digestive upset. To Melanchthon he wrote in July, "I should be ardent in the spirit but I am ardent in the flesh, in lust, laziness, leisure, and sleepiness. . . . Already eight days have passed in which I have written nothing and neither prayed nor studied. I am attacked partly by temptations of the flesh and partly by other worries." He was a monk in the midst of knights, men of the world. A few pills sent from Wittenberg soon settled his stomach. But being put on the shelf did not sit well with him. "Maybe," he wrote, "the Lord burdens me so in order to push me out of this hermitage and into the arena."[3]

But Luther was not going anywhere, and so he set to work. He had managed to snatch his Hebrew Old Testament and his Greek New Testament just as he himself was being snatched from the wagon. So he began his stay at the Wartburg by reading them daily, even without a dictionary. In spite of his remarks to Melanchthon, these proved to be among the most productive months of his life. Before they ended he had published a dozen books and translated the entire New Testament into German. Before three weeks had passed, he had finished the first of these new books and sent it off to Wittenberg for publication. Yet he still wrote to Spalatin, "Here I sit all day long, lazy and full of food."[4]

True laziness was something Luther never knew. What he meant was rather that at the Wartburg he was literally above the day-to-day struggles that he himself had unleashed. Sometimes he insisted that he was resigned to the fate God had in store for him. Nonetheless, he plotted ways to come down from his tower, even to the point of perhaps seeking a post at another university. But he had no choice in the matter. On the few outings he was eventually allowed, he was warned not to show interest in printed materials, because to do so might give away his disguise. Completely without distractions, he could spend his time only reading, thinking, and writing. The subject of the exile's first book is therefore a key to the true state of his mind and his intentions. It was a commentary on Psalm 68, written in German for the laity. The

writer of that psalm cried out in his distress and begged God to destroy
his enemies.

This sense of being deserted and of begging for vindication lay heavy
on Luther during his months at the Wartburg. It was also rooted in the
thinking he had done about the nature of the church some eight years
earlier in his first series of lectures on the Psalms. Both his feelings
and his thinking came forth most clearly in his *Commentary on the
Magnificat,* which he also began immediately on his arrival. In the
choice of Mary to bear the child Jesus he found a powerful example
of how God turned the world upside down. God exalted her precisely
because she was so genuinely lowly, a person of no account. And
because she was so lowly, she could do nothing except trust in God's
graciousness. Luther was quick to draw the lesson for his own time
and situation. Where Mary sang of God's humbling the mighty, Luther
commented that God allowed evil people "to become great and to put
themselves mightily forward." But, he added, "When their bubble is
full of air and everyone thinks that they have become victorious and
have surmounted every obstacle, and even they are satisfied with their
own achievements, then God sticks a pin in the bubble, and everything
is finished."

Here Luther's understanding of the life of faith also turned the traditional view of Mary upside down. The role of Mary was especially
important in the piety of the late Middle Ages. For Luther, Mary was
indeed to be praised above all human beings. "We ought to call on
her," he wrote, "so for her sake God may grant and do what we ask."
But, he added, "she does nothing; God does everything." Mary stood
as a lesson to all Christians not because she was so pure but because
she was so impoverished, a woman who was pregnant but not married.
The lesson was obvious: "You must not only think and speak in a
lowly manner," he concluded, "but actually become impoverished and
be completely wrapped up in poverty so that, without any human help,
God alone may do the work."[5] Mary was far from a saint whose great
worthiness Christians should copy. She was an example of utter worth-
lessness, blessed by God.

The idea that God empowered the weak was a great comfort to Luther
while he sat in the Wartburg. He himself was utterly dependent on
Elector Frederick, his castle, and the castle warden. But his sojourn
in the kingdom of the birds did not entirely withdraw him from im-

mediate and very demanding obligations. Even apart from his normal
routine, Luther remained a man of controversy. He felt empowered to
do work of his own to humble the mighty.

A condemned man

The Edict of Worms, issued by the emperor shortly after Luther left
the city, declared him an outlaw. Legally, anyone could strike him
dead and not be punished for murder. In addition, his teachings had
by now been condemned by the theological faculties of the universities
of Paris, Louvain, and Cologne. They would certainly not support an
appeal to a future council, even if they agreed in principle that such
a thing was proper.

Luther scarcely replied to these condemnations. "Who," he asked,
"can imagine that the Scriptures still carry any weight when one is
obligated to assent to professors who concoct their arguments without
reference to the Scriptures?" But the attack of James Latomus, which
he received from Melanchthon shortly after arriving at the Wartburg,
and which did allege proofs from the Scriptures, was a different matter.

In his response to Latomus, which he completed within a month,
Luther came as close as he ever did to a full treatment of his doctrine
of justification. Employing a point-for-point style of argument that he
would use against opponents throughout his career, he nonetheless
presented one central message. There was no part of the human being
that stood above or beyond sin. The whole person was condemned and
therefore the whole person was saved. "Whoever is subject to wrath
is entirely subject to the entirety of wrath, and whoever is subject to
grace is entirely under the entirety of grace, for wrath and grace concern
the person" as a whole.[6] There was for Luther therefore no room to
speak of a spark of goodness that might incline a Christian to do
partially good works, such as purchasing indulgences. Even to think
of doing so was simply to fool oneself. There was no way to attain
salvation through doing works of any kind.

Luther wrote as a controversialist, as he did so often during these
months. In July he wrote a reply to the canon at Meissen, Jerome
Emser, in which he faked a recantation of all his supposed errors. But
at the same time he pressed the idea that all Christians were priests to
one another. Emser apparently did not appreciate the little joke, so he
continued to write against Luther while Luther happily referred to him

simply as "the goat." Eck rejoined the fray also. In private, Luther's favorite term for him was *Dreck* or "dung."

Luther was a master polemicist; at name-calling he had no peer, as many discovered to their regret. But he reserved such tactics for opponents who were, or at least claimed to be, teachers of the church. With them he never thought himself involved in a polite discussion. No holds were barred when it came to those who taught contrary to the doctrine of Christ.

Defending the truth against such error was a task to which Luther felt directly called. But his heart really lay with the uncommitted, the wavering, the confused, and those directly affected by the powerful changes that were underway. As he had put it a year earlier in *On the Freedom of a Christian,* he sought to transform such persons into people taught by God. So he wrote books for them as well. In these he turned once again to the task of spelling out the practical consequences of his theology for the day-to-day conduct of Christian life. The first of them, completed by June 1, was *On Confession: Whether the Pope Has the Power to Require It.*

His answer was a flat no. Since the Fourth Lateran Council, three centuries earlier, the church had required all the laity to confess their sins to a priest at least once a year, usually during Lent. Now Luther declared that this rule was a monstrous burden laid on the consciences of ordinary people. It was not necessary, he insisted, to confess one's sins to a priest, because Christ himself ordered only that Christians confess to one another. "Therefore," he urged, "let us candidly and from the heart . . . confess, counsel, help, and plead with one another about whatever lies secretly on our hearts, whether it is a sin or a deep ache, and then without doubts about the bright, clear promise of God, and on this account, go freely and happily to the sacrament and die [to ourselves] in it."[7]

Practical concerns

These practical works that he wrote for the laity best reveal the driving force behind Luther's immense productivity at the Wartburg. From the moment of his arrival, his fundamental concern was pastoral. The core of his own theological development was complete. What remained was to spell out its impact on the daily conduct of the Christian life. In this regard the first and the highest task was to ease the consciences of the faithful. His own conscience had been tortured by the religious world in which he became an adult, and now he sought to warn others away from this agony. He started on the path to reform when Tetzel's indulgence sale contradicted his teachings as a professor and threatened his concerns as a pastor. Now these same concerns thrust him back into the fray, even if from afar. By explaining the practical consequences of his theology, he took responsibility for all he had earlier said and done.

Wittenberg was a small, dirty town that was blessed, or cursed, with the presence of many restless minds. Very soon Luther learned that some were beginning to act on his convictions, at least as they interpreted them. As early as May he heard that one of his Augustinian friends had left the order and had married. Luther neither condemned nor blessed the act. In August he advised Melanchthon against a set of theses from Carlstadt in which his fellow professor declared that not taking both the bread and the wine in the sacrament was a sin. That same month he received yet another of Carlstadt's essays. This time the restless spirit was arguing that vows of celibacy were themselves sinful and had to be broken. Luther declared that his friends "will never force a wife on me!"[8]

The issue of monastic vows was one thing. It directly affected only those who had taken them. But the sacrament was a matter that touched every Christian. After a number of exchanges within the Wittenberg community on the subject, the university held a formal disputation on the Mass. Shortly thereafter, in September, Melanchthon and several students participated in the first Evangelical Lord's Supper, in which everyone received both the bread and the wine and the emphasis was on God's work with his people. In the middle of October, Luther's own Augustinian cloister suspended private celebrations of the Mass on the grounds that they blasphemously masqueraded as a good work.

The religious world of the late Middle Ages was disintegrating in Luther's own hometown. The changes were regarded as such a scandal that Frederick the Wise wrote the theological faculty at his little university and asked them for an opinion on what was happening. On October 20 the professors held a solemn discussion, and after much wrangling they declared that the Mass, when conceived as a sacrifice, was idolatry. Therefore it could not be celebrated in private, as in the case of masses for the dead. Moreover, withholding the cup from the laity suggested that the priest was somehow closer to God than they were. The Mass could no longer be tolerated.

Luther was forced to intervene. He himself had more than implied the need for such changes in his three treatises of 1520. The most pressing problem was the Mass. He and his colleagues had always been taught that it was a good work, done by the priest for the lay people. It was pleasing to God in and of itself, even when conducted by a priest in private (without a congregation present). Luther himself had conducted just such masses while he was in Rome. Now brothers in his own order had ended the practice.

Luther's reply to these developments was *On the Abolition of Private Masses*, which he translated into German for the laity as *On the Misuse of the Mass*. He knew that far-reaching changes in the Mass would be deeply unsettling to people who had been taught to find their salvation in it. He also knew that those who actually made the changes could suffer from grave doubts about what they were doing. In this work he confessed that he had often asked himself, "Are you alone wise? Can it be that everyone else is in error and has been in error for so long? What if you are wrong and lead into error so many people who might then be eternally damned?"[9]

For Luther, establishing whether a practice was right or wrong was far more than an exercise in reading, thinking, and coming to the proper conclusion. Above all, he insisted that "consciences must be treated with faith and trust." He therefore gave his colleagues solid arguments so that they might be confident in their actions. But at the same time he charged them to coerce no one. It was true that the New Testament did not speak of a special priesthood that was empowered to handle the mysteries of God in a magical way. Nonetheless, for the present at least, nothing should be said against a brother who wished to celebrate the Mass in the old way for the nourishment of his own soul. Luther refused to require anyone to commune in both kinds. Just because it was preferable for all to be offered both the body and the blood of Christ did not require anyone to take them both.

If Luther had been an ideologue, he would have reacted to the question of the Mass rather differently. He would have demanded strict and immediate adherence to the exact truth of the matter. But his first concern was for the care of souls and consciences. Therefore he urged his colleagues to proceed with caution. As a consequence, when he began to wrestle with the issue of vows of celibacy he proceeded in the same manner as he had with respect to the Mass.

The question of monastic vows

Monastic vows posed a particularly difficult question for Luther. As late as December 1521, he wrote the vicar-general of his order (who was now his old friend Linck), "I will remain in this cowl and way of life unless the world changes." But as early as August the same year, he had confessed to Melanchthon, "If Christ were here, I do not doubt he would dissolve these chains and would annul all vows." [10]

Luther therefore had to think this question through with great care. In his *Address to the Christian Nobility* of a year earlier, he had declared that celibacy should not be mandatory for secular priests who worked daily with the laity in the world. But monks and nuns were different, because they had taken their vows freely and had not had them imposed on them from without. Luther finally began to unravel the problem when he approached it from the point of view of consoling troubled consciences. If the vow had been taken in order to make the taker more righteous, and if it still served this purpose, then it was idolatrous. But if a Christian was able to serve freely within monastic vows, then there was no compulsion to reject them. He therefore insisted that "According to Paul, the law is not law when you keep it of your own accord; so too the vow is not a vow when you keep it freely." Luther sent these considerations to Wittenberg in two separate documents that totaled 280 theses. When he read them, Melanchthon commented, "This is the real beginning of the freeing of the monks." [11]

It was, however, no more than a beginning, and Luther knew it. On November 11 he informed Spalatin, "I have decided to attack monastic vows and to free the young people from that hell of celibacy, totally unclean and condemned as it is through its burning and pollutions." [12] One day later, 13 of his fellow monks left the Augustinian cloister in Wittenberg. Luther feared that they had not done so "with a sufficiently secure conscience" and hoped that his *On Monastic Vows* would help.

The book (120 pages long and written in only 10 days) was in one way an intensely personal undertaking. Luther dedicated it to his father. He candidly recalled how Hans Luder had strongly opposed his decision to become a monk. He related Hans's continued objections just after Luther had celebrated his first mass. And he freely admitted that Hans had been right when he had asked if perhaps Luther had not been hearing the devil in the thunderstorm. "You," he now wrote, "quickly came back with a reply so fitting and so much to the point that I have scarcely in my entire life heard any man say anything that struck me so forcibly and stayed with me so long." But good had come of it, for now "the wind that blows over these vows of grass and their bloom will dry up the grass and wither the blossoms."

On Monastic Vows did not go far beyond the views Luther had already expressed in his theses and his private correspondence. He did, however, now organize these earlier ideas under the themes of Christian liberty and love for one's neighbor that he had developed in *On the Freedom of a Christian* more than a year earlier. As a result, he declared that vows of this kind could be freely taken, but were not to be legally binding. Above all, such vows went against the law of love, and in particular love for one's parents. By being in a monastery and withdrawing from the world, he could do nothing to help others. "Therefore," he concluded, "we may keep our vows, but we are not obligated to do so, because love is our only obligation." He closed with the advice that those who were thinking of leaving a monastery or convent should first examine their consciences. If they had taken those vows because they then thought they would be pleasing God but now thought they could serve God's creatures better in the outside world, they should freely leave.[13]

Even from exile, Luther's words had impact. In the case of the Mass and in that of monastic vows, they powerfully encouraged his colleagues at Wittenberg. In another case, they put a stop to a renewed sale of indulgences. With Luther out of sight, the archbishop of Mainz thought he could get away with opening a new collection of relics at his residence in Halle. When Luther heard of it he was furious. He responded with a little essay, *Against the Idol at Halle,* whose very title suggested that the idol was not just the relic collection but the good archbishop himself! Intense negotiations among Spalatin, Melanchthon, and the archbishop's representatives finally persuaded Spalatin to gag Luther. He simply held up publication of the book. But the mere threat of a blast from the Wartburg was enough to put an end to the new reliquary. Luther also wrote to the archbishop's representative, Wolfgang Capito, who had earlier been such a supporter while in Basel, "The most important thing of all is to declare what is right and what is not right. . . ."[14]

A visit to Wittenberg

In spite of being vitally involved in so many practical issues, Luther was now both restless and lonely. Throughout November he complained of being attacked "by many devils" at whom, he said, he "laughed." In fact, he was suffering from the very doubts that he had tried so hard to overcome among his friends. With no one of a similar mind around him, he finally could bear the solitude no longer. On December 2 he stole out of the Wartburg, commandeered a horse, and left for Wittenberg. He had to see with his own eyes what was happening and hear with his own ears what people were thinking.

Luther must have had a very good horse and must have ridden the beast very hard. By the next afternoon he was having lunch at a tavern in Leipzig about 100 miles to the east. He must have said something that gave him away. Perhaps he just showed too much interest in gossip from Wittenberg. Afterward his host was interrogated by the local authorities on orders from Duke George. But Luther was already in Wittenberg, another 30 miles to the north.

He stayed little more than a week. Because his disguise was good but not perfect, he did not visit his fellow brothers in the monastery. But when he arrived to lodge with Melanchthon, who was himself living in the home of Amsdorf, even these friends did not recognize him. Having learned who the visitor was, they then decided to play a little joke on Lucas Cranach. They invited him to come and do a portrait of a famous visiting knight. Even Cranach, with the eyes of an artist, did not recognize him.

For Luther, the visit was a tonic. He saw exactly what was happening as a result of his teachings, and most of his fears evaporated. "Everything I see and hear pleases me immensely," he wrote Spalatin. "The Lord brings courage to men of good will." Yet one matter was troublesome. Luther noted that "on the road [to Wittenberg] I was disturbed by various rumors of a certain ill-will among our people" toward those who were not in full agreement with him.[15] He returned to the Wartburg with the determination to write yet another book.

The result was an *Admonition to All True Christians to Guard Themselves against Sedition*. Here Luther turned his pastoral concern for weak consciences into an attack on all partisanship. He declared that any public uproar was "a precise and certain sign of Satan's intervention." Above all, he insisted, "There are no grounds for insurrection,

Luther as Junker Jörg (by Cranach).

because it almost always harms the innocent more than the guilty. . . ."
For those who took his name in defense of their actions he had nothing
but scorn. "How did it come about," he asked, "that I, a poor, stinking,
bag of dung, should come to the point that anyone could give the
children of Christ my godless name?"[16]
    With such concerns Luther might well have leapt into the fray him-
self. But he was still under the imperial ban (as he would remain for
the rest of his life), so he could not play a direct role in the day-to-
day direction of what had become a popular movement. Rather, he
stayed at the Wartburg and took up the translation of the New Testament. If he could put the Scriptures and a guide to reading and understanding them in the hands of every Christian, then they could all
become *theodidacti,* people taught by God.

Translation of the New Testament

    Luther translated the entire New Testament into German within 11
weeks. Like a man possessed, he worked at the rate of more than 1500
words per day. What he produced was so masterful that in time it did
much to create the modern German language. He was determined to
do as good a job as possible and to prove to the world that "German
nightingales can sing as beautifully as Roman goldfinches." In so doing
he took great care to use the language of the people. To Spalatin he
wrote of the work, "We shall employ you sometimes to find the right
word. But give us simple words and not those of the court or a castle,
for this book should be renowned for its simplicity." During the midst
of the work he declared, "I have undertaken to translate the Bible into
German. This was good for me; otherwise I might have died in the
mistaken notion that I was a learned fellow."[17] Together with his colleagues in Wittenberg, Luther spent the rest of his life preparing and
refining both testaments of his German Bible.
    In this last of his works at the Wartburg, Luther was once again the
theologian and pastor, seeking to create *theodidacti.* Translating the
Scriptures was therefore a theological act, another of Luther's labors
as a professor of theology. He made his intentions obvious when he
declared in the introduction that the situation "calls for some sort of
guidance by way of a preface [to the Scriptures], to free the ordinary
person from false, albeit familiar, ideas, to lead him onto the straight
path, and to give him some instruction." In the *Preface to the New*

Testament he insisted that the reader "must be shown what to expect
in this volume, that he might not search through it for commandments
and laws, when he should be looking for the gospel and promises of
God."

Luther obviously did not think that Bible reading by itself would
necessarily lead anyone to a saving knowledge of God. As in his
Postillae (meditations on the appointed scriptural texts for the day),
which he wrote sporadically throughout this period, Luther saw this
work as a preparation for reading the Scriptures themselves. Perhaps
he recalled his own struggles with the "righteousness of God." Now,
like the satisfied reader of a mystery novel who excitedly gives away
the ending, Luther wanted there to be no mistake. He admonished his
readers to "beware lest you make Christ into a Moses and the gospel
into a book of law or doctrine, as has been done before now. . . ."
"Properly speaking," he continued, "the gospel demands no works of
us to become holy and redeemed. Indeed, it damns such works and
requires of us only that we trust in Christ, because he has overcome
sin, death, and hell for us. . . ."[18]

The law, commandments, and regulations had their place. Their chief
task was to condemn everyone at all times. "How," he asked, "can
anyone prepare himself to be good with works when he never does a
good work without some reluctance or reticence inside him? How can
it be possible for God to delight in works that grow out of reluctant
and resisting hearts?" For Luther the Scriptures, and in particular Paul
in his letter to the Romans, were absolutely clear about the law and
right living. "To fulfill the law is to do its works happily and in love,
and freely without the compulsion of the law to live godly and virtuous
lives as if there were no law or punishment."[19] No one, not even the
most pious Christian, could fulfill this requirement—ever.

Therefore the law was also a hammer that smashed down human
pride and prepared Christians to hear the gospel once again, because
"to know [Christ's] works and the story of his life is not the same
thing as to know the gospel, because it does not mean that you trust
that he has vanquished sin, death, and the devil." Moses, Luther declared, "urges, drives, threatens, strikes out, and punishes severely."
By contrast, the gospel, even in the Beatitudes, "does not constrain
us but invites us in a friendly way." As he commented in the *Preface
to Romans,* "if the law is rightly understood, and if it is construed in

the best way, all it does is remind us of our sins, uses them to kill us, and makes us guilty, subject to everlasting wrath."[20]

With the law God was working in a hidden way, as if behind a mask. For under the horrible face of the law and God's demands there lay his gracious work of preparing sinners (and all Christians were sinners) to receive grace. Hearing the law had to lead to one conclusion, that "a person must have something other than the law, more than the law, to make him righteous and save him." Consequently Paul moved from his treatment of the law to the gospel, where he "assures us that we are still God's children, however hard sin may be raging within us, so long as we follow the Spirit and resist sin in order to slay it." The law started and restarted Christians on their pilgrimage, while the gospel "comforts us in our sufferings by assuring us of the support of the Spirit, of love, and of all created things, namely that the Spirit sighs within us and the creatures long with us that we may be without the flesh and sin."[21]

A biblical theology

Luther found his entire theology in the Scriptures. Here was what he meant when he said at Worms that he would stand by the Scriptures "and evident reason." For him the Bible was not first and foremost a book of doctrines or collection of laws with respect to what one must believe in order to be saved. Rather, it proclaimed Christ and him crucified, that is, the back-and-forth of law and gospel which repeatedly condemned and saved sinners.

This understanding allowed Luther even to declare that not all books of the Bible had equal authority in the Christian life. "You," he addressed his readers, "are now in a position to differentiate properly among all the books [of the Bible] and decide which are the best." Among these he included the gospel of John, the letters of Paul, and the first letter of Peter. "You will not find much said in these books about the works and the miracles of Christ," he admitted, "but you will find a masterly treatment of how faith in Christ conquers sin, death, and hell, and gives life, righteousness, and salvation."[22]

Indeed, Luther held, "it is not yet knowledge of the gospel when you know the doctrines and commandments, but only when the voice comes that says, 'Christ is your own, with his life, teaching, works, death, resurrection, all that he is, has, does, and can do.' " The gospel was not a distant abstraction but an intensely personal matter. Thus, he added, "If I were ever compelled to make a choice, and had to do without either the works or the preaching of Christ, I would rather do without the works than the preaching, because the works do not help me at all, while his words give life, as he himself declared."

Consequently, those portions of the Bible that did not emphasize the gospel, the saving message, were of relatively little importance for Luther. Of the books he recommended he declared, "They teach everything you need to know for your salvation, even if you were never to see or hear any other book or hear any other teaching. In comparison with these, the letter of St. James is full of straw, because it contains nothing about the gospel." Set beside John, Luther thought even Matthew, Mark, and Luke were inferior because "they record many of [Christ's] works but few of his words."[23] For Luther, the gospel was the one authority for Christian life and the one message he wished to convey.

TEN

Return to the Fray

*E*vents at Wittenberg soon took a turn directly contrary to Luther's pastoral intentions. Even before he had left for Worms, the professors, pastors, and monks were beginning to divide over the practical issues of Evangelical religion. Then on Christmas Day 1521, Carlstadt celebrated the Mass without wearing the traditional robes, delivered the sacred liturgy in German, and distributed both the bread and the wine to the throng of Christmas worshipers. Later that night mobs disturbed the services held in the traditional manner at each of the churches. Two days later, three men arrived from the town of Zwickau, which was located well to the south. They claimed special revelations from God and were quickly dubbed "The Zwickau Prophets." Elector Frederick was not impressed. He had Melanchthon and Amsdorf brought before him and told them to have nothing to do with such disturbers of the peace. Nor would he agree to their request that Luther return.

Carlstadt and the popular movement that followed him were forcing the issues. Tensions increased throughout the winter as people began to act on the assertions Luther had made in his writings. Within weeks most people in Wittenberg had communed in both kinds. On January 19, 1522, Carlstadt married, and when it became known that Luther approved, others followed him. Earlier that month, the German Augustinians, as represented by several different cloisters, met in Wittenberg and declared that anyone who wished to remain in the order might do so but that all were free to leave and to take up useful occupations in the world. Even those who held to their vows would now spend their time in preaching, physical labor, and caring for others.

These changes flowed directly from arguments that Luther had set forth in his three treatises of the previous year. Therefore he did not object to any of them in principle. Yet the spirit in which some of these reforms were carried out concerned him greatly. He was also troubled by episodes of violence, as when a group removed the side altars from the church and burned its pictures and sacred oil. On January 25, under the advice of Carlstadt, the city council decreed that all monies for charitable purposes would henceforth be taken from the churches and deposited in the common, public chest for the care of the poor. The city fathers would no longer tolerate begging, even by mendicant friars, on the grounds that nei-

A Pietà *defaced in religious riots.*

ther poverty nor the giving of alms improved the status of anyone's soul. Moreover, the order of worship that Carlstadt had used on Christmas was now to be the standard. Iconoclastic riots followed this decree. Next a few individuals began to raise questions about the baptism of infants. Coercion was becoming the order of the day.

A cross for the elector

By now Luther could no longer remain silent. He wrote Melanchthon that the Wittenbergers were to test the spirits, and in particular the Zwickau Prophets, to see if they were from God. Questions about infant baptism he attributed to the work of the devil. When the city fathers themselves in mid-February begged him to return, he knew that the situation was grave. In addition, he was at the point in his translation of the New Testament where he needed the assistance both of books and of other scholars. So he decided to return, regardless of the consequences.

This decision created a problem for the elector. Luther was still an outlaw. And Frederick was under great pressure from his cousin, Duke George (who had hosted the Leipzig Debate), to put a stop to the reforms that were being made. In late January the duke even secured from the imperial authorities in Nuremberg an edict that forbade changes in the Mass and any breach of monastic vows. It also required the princes to proceed with force against all who violated this mandate.

Luther was aware of the situation and did everything he could to accommodate his prince. First, he used a light touch to announce his intention to return. Knowing Frederick's continued attachment to sacred relics, he declared, "Grace and joy from God the Father on the acquisition of a new relic! . . . Without cost or effort, God is now sending Your Grace an entire cross, complete with nails, spears, and scourges. . . . Be glad and be thankful."[1]

The new cross was Luther, but there is no evidence that the elector was amused. Through his official at Eisenach, the town at the foot of the Wartburg, he acknowledged Luther's intentions and tried to persuade him to remain. He admitted that he personally was uncertain about the right course of action but added that the Wittenbergers did not know "who is cook and who the keeper of the wine cellar." As for himself, he was willing to defer to Luther's "understanding," for Luther was "experienced in such high matters."[2] But above all, Luther was not to act on his intention to come visit the elector and talk matters over face-to-face. Frederick the Wise was willing to suffer—if this were truly God's business—but there was no sense in tempting their mutual enemies.

Luther was delighted. The elector had not said "no," so he began his return trip on March 2. Two students saw him at the Black Bear Tavern in Jena while en route, engaged in spritely conversation with two merchants. When these students later passed him going in the same direction, he gave them a message: "Say that he who is coming greets you." To Elector Frederick he replied, "I have written this so Your Electoral Grace might know that I am going to Wittenberg under a far higher protection than the elector's. I have no intention of asking Your Electoral Grace for protection. In fact, I suspect that I will protect Your Electoral Grace. . . [for] he who trusts the most can protect the most."[3]

The exile returned on March 6. His first task was to reply to yet another letter from the elector. He wished Luther to write him in such a way as to make it clear that the elector had nothing to do with his return. The task required several revisions and much help from the politically astute Spalatin, but Luther managed it. He managed it so well that when Frederick showed the letter to his cousin, even Duke George swallowed the semi-fiction.

Preaching the law

Back in the black cowl of an Augustinian monk, Luther mounted the pulpit on March 9, 1522. The message could hardly have been what his followers expected. "The summons of death comes to us all," he began, "and no one can die in the place of someone else. Everyone must fight his own battle with death by himself, alone." For Luther the time had come to preach the law. Without compromise he declared that "a faith without love is not enough. Indeed, it is no faith at all; in fact it is a false faith, just as a face seen in a mirror is not a face but merely the image of one." Love did not coerce others. It served them. Rome was condemned because it forced Christians to fast, to receive only the bread in Communion, without touching it with their hands, and to confess their sins to a priest. But now the Wittenbergers were doing the same thing. The only difference was that they were coercing the faithful to do the opposite of what Rome demanded. Luther declared that he was ready

Luther after his return to Wittenberg (by Cranach).

to leave them forever. "No foe, regardless of how much pain he has inflicted on me, has so put the screws to me as you have right here."[4]

Seven more sermons in the same vein, followed by a series on the Ten Commandments, made the point to everyone present. The gospel had to be preached and people carefully taught before any changes could be mandated. The first concern had to be for the well-being of the weakest member of the body of Christ. Just as traditional believers could not claim they were superior on account of their works, so too those who had heard the gospel could not declare themselves better Christians because they communed with both the bread and the wine. The law condemned everyone. People should not think of themselves or their group as being more "spiritual" than others. Anyone who did so was lying, because faith was hidden.

The impact of these sermons and of Luther's first days back in Wittenberg was immediate. Two months after his return, he wrote Spalatin, "Here, one can find nothing but love and friendship." In March, one of the students wrote that, by contrast with Carlstadt and "like Paul, Martin knows how to feed [the people] with milk until they have matured and are ready for solid food. To judge him by his face, Luther is a kind man, mild and good-natured. His voice is pleasing and impressive, and you must be amazed at his winning way of speech." Another student declared that "All week long Luther did nothing other than to put back in place what we had knocked down, and he took us all severely to task."[5]

Simply by preaching both law and gospel, Luther succeeded in restoring order. Capito, the representative of the archbishop of Mainz in the business over the reliquary at Halle, visited Wittenberg as soon as he heard that Luther had returned. During 1521 and early 1522 he had repeatedly complained that Luther's writings and followers helped incite revolution and bloodshed. During the negotiations with Spalatin and Melanchthon in late 1521, he had also questioned various aspects of Luther's theology. He had even befriended one of the students at Wittenberg and in effect recruited him to be a spy.

From all accounts, even Capito was amazed at what he saw after Luther's return. One student reported,

On March 14, Fabricius Capito came to Wittenberg to reconcile himself (or so they say) with Luther, whom something in his letters had offended to such an extent that (again they say) he was called a virulent beast by Martin. Yes, there is already a beautiful harmony between them. . . . Whatever displeased Capito is beginning to satisfy him. By chance, we caught sight of him listening to Martin preach in the Wittenberg church.

On his way back to the archbishop, Capito wrote to a friend,

> Learned men had written to Luther; they urged him to continue in a
> candid and steadfast manner. He is therefore now in Wittenberg. He is
> preaching daily and he plucks at his followers. He is rebuking those who
> did not maintain respect for the simple folk. At the same time he is not
> forgetting to contribute what he contributed in the beginning. Already,
> the people are flowing together as if into a procession and then continuing
> on into the liberty of Christ.[6]

Within a year, this official from Mainz had moved to Strasbourg and
become a leader of the Evangelical movement there.

Building a team

Luther's actions had immediate effects both on ordinary people and
on those of greater sophistication. At the same time (and at first perhaps
without realizing it) he began to build a team that would labor with
him at reform for the remainder of his life.

The first step in this process had occurred well before the Diet of
Worms and the exile to the Wartburg. Through his first lectures on the
Psalms and then on Romans, he had gradually begun to convince his
colleagues of the truth of what came to be known as the "Wittenberg
Theology." An age that was enamored of schools of thought had found
a new one. With its emphasis on the Scriptures, this school had appeal
far beyond the boundaries of Electoral Saxony. It spread through the
humanist circles in Basel, Nuremberg, Strasbourg, and elsewhere.

The actors in this first phase comprised an unlikely team. First there
was Carlstadt, who was several years Luther's senior by virtue of his
tenure as a professor at Wittenberg. He was a thoroughly scholastic
theologian, one who usually thought in terms of systems, theses, and
their logical consequences. Well before the Leipzig Debate in mid-
1519, he joined the developing struggle with the argument that only
the Scriptures were authoritative in matters of faith. It was also he who
led the movement in Wittenberg to apply Luther's basic ideas to practical matters such as the Mass, monastic vows, the marriage of the
clergy, and the care of the poor.

By contrast, during these early years there was also the figure of
Melanchthon. He was much younger than Luther and was a student

1526

VIVENTIS·POTVIT·DVRERIVS·ORA·PHILIPPI
MENTEM·NON·POTVIT·PINGERE·DOCTA
MANVS

Philip Melanchthon (by Dürer).

of the ancient languages rather than a theologian. He was also less decisive when it came to the immediate application of doctrine to daily practice. He did participate in the first Evangelical Lord's Supper, in which university students received both the bread and the wine. But these students were technically part of the clergy, and he left it to Carlstadt to extend the practice to the laity. Melanchthon's first important contribution was rather to help Luther understand just how far he had come theologically. It was also Melanchthon who in 1521 initially put Luther's theology in systematic form with his *Commonplaces of Evangelical Theology* or *Loci Communes.*

John Bugenhagen, who arrived while Luther was still at the Wartburg, proved to be a particularly important member of the team. He had encountered Luther's writings as a schoolteacher and was, like Melanchthon, trained in the liberal arts and the ancient languages. His first reading of *On the Babylonian Captivity,* where Luther reduced the number of sacraments to two and radically altered their character, made him think of Luther as the greatest heretic of all time. However, with more thought he came to declare, "The entire world is blind, for this man is the only one who sees the truth." With Melanchthon he assisted in the translation and retranslation of the Bible. He also became one of the chief reformers of northern Germany, one who was "loaned" to various territories and even to the king of Denmark. But Luther valued him most because Bugenhagen became the man to whom he turned daily to confess his own sins. Luther recalled that in one dark moment Bugenhagen had said to him, "God must surely be asking himself, 'What can I still make of this man? I have given him so many superb gifts, but now he questions my grace.' " Luther added that, "For me, this was an immense comfort, like the sound of angels echoing in my heart."[7]

Strife, however, was the order of the day. Even within Luther's closest group there were clashes. The most volatile problem was with Carlstadt, whom Luther sharply rebuked on his return. Carlstadt reacted with deep resentment. He continued to lecture at the university, but within a year he moved to a pastorate at the town of Orlamünde, some 100 miles to the south. A real parting of the ways followed. Carlstadt was but the first of many who, although opposed to Rome, found themselves opposed to Luther as well.

The spread of reform

The same process of building teams of reformers was occurring all over Germany. Sometimes Luther was directly responsible. In April and May he responded to several invitations and visited a number of towns in which he essentially repeated the work he had already done in Wittenberg. He preached, he encouraged, and he advised. Above all, he made clear that the "Wittenberg Theology" did not necessarily bring revolution in its train. The town of Altenburg even asked him to send them a preacher, and he did so. This act was the first installation of a new Evangelical pastor.

In most cases, however, Luther's influence in spreading reform was more indirect. Given the distances and the difficulties of communication in those days, it could hardly have been otherwise. Nonetheless, reform movements began to spring up in towns and principalities all over the empire. Of Nuremberg, a papal legate declared that, "In this town the people regard Martin as their enlightener." In Augsburg the cathedral preacher Urbanus Rhegius was struggling with his superiors over the question of indulgences. In Switzerland Ulrich Zwingli was writing a friend that the people in Zurich had so far been feeding on milk; soon, he declared, "they will be ready for solid food."[8] John Oecolampadius, who had attacked private confession before Luther had done so, was now established in Basel. Martin Bucer, who had first encountered Luther at Heidelberg five years earlier, now joined Capito in Strasbourg. They immediately came to the defense of a popular preacher who had come under attack for expounding Paul's letter to the Romans.

Throughout 1522 and 1523 the movement spread rapidly and took root. Moreover, those who took these first steps were themselves men of learning and position. They had decided that Luther was right, and the masses followed them. As Luther wrote to the city council at Altenburg, "Now everyone must know and believe for himself what faith is true and what is untrue."[9]

Two kingdoms

In March 1523 one of Luther's opponents accused him of having no regard for the time-honored, established customs of the church. With scorn he replied, "Our God does not impose 'custom' on us but the truth. Certainly our faith does not trust in custom but in the truth that is God himself." [10] It was nonetheless true that the bonds of tradition were losing their hold on people. Luther recognized this situation for what it was and admonished his followers to educate their parishioners before making radical changes. Many, however—such as Carlstadt and the Zwickau Prophets—acted urgently and without regard for the wishes of either Luther or their temporal lords. So in the same month that Luther condemned slavish adherence to custom, he also composed a treatise in which he rejected stirring up the populace, even if strict conformity to the truth might seem to require it.

In this essay, *On Temporal Authority, the Extent to which It Should Be Obeyed,* he insisted that no one had the right to rebel against those whose task it was to govern. God, he said, had created two kingdoms in this world. In one belonged the righteous, and over them God ruled with the love of the gospel. To the other belonged sinners. Over them God ruled through the might and terror of the secular sword. Without the sword, he declared, "men become beasts."

Love and the sword stood side by side. Yet Luther had no difficulty stating that Christians, too, owed allegiance to the secular authorities. Love for one's neighbor required such loyalty, "so that good order may not perish" and people live in fear for their lives. Emperor, king, prince, city council—all held authority directly from God, and Christians were to obey them. Moreover, Christians themselves remained sinners and required the constraints of judge, jailer, and executioner. No matter how just their cause, Christians could resist only if the authorities acted with manifest injustice and against the gospel. Even then, resistance ought to take the form of passive disobedience, grow out of love for one's neighbor, and stand in full readiness to suffer the consequences of imprisonment and death. Never were private citizens to seize the sword of rebellion or act against the authorities simply in defense of what they took to be their own rights. To do so was in every instance selfish and contrary to the law of love.

In many respects, the thinking and the concerns in this new work were the same as those that guided Luther in the *Admonition against Sedition* that he wrote shortly after his brief visit to Wittenberg 18 months earlier. But when it came to condemning Carlstadt, the Zwickau Prophets, and those he generally called *Schwärmgeister* (or "spirits who swarm about" in the manner of a beehive gone mad), Luther's own actions presented him with a problem. He himself had defied the authorities on a matter of principle. How could he consistently condemn those who appeared to follow his example? Yet condemn them he did. He was particularly infuriated with Carlstadt, whom he had taken to be a loyal member of the Wittenberg team. Carlstadt had now moved to Orlamünde and there soon began to introduce the same changes that had caused such an uproar in Wittenberg. As a symbol of what he took to be Luther's understanding of the priesthood of all believers, he abandoned all clerical garb and conducted services in the plain, gray clothing of his peasant parishioners. He also began publishing treatises in which he criticized Luther's understanding of the Lord's Supper, his retention of traditional services, and his unwillingness to strip the churches of their ornamentation. He even began to raise questions about infant baptism. He signed his works as, "the new layman."

Thomas Müntzer

At the same time, Luther began to associate Carlstadt with a *real* revolutionary, Thomas Müntzer. Müntzer had been one of Luther's earliest, self-proclaimed followers, but he caused a public outburst wherever he went. In April 1521 he was forced to leave the town of Zwickau after fighting with the city council and disrupting the sermons of the other pastors. Leaving the Zwickau Prophets behind to carry on his work, he moved to Bohemia, where he made contact with the Hussites. To them he declared that "God himself has hired me for this harvest," a harvest in which the wicked would be destroyed.[11] A mystic who was given to personal revelations, he wrote Melanchthon and Luther that they, too, had to learn to prophesy. By 1522 he was back in Germany and had secured a post at the town of Allstedt. In March 1524 a group of his followers put the torch to a small chapel nearby.

Thomas Müntzer, according to a 17th-century rendering.

To Luther, Müntzer personified the *Schwärmgeister*. Two years earlier, Luther had declared, "I did nothing; the Word did everything. If I had wanted to stir up trouble, I could have brought immense bloodshed on Germany. In fact, I could have started such a game that even the emperor would not have been safe." But, he repeated, "I did nothing. I let the Word do its work." Later he said, "I simply taught, preached, and wrote God's Word. . . . And while I slept or drank Wittenberg beer with my friends Philip and Amsdorf, the Word so greatly weakened the papacy that no prince or emperor ever inflicted such losses on it. I did nothing. The Word did everything."[12] By contrast, the likes of Carlstadt and Müntzer were trying to force events by manipulating people.

This distinction between himself and his ever-greater numbers of anti-Roman opponents became increasingly important to Luther as the years passed. Words became the bullets in this war. Luther was not seeking to establish his personal authority over others. Rather, even in pointing to himself as an example, he was underlining the authority of his message. He never tired of reminding people that he did not seek to become a doctor of theology but was compelled by Staupitz. "Therefore, my dear brethren," he declared, "follow me. I have never been a destroyer. And I was also the very first that God called to this work."[13] In conflict with his anti-Roman opponents, Luther continued to see himself as a teacher of the church, one who led both by word and by deed.

Müntzer quickly and utterly discredited himself. In 1525 he became a local leader of the Peasants' War. For Luther this war and Müntzer's behavior in it were immensely painful, precisely because they provided clear illustrations of all he had warned against.

The Peasants' War (1524–1525) was first and foremost a reaction against real oppression. Even landlords were losers in a time of declining population, when disease and hunger ravaged the countryside. They lost workers who could pay taxes and perform useful services. So they resorted to the tactics of tying peasants to the land or turning them into serfs and extorting ever greater dues from them. When the countess of Lütphen compelled her peasants to pick strawberries for a great banquet, they rebelled. Others in nearby areas followed. Little by little, the rebellion spread. Müntzer, then located in the town of Mühlhausen, urged them on. He declared that the kingdom of God was at hand, and he assured the peasants that he had received a special revelation from God, according to which the princes' bullets would be caught in the sleeve of his coat. But Müntzer's sleeves did not work. His peasant army was massacred at the Battle of Frankenhausen. Müntzer was found hiding in a bed, was tried, retracted all his errors, and was executed. Sporadic violence and bloodshed continued all over Germany for several months.

Luther and the Peasants' War

Luther was forced to take a hand in the matter. He was so well-known and his authority so great that one of the most widely circulated lists of peasant demands, the *Twelve Articles of the Swabian Peasants,* even named him as an acceptable arbiter. He responded in writing with *An Admonition to Peace.* First, he addressed the princes and the lords. He condemned them for their unjust treatment of the peasants and declared that the authorities were bringing revolt on themselves. Second, he addressed the peasants. He granted that many of their demands were just, but repeated his universal rejection of rebellion. Above all, he condemned as blasphemy their appeal to Christian liberty and the gospel as justification for self-serving violence. Christ brought forth love, not selfishness. Both sides ought to negotiate.

The reformer also did his best in a practical way to improve the situation. He spent much of late April and early May 1525 traveling about the countryside and admonishing crowds of peasants to keep the peace. Although he had earlier been viewed as their friend, now he himself was rejected, jeered, and threatened. Elector Frederick the Wise, Luther's one sure supporter, died on May 5. Dejected and fearful of the future, Luther returned to Wittenberg.

Another treatise then exploded from his pen. *Against the Murderous and Thieving Hordes of Peasants* had a different tone than the earlier work. Luther was bitter. "These are strange times," he wrote, "when a prince can win heaven with bloodshed better than other men can with prayer!" Now the princes ought to act quickly. As a last resort, they should "offer the mad peasants an opportunity to come to terms, even though they are not worthy of it." If the peasants did not lay down their arms, then the princes were to "smite, strangle, and stab [them], secretly or openly, remembering that nothing can be more poisonous, hurtful, or devilish than a rebel. It is just as when one must kill a mad dog: if you do not strike him, he will strike you and a whole land with you." [14] Even while Luther was writing those words, the princes were already doing as he recommended.

Luther was deeply criticized for this book at the time, just as he is criticized for it today. The criticism was so loud that in June he wrote *An Open Letter on the Harsh Book against the Peasants.* But he took back scarcely a word. He did point out that he had had nothing to do with the brutality of the princes, who massacred even those who had surrendered or been taken prisoner. He was certain that these "senseless tyrants" were bound for "hellfire." But to him there was still nothing worse than a rebel—except one who claimed the Word of God as justification for rebellion. The

A peasant being "burned" at the stake. Death came from smoke inhalation.

peasants, with Müntzer at their head, were both. Luther insisted that he was bound to defend the Word. He added, "When I have time and occasion to do so, I shall attack the princes and lords too, for in my office of teacher a prince is the same to me as a peasant." [15]

PART FOUR

The True Church

ELEVEN

"False Brethren"

T he Sacramentarian Controversy, which began before the Peasants' War and continued long afterward, proved to be one of Luther's most painful tests. The issue was both simple and complex. What did Jesus intend the night before his crucifixion when he said, "This is my body," and "This cup is the new covenant in my blood"? Were these words to be taken literally or were they, as with "I am the vine," to be understood figuratively?

As with so many issues that may now seem to be trivial, the answer given to this question had enormous practical consequences for the conduct of Christian life. On the one hand, as in *Against the Heavenly Prophets* of January 1525, Luther insisted that iconoclasm and rapid, compulsory changes in the forms of worship, (which proceeded from a new theological understanding) were acts of sedition of the same type as the Peasants' War. On the other, Luther himself had theological questions about the Mass. He and his contemporaries had been taught that when the priest uttered the Words of Institution, he suddenly and substantially changed the bread and the wine into the body and blood of Christ. This transubstantiation, as it was called, was the basis for the idea that the Mass was a sacrifice, and therefore a good work that was meritorious for salvation. In this act also lay the distinctive authority of the priest, for only he could perform it. Further, the elements of bread and wine that were now the body and blood of Christ were so holy that the laity could not touch them. They were literally to adore them, as in the processions of the Festival of *Corpus Christi* (the body of Christ). Some changes were required in order to bring practice into harmony with doctrine.

A symbolic understanding

The seeds for the disagreements Luther faced within the movement had been planted long before. More than a century earlier, the Englishman John Wycliffe had argued that the bread and wine were symbols of the body and blood rather than the things themselves. Therefore priests had no special power over the laity. Jan Hus, the Bohemian, concurred, and his followers declared that the laity could indeed handle the sacred elements and should receive both the bread and the wine.

Carlstadt began to espouse some of these ideas even before Luther returned from the Wartburg. This symbolic understanding of the Words of Institution lay behind his offering of both the bread and the wine to the laity and his decision not to celebrate the Mass in the traditional vestments or with the customary liturgical ceremony. He went so far as to insist that the laity *had* to hold the bread in their own hands.

When Carlstadt laid down yet another rule for worship, Luther saw just one more misapplication of the law. But the fact that he himself was called a Hussite forced him from an early date to think about the root problem: precisely what the bread and wine were, or became, during the celebration of the Lord's Supper. He treated this question as early as 1519 in a published *Sermon on the Body of Christ*. There he simply assumed the physical presence of Christ's body and blood and emphasized the gift of God's grace in the sacrament. At the same time, he pointed to Paul's words in 1 Cor. 10:16-17 and underlined the idea that in the Lord's Supper all Christians were "one loaf, one bread, one body, one drink, and everything is in common."[1] He therefore based his insistence that all might partake of both the bread and the wine on this passage rather than on a reinterpretation of the Words of Institution. At the same time he assumed that Jesus' words meant precisely what they said, that the bread became the body of Christ and the wine his blood.

Luther was soon forced to think more carefully about the matter. In 1522, still two years before the Sacramentarian Controversy, his friend Paul Speratus asked him for an opinion about the teaching that the bread and the wine were only symbols of Christ's body and blood. As it would be in 1523 when he responded to much the same question from Margrave George of Brandenburg-Ansbach, the issue was whether to venerate the consecrated bread and wine. On each occasion Luther gave the same answer. In their sacramental use, the bread and wine were Christ's body and blood, but whether one venerated them was an indifferent matter. No one was to be compelled either to do so or not to do so. Nonetheless, he insisted, those who "contort the little word 'is' into 'signifies' " did so "frivolously and unsupported by the Scriptures."[2] The question of what Jesus intended by "This is my body" and "This is my blood" was therefore present from an early date. Only an accident was necessary to bring it into the open. The accident was Carlstadt.

In August 1524 Luther and Carlstadt met at the Black Bear Tavern in Jena to discuss their differences over the pace and necessity of dramatic changes in worship practices. After a heated exchange, Luther tossed Carlstadt a coin and challenged him to a literary duel. Carlstadt took the challenge and began to publish against Luther. He continued to do so even after the authorities expelled him from his parish for being a troublemaker. His wanderings took him to the west and the south, first to Strasbourg and then to Basel, and eventually to Zurich in Switzerland. By the time he arrived in Zurich, he had published 13 treatises on his difficulties with Luther. The meaning of the Words of Institution figured prominently in their pages.

"External things"

In his travels Carlstadt watered seeds of dissension that had already been sown and were ready to sprout, even if they could not yet be seen above soil level. His trip unsettled many, partly because he had been so close to Luther. It was particularly damaging to Luther's relationship with Bucer and Capito, the reformers in Strasbourg. They certainly had little love for Carlstadt or his behavior. Capito even referred to him in print as a "glory boy."

In fact Capito and Bucer already held opinions about the elements in the Lord's Supper that differed from Luther's, but they decided to seek advice from others. In November 1524, just after Carlstadt's unwanted visit to their city, the two asked both Luther and Zwingli for guidance on the meaning of the Words of Institution. The critical portions of these two letters were virtually identical. To each of their colleagues they recounted what they had heard about Carlstadt's teachings and then added a description of how they understood the matter. To Zwingli they wrote:

> The bread and the cup are external things (whatever they may be) and by themselves they accomplish nothing for salvation; but the memory of the Lord's death is both beneficial and necessary. Therefore, we admonish our [parishioners] to eat the Lord's bread and to drink the cup for this purpose while passing over other things.

To Luther they wrote:

> The bread and the cup are external things and, however much the bread may be the body of Christ and the cup his blood, they nonetheless provide nothing for our salvation, seeing that the flesh, in sum, is of no profit [John 6:63]. But on the contrary, to remember the Lord's death, for this purpose, here is the only thing that brings salvation.[3]

Martin Bucer.

Johannes Oecolampadius.

From Zurich, Zwingli quickly replied to the Strasbourg pastors that he thought the three of them were in essential agreement. The bread and the wine were symbols of Christ's body and blood, and the real benefit from the Lord's Supper came in remembering Christ's death and resurrection. The position that Luther's opponents took in the Sacramentarian Controversy was therefore largely developed before the conflict began.

ANNO AETATIS EIVS XLVIIL

Ulrich Zwingli.

"This is my body"

Luther's position, as well, was already well-formed. His reply to the Strasbourg reformers differed sharply from that of Zwingli. This was one of his many letters that somehow made its way into print before the addressees received it. The *Letter to the Christians in Strasbourg against the Enthusiasts* showed Luther in his most polemical form. Carlstadt, he declared, was the cause of all the problems. Luther labeled his teachings "a smoke-screen." The Strasbourg theologians ought to guard themselves against them. "For me, the text ["This is my body"] is too powerful. I cannot get away from it."[4] Anyone who sought to turn the bread and the wine into symbols of Christ's body and blood was an instrument of Satan.

A careful reading of the letter from Strasbourg revealed that Capito, Bucer, and Zwingli were already appealing to John 6:63 as support for their understanding of what the bread and the wine were or became. When Jesus said, "Do you take offense at this? . . . It is the spirit that gives life, the flesh is of no avail," they understood him to be setting forth a principle that could be applied to the bread and the wine in the Eucharist. Therefore the bread remained bread but served as a powerful symbol of Christ's body, while the wine remained wine and symbolized Christ's blood. Physical things did not convey spiritual realities.

By contrast, as early as 1520 (when he found himself accused of being a Hussite or Bohemian), Luther had remarked in passing that the entirety of John 6 in no way applied to the declaration of Jesus, "This is my body," "This is my blood." In an *Explanation of Certain Articles on the Holy Sacrament* he insisted "that the Lord is saying nothing about the sacrament in this passage. On the contrary, he is talking about faith in the Son of God and the Son of man, who is Christ." A few lines later he declared, "These [particular] Bohemians I regard as heretics. May God have mercy on them!"[5] Four years before his future opponents appealed to it, Luther had concluded that this very passage of Scripture could not be brought to bear on the Words of Institution.

Soon after Luther replied to the query from Bucer and Capito, he learned of Zwingli's teaching that references to eating Christ's body in the Lord's Supper meant only that Christians were "to believe that his body was given over to death for us." In November 1524 a friend sent Luther a copy of a letter in which Zwingli declared that he admired Carlstadt's boldness on the subject of the Eucharist. The following March, Zwingli published a *Commentary on True and False Religion* in which he declared that Christ was not physically present in the bread and the wine. Luther's colleague, Bugenhagen, countered in mid-July. Oecolampadius replied to Bugenhagen, and then another of Luther's followers replied to Oecolampadius.

The battle was joined. But this controversy proved to be rather different from Luther's struggles with his Roman opponents. In the first place, aside from *Against the Heavenly Prophets,* in which he opposed religious radicalism in general, he personally remained aloof from the early exchanges. He did so in part because others were acting in his stead. But he was also distracted by other matters.

Luther's initial problems with Carlstadt had occurred in 1524. Then in early 1525 the Peasants' War raged. Later the same year Luther found himself preoccupied once again with Carlstadt, but in a much different way. Carlstadt had wandered around Germany through early 1525. Together with his wife and child, he found himself destitute in Frankfurt am Main. He wrote to Luther and begged him to intervene with the Saxon princes so that they would allow him to return to Orlamünde. Luther honestly tried to do so, but was unsuccessful. Then Carlstadt sent his wife to Luther, and at last the reformer agreed to provide his opponent secret lodgings in Wittenberg for eight weeks during the summer months. As Luther's guest, Carlstadt wrote one more book in which he retracted much of what he had previously written. Luther even provided a foreword in which he exonerated Carlstadt of all involvement with the Peasants' War, and a preface in which he underlined how Carlstadt was changing his views on the Lord's Supper. Even so, Luther made it clear that he had no illusions about Carlstadt's reliability.

Marriage

One other unexpected matter distracted Luther from the growing struggle with the Swiss theologians. On June 13 he was betrothed to Katharina von Bora. Katie, as he came to call her, was one of a group of nuns who had arrived on Luther's doorstep one April day two years earlier. They had fled their Cistercian convent in barrels that had once contained beer or herring, and now something had to be done with them. By 1525 Luther had found places, and in many cases husbands, for all the others. Only Katie, a handsome woman of noble descent, remained. She refused all of Luther's permanent arrangements for her, including potential suitors. Tradition has it that she would agree to marry only Luther himself, or perhaps his colleague Nicolaus Amsdorf. To a friend Luther wrote, "Suddenly, unexpectedly, and while my mind was on other matters, the Lord has snared me with the yoke of marriage."[6]

Most of Luther's colleagues were equally surprised. Katie had been in their midst for two years and not one of them had the slightest idea that Luther was attracted to her. Nor did Luther divulge his plans to them, if he had any. They also had grave misgivings about the public relations aspects of the match. In fact, some did not much like Katie, for she had a mind of her own and was not at all reticent about letting others know her views.

Katie's wedding band.

Luther declared that he had married to provide old Hans with grandchildren and those who wavered with an example. As well as he could identify them, these probably were his real motives. Only months

Katharina von Bora Luther (by Cranach).

earlier, while he was touring areas of peasant unrest, Luther had talked with his father and Hans had repeated his wishes for more heirs. Also, Luther had encouraged many others who were considering marriage. Now he declared, "I wanted to confirm what I have taught by practicing it, for I find so many timid people in spite of such great light from the gospel. God has willed and brought forth this action, for I am not 'in love' or burning with desire. But I do love my wife."[7]

For Luther it was a shock to wake up in the morning and find pigtails on the pillow next to him. He was 42 years old when he married. As he wrote a friend, "God likes to perform miracles in order to mock and trick me and the world." To another he wrote, "It is all so strange to me that I can scarcely believe it. Yet there were so many witnesses that for their sakes I have to believe it."[8] Even Luther's colleagues were finally won over. Melanchthon, for one, suggested that perhaps marriage would cure Luther of his love for coarse jokes. He was wrong.

The marriage turned out to be a good one. Genuine affection developed between the two, and they had six children. The one source of continuing tension was that Luther thought money was for spending or giving away. "Ah, Kate," he once remarked, "when the money is gone, the goblets will go next."[9] Katie, however, managed affairs with a firm hand. For extra income, and perhaps at her urging, Luther once toyed with taking up carpentry. He did prove to be a capable gardener. But the couple was fortunate in their household finances. Elector John, the successor to Frederick the Wise, sent a handsome gift of 100 gulden and raised Luther's salary so he could meet his new obligations. The archbishop of Mainz himself sent 10 gold gulden. Luther commanded that the gift be returned. Katie disobeyed and kept the money, only to produce it the first time the cupboard became bare.

Debate with Erasmus

The Peasants' War, dealing with Carlstadt, and marriage—all kept Luther from leaping into the growing controversy over the Lord's Supper. Yet there was one more matter that came in the way: his debate with Erasmus. Luther found this particularly painful because he had counted on Erasmus for at least benevolent neutrality.

The debate with Erasmus was another controversy that had been long in the making. In early 1517 Luther had written to one of his friends, "I am reading Erasmus and my esteem for him diminishes daily. . . .

Though I prefer not to judge him, I admonish you not to read all his works, or rather, not to take them in without care." [10] A year later, Erasmus objected when he learned that his followers had used his publisher to print an edition of Luther's works in Latin. Yet during these early years the two giants had corresponded politely, or at least without rancor. To Erasmus, Luther wrote as "your little brother in Christ," and Erasmus reciprocated by praising Luther to Frederick the Wise against the machinations of Aleander, the papal ambassador.

Mutual friends and supporters worked hard to maintain proper relations between Erasmus and Luther. But the two principals could scarcely have been in more fundamental disagreement. For Erasmus, true religion was basically a matter of the inclination of the heart, the wisdom that filled the mind, and an attitude of love for one's neighbor. True doctrine played little part in it. He despised Luther's teachers, the scholastic theologians, not because they taught false doctrines but because they taught too many doctrines. To him true religion was present when the plowman and the weaver chanted psalms at their labors. Meanwhile Luther was discovering in the Psalms and Romans a radically new doctrine of the righteousness of God. While Erasmus was promoting learned piety, Luther was starting down a path of doctrinal development that led to the Reformation. And Erasmus watched while one after another of his own followers turned to Luther.

It is no wonder that Erasmus became increasingly convinced that Luther's movement was destroying the rebirth of good learning and genuine religion. So he began to look for an issue on which he could distance himself from Luther. Matters of doctrine did not come naturally to him. Thomas More, soon to be Lord Chancellor under Henry VIII of England, suggested the freedom of the will, and this was the subject on which Erasmus wrote—even if he did not have much taste for it. In September 1524 he attacked Luther in a book he called *A Diatribe on the Freedom of the Will*.

Erasmus began by declaring that he preferred the position of a skeptic in such matters unless compelled by the church or the Scriptures and the testimony of the ancient Fathers. True to himself, he then argued that the question could not finally be resolved. The Scriptures were unclear, so one had to have recourse to experience and reason. He concluded that because human beings made choices between good and evil, or between better and worse, and because they were commanded to do so, they had to be *able* to do so. Therefore they had to have free will.

The bondage of the will

Doctrinal arguments were distasteful to Erasmus. Nonetheless, he had put his finger on the fundamental theological difference between Luther and his Catholic opponents, and Luther thanked him for it. In his published reply he told Erasmus "that you alone among all the others have seized on the matter itself, the core of the question, and you have not involved me with foreign questions on the nature of the papacy, purgatory, indulgences, or other such things. . . . You and you alone have seen through to the nerve-center of the matter and have put the knife to the jugular. Therefore I give you my heartfelt thanks."[11]

Even so, Luther was appalled by what he read. Erasmus's work had been published in September. In November, Luther wrote to friends who were pressuring him to reply immediately, "I cannot describe how terrible I feel about this little book on the freedom of the will. . . . It is very difficult for me to answer such an unlearned book from such a learned man."[12] So Luther put it off. He did not publish his *On the Bondage of the Will* until December 1525, some 15 months later.

For this task, the reformer marshaled all his skills as a professional theologian and a polemicist. *On the Bondage of the Will* is difficult for modern readers precisely because Luther so vigorously wielded all the weapons of 16th-century theologians. These required first and foremost a point-for-point refutation of everything the opponent maintained. Erasmus had used more than 200 scriptural citations to demonstrate that there was no final answer to the question, but that it appeared that the human will could claim some measure of freedom. Luther replied to every citation in detail. He granted that "free choice is allowed to man, [but] only with respect to what is beneath him, and not to what is above him." Human beings did have dignity. "God did not create the kingdom of heaven for geese."[13]

But everything that related to the divine was another matter. The human will could not "move toward the righteousness of God." True freedom of the will was a divine attribute "that can no more justly be attributed to human beings than can divinity itself." He borrowed from Augustine to illustrate his meaning: "The human will is like a beast between [God and Satan]. If God sits on it, it wills and goes where

God wills to go. . . . If Satan sits on it, it wills and goes where Satan wills. Nor does it have the power to choose which rider it will go to or seek, but the riders struggle over which of them will have it or rule it."[14] Not even the most faithful people had any choice in the matter. Even so, the outcome of this cosmic struggle was never in doubt. In Christ, God had won the victory.

Never simply the stuffy theologian, Luther also leaped on opportunities Erasmus left him to employ the ancient tactic of ridicule. Erasmus had begun his treatise by granting that he was not a theologian and that "I am so far from delighting in 'assertions' that I would readily take refuge in the opinion of the skeptics, wherever this is allowed by the inviolate authority of the Holy Scriptures and by the decrees of the church. . . ."[15]

This declaration appalled Luther. "I assume, as in courtesy bound," he replied, "that it is your charitable mind and love of peace that prompts such sentiments. If anyone else were to express them, I would likely fall on him in my usual way!" For Luther there could be no Christianity without "staunchly holding your ground, stating your position, confessing it, defending it, and persevering in it unvanquished." It was the work of Satan to say that there could be no final answer to such an important question as the freedom of the will. Above all, Luther insisted, the Scriptures were perfectly clear on all matters essential to salvation. The question of whether God was the author of salvation or whether human beings with their "free will" were was just such a matter. Here Luther's attempt to be polite utterly failed him. He asked, "What more ungodly assertion could anyone make than that he wished for the liberty of asserting *nothing* in such cases?"[16]

On the Bondage of the Will hurt Erasmus deeply. He replied twice. For Luther, his own single contribution to the debate was enough. He fully intended the implication that Erasmus was not a Christian. It was not just that Erasmus was in error, but also that he was putting himself forth as a teacher of the faithful. In such a situation no holds were barred.

The Sacramentarian Controversy

"Thus have I declared that I write not against flesh and blood, as St. Paul teaches, but against Satan and his followers," is the way Luther finally directed his attack against Zwingli, Oecolampadius, Bucer, and

Capito. When he at last locked horns with them, he did so in the conviction that they were just as wrong as Erasmus was, and on an issue of equally high and holy significance for all Christians. As Luther put it, "We intend to shun, condemn, and censure them . . . and to pray for them and admonish them to stop." Like Erasmus or the defenders of Rome, these adversaries as well were the instruments of Satan. And to Satan, as he once remarked, one "must give the backside." [17]

His opponents in this struggle found themselves both embarrassed and at a substantial disadvantage. On the one hand, they were embarrassed by the violence of Luther's polemics in the same way that many people still find them embarrassing. On the other hand, they felt constrained to admit their own deep indebtedness to the man who was now so vigorously attacking them. Oecolampadius, a mild-mannered and scholarly person, wrote in a reply to Luther's *Against the Heavenly Prophets,* "These are the words of an angry man." But he added, "I do not willingly oppose you, whom I recognize as a worthy and cherished servant of the gospel through whom God has opened the eyes of many to recognize the veritable path of truth." [18]

These expressions of gratitude and admonitions to proceed less intemperately mattered not one whit to Luther. To him the question of whether Christ was physically or only spiritually present in the bread and the wine had implications that extended far beyond the Eucharist. Oecolampadius, for instance, joined Zwingli in depending on John 6:63 for his understanding of the Words of Institution. But he added that because Christ was resurrected and seated at the right hand of the Father, he could not be physically present in the elements of the Lord's Supper. To Luther, such an argument amounted to "mere physics." On the contrary, he replied, "the Word says first of all that Christ has a body, and this I believe. Secondly, that this same body rose to heaven and sits at the right hand of God; this too I believe. It says further that this same body is in the Lord's Supper and is given to us to eat. Likewise I believe this, for my Lord Jesus Christ can easily do what he wishes, and that he wishes to do this is attested by his own words."

If nothing else, Oecolampadius convinced Luther that any argument against the simple meaning of the Words of Institution turned on assumptions that came from human logic. In addition, Luther saw that any of these assumptions could then be turned against other articles of the Christian faith, such as the incarnation, the Trinity, or the nature of Christ himself. As he put it, "We hold the flesh of Christ to be very, indeed to be absolutely, necessary. No text, no interpretation, no use of human reasoning can take it away·from us."[19]

For Luther, the core issue in the Sacramentarian Controversy was the understanding of the place of human flesh itself. To his mind, the great error came in the argument that according to John 6:63, physical things could not, by their nature, carry spiritual benefits. In a work prepared for the Frankfurt book fair in the spring of 1527, he insisted that "everything our body does outwardly and physically is in reality and in name done spiritually if God's Word is added to it and it is done in faith. Nothing can be so material, fleshly, or outward but that it becomes spiritual when it is done in the Word and in faith. 'The spiritual' is nothing more than what is done in us and by us through the Spirit and faith, whether the object with which we are dealing is physical or spiritual." By contrast, he argued, "Our fanatics . . . think nothing spiritual can be present where there is anything material and physical, and they assert that the flesh is of no profit [John 6:63]."[20]

To Luther's mind, the claims of his opponents in the Sacramentarian Controversy therefore struck at the heart of his theology just as strongly as had Erasmus's arguments in *On the Freedom of the Will*. Each allowed human reason to intrude on the plain words of the Scriptures. Each required Christians to bring something of their own to their salvation. Each limited the work of God to that which was already in some sense pure. Each brought to mind exactly the struggles he found in the monastery. Luther found no reason to be more charitable with the "false brethren" than he was with his opponents from Rome.

Public man, public issues

The testimonies of the "false brethren," who could never bring themselves to reject Luther utterly, grew in part from the fact that by the mid-1520s he had become even more of a public figure than before. One antagonist, who later became a bishop, reportedly remarked to tourists that "Those who have not seen Martin Luther and the pope have seen nothing." Wittenberg became a stopping place on the itineraries of many people, including the politically unfortunate King Christian II of Denmark, who lost his throne. Luther later commented that this man was proof that "God takes kings with the same seriousness as children give to card games."[21]

At the same time, the reform movement was becoming so much a public issue that by 1525 it was no longer possible to distinguish between politics and religion in Germany. Local resistance had made many rulers reluctant even to try to implement the Edict of Worms against Luther and his followers. In 1522 a new pope, Adrian VI, came to the throne and demanded a decree of enforcement from the Diet that was then meeting at Nuremberg. How far things had come was evident in the edict to which the politicians finally agreed a year later. Everyone was to preach "only the holy gospel" and to "avoid debatable subjects . . . that await the determination of the proposed council of the church."[22] Now it was the politicians who were appealing to a council of the church!

Matters only became worse from the point of view of Charles V and the representatives of Rome. A new diet met at Speyer in late June 1526. Again the demand was made to promulgate and enforce the Edict of Worms. Again the princes and city councilmen appealed to a future council. This time they defiantly added that each would act with respect to the edict according to their own understanding of their responsibilities to God and to the emperor.

On the surface all seemed to be going well. Luther's enemies on the Roman side were unable to proceed against him and most of his followers. Against the "false brethren" he had decisively clarified the truth of the gospel as he saw it with respect to civil unrest, the ceremonies of the church, and the nature of the Lord's Supper. He had married and his family was prospering. On June 7, 1526, his first child was born. He was named Hans in honor of Luther's father. Ten days later Luther wrote his old friend, Spalatin, "I have planted a garden and built a wall, both with marvelous success. Come visit, and you will be crowned with lilies and roses!"[23]

However, Luther's life had by no means become a bed of roses. In 1523 the Reformation had seen its first martyrs. Two Evangelicals were burned at the stake in the Low Countries. The struggles with Carlstadt, the peasants, the Swiss, and Erasmus all took their toll on Luther. In addition, many of those who claimed to be his followers were forced to pay the price of their convictions. Duke George hunted down monks and nuns who had left their orders as if they were criminals (which, according to the law, they in fact were). The duke and his allies also sought to strip Luther's new prince, Elector John, of his title. The question, "Are you alone wise?" came back to haunt Luther more than once.

Physical and spiritual testing

The life of physical deprivation that Luther had led as a monk also began to exact its penalties. Times of stress, as at Augsburg or Worms or the Wartburg, commonly upset his entire digestive tract from the neck down. In 1527 he began to be afflicted by more severe illnesses, and these proved to be chronic. On April 22 spells of dizziness and fainting caused him to give up preaching for a time. Around nightfall on July 6 he fell into such a terrible feeling of weakness that he was certain he was about to die, and he called Katie and his friends to his side. In August the Plague came to Wittenberg, and many students and faculty fled. The elector urged Luther to flee as well. But he chose to stay, even though his lecture hall had almost no one in it. As late as November he wrote that he and his family were living "suspended in the midst of all sorts of fears."[24]

The threat of the Plague was so common in the 16th century that in early November Luther wrote a book with the title, *Whether One May Flee from Death*, to comfort those who had already done so. To flee obvious danger was natural, he said, and even a God-given reaction. Only pastors and the civil authorities were not to flee, for their God-given offices required them to stay and help the afflicted. (A common story of the time had it that when the Plague struck, doctors were the first to flee, because they recognized the symptoms.) In a time when quarantine was the standard defense, Luther recommended that every parish should establish a home for the sick, "so that not every citizen must turn his own home into a hospital."[25] He was speaking from experience. He and Katie had taken in so many who were stricken that their home remained under quarantine even after the Plague left the city.

These physical dangers were nothing to Luther by comparison with the depression into which he fell during the same months. As had been true when he was a monk, this was far more than mental depression. Of the night he thought he would die he wrote, "I despaired. . . ." To Melanchthon, who had fled the Plague, he reported yet another bout with illness: "I spent more than a week in death and in hell. My entire body was in pain, and I still tremble. Completely abandoned by Christ, I labored under the vacillations and storms of desperation and blasphemy against God. But through the prayers of the saints God began to have mercy on me and pulled my soul from the inferno below."

From his description, he was perhaps suffering from a vicious disease known then as the English Sweats. The references to weakness, tremors, and the fires of hell would suggest as much. But he candidly admitted that the experience shook even his faith. Like many people in the depths of a severe illness, he felt abandoned. The prayers of his friends and wife saved him, he reported, but not from the illness. They ministered to his despair. And so he told Melanchthon, "You, too, must not give up praying for me, just as I pray for you. I know that my agony applies to others as well."[26]

In the midst of these trials, Luther's trust in a gracious God endured. His assurance did not depend on his outward well-being. During these

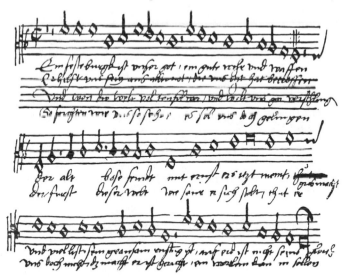

Luther's manuscript of his hymn, "A Mighty Fortress Is Our God."

very months he wrote a hymn that became immortal under the title, "A Mighty Fortress Is Our God." Its text is timeless, but at least its third and fourth verses were deeply rooted in Luther's own experiences of the moment:

And though this world with devils filled
should threaten to undo us,
We will not fear for God has willed
his truth to triumph through us.
The prince of darkness grim? We tremble not for him.
His rage we can endure, for lo! His doom is sure.
One little Word shall fell him.

Luther composed the music as well, and he chose a stately tune in a triumphant major key. The "little Word" was Christ.

That Word abides o'er earthly powers,
no thanks to them be given.
The Spirit and the gifts are ours,
through him who stands beside us.
Let goods and kinfolk go, this mortal life also.
The body they may kill, God's truth undying still.
His kingdom is forever.[27]

TWELVE

Pastor and Teacher

By late 1527 the great, heroic moments that are associated with Luther's life were behind him. His teachings and their practical implications were clear. A powerful movement had begun to establish itself as a historical force. The Indulgence Controversy, the Heidelberg Disputation, the confrontation with Cajetan, the Leipzig Debate, Worms, the Wartburg, the translation of the Bible, Wittenberg and the radicals, the Peasants' War, the break with Erasmus, marriage, the Sacramentarian Controversy—all had come rushing in on him in 10 short years, and they had taken their toll on the man. Luther had faced these crises with great energy and decisiveness. It is not surprising that he occasionally became tired or even depressed.

But Luther was now only 44 years old, and he lived for almost two more decades. Chronic illnesses and increasing age had an ever-greater effect on him. The average life-expectancy at that time has been calculated to have been about 40 years, and from that point on a man would commonly refer to himself as *senex,* or an elder. Even so, Luther remained immensely productive. The essential difference between the early years and these later ones was that external circumstances and the requirements of the Evangelical movement ushered in a new and somewhat different phase of life. He was still creative, but in a far more official way. He became less the professional and academic theologian and more the churchman, pastor, bishop, and even defender of the faith.

True liberty

In late 1527, Luther's new prince, Elector John, proposed to conduct a visitation of all the churches in his territories. The purpose of these visits was to determine the exact status of each parish. Luther was intensely interested in this work. In early August he reviewed the orders (which he had helped write) under which the visitors would carry out their mission. After several revisions, he finally approved these "articles," as they were called. In a preface to their published version, he urged everyone to cooperate with the visitors. He also took the time to write a private letter in which he assured one of the project's chief critics that "Christ will make certain that everything transpires properly."

This critic was John Agricola. He had earlier been one of Luther's favorite students and was now rector of the new Evangelical school in Luther's hometown of Eisleben. Agricola argued that the visitations violated freedom of the conscience and Christian liberty. Had not Luther himself chastised Carlstadt and the city council in Wittenberg because they were coercing people into following Evangelical practices with respect to the Lord's Supper, forms of worship, and the like? How could the man who had restored order in Wittenberg simply by example and by preaching the Word now turn to the coercive power of the civil authorities? Did this not amount to tyranny?

Luther had never imagined, let alone advocated, religious liberty in the modern sense of the term. A true Christian must insist on "the freedom of consciences," he wrote, "even if the tyrants make plans to the contrary." But Luther viewed Paul as the true model of Christian freedom. Paul had circumcised Timothy because Timothy "would be preaching to the Jews," but he "reprimanded Peter because he was judaizing the Gentiles" by requiring all male believers to be circumcised. Luther then reminded Agricola that "the tyrants are not [objecting to the visitation] so that the weak may be taught, but so that the servants of the pope and the ministers of Satan may see our liberty extinguished." This liberty "consists of the blood of the Son of God and was procured for us" by Christ. In the current situation, Luther declared, "If you admit one iota of tyrannical [i.e., Roman] teaching, you deny all of Christ."[1] The visitations would simply guarantee that Christ was preached in the elector's lands.

Luther declared in this letter that nothing he was then doing contradicted the principles he had earlier laid down. In this he was correct. He had called on the civil authorities to reform the church as early as 1520 in the *Address to the Christian Nobility.* He had done so with the argument that a Christian who held secular office was still a Christian and as such was equally obliged to serve the well-being of the church as was any priest, bishop, cardinal, or pope. On the other hand, in the midst of the Peasants' War he had also declared that people must be allowed to believe and teach as they wished, even if it were utter nonsense.

Circumstances had changed, and Luther's intentions changed with them. In the years that had elapsed, what he had said in 1522 had come true: "There should be no changes made until the gospel has been thoroughly preached and confessed."[2] By now it had. In addition, those princes who had most warmly supported Luther earlier had done little more than to protect him and, within limits, to allow him to go his own way. They were not fully the "emergency bishops" whom Luther pictured in the *Address.* Now a new generation was in power, men like Elector John and Landgrave Philip of Hesse. They thought Luther was right on the religious issues, and they had decided to act. Luther applauded this decision and only added the condition that, when they acted, they should do so not as princes but as members of the church. Therefore they ought to act with love and not with the sword. True liberty would be the result.

The visitations

Even in the midst of his illnesses and depression in late 1527, Luther followed the early visitations with growing impatience. He received the articles on August 18, and only two days later he wrote Nicolaus Hausmann, the pastor at Zwickau, "The hope is that the visitation will proceed easily," because the work "is necessary for the churches." But the revised articles did not come back to him until early October. On the 12th he returned them with a few comments from himself and Bugenhagen and the remark that "practically all of it pleases us, because it is organized in the simplest way possible for the sake of the common people."[3] Even so, the articles were not finally published until late winter, and the first visitation was not announced until July 1528.

The earliest reports reached Luther in the fall. On November 8 he wrote Spalatin, "Our visitation is proceeding apace. What miseries we see here!" Three days later he reported somewhat more fully: "In our visitation of the area around Wittenberg, we have discovered so far that all the pastors are living in harmony with their peasants, but the people are lazy when it comes to Word and sacrament. Pray for us." When his health and the situation in Wittenberg finally permitted, Luther himself served as a visitor. In January 1529 he wrote Elector John, "We maintain, believe, and know that Your Electoral Grace can have ordered no better work than the visitation; there is therefore nothing that we will withhold from it." A few days later, the new direction of Luther's career was clear. To a pastor at Braunschweig he wrote, "I am busy with preparing a catechism for the raw pagans."[4]

The results of these and other visitations appalled reformers all over Europe. Then, as now, the educated and urban classes amused themselves at the expense of those who worked the land and whom they variously called "hayseeds" and "barbarians." What most of the reformers discovered was that much of the 16th-century version of this stereotype was true. The peasants were a harsh, crude folk who far preferred fairs and hard drinking to church services. Luther himself once remarked that the workers he knew kept time not with a clock or by the sun but by the number of empty tankards lying about them.

Luther also despised do-nothings, drunkards, wife-beaters, promiscuous youth, and scoundrels of all kinds. His scorn knew no bounds, particularly if an individual offender were highly born. To one such person (in this case a woman) he wrote, "You of the nobility and high estates should of necessity all be pious, for there are few of you. Yet you are debauched. It is no wonder that the great multitude of the common people is dissolute."[5]

Moral turpitude, even gross public immorality, came nonetheless as no great surprise to Luther. But as a man who was trying to create *theodidacti*—people taught by God—he was horrified by the religious ignorance of the common people. In his preface to *The Small Catechism,* which appeared in May 1529, he reported what he had discovered in the visitation:

Good God, what wretchedness I beheld! The common people, especially those who live in the country, have no knowledge whatsoever of Christian teaching, and unfortunately many pastors are quite incompetent and un-fitted for teaching. Although the people are supposed to be Christian, are baptized, and receive the holy sacrament, they do not know the Lord's Prayer, the Creed, or the Ten Commandments, they live as if they were pigs and irrational beasts, and now that the gospel has been restored they have mastered the fine art of abusing liberty.

"Woe to you forever!" was Luther's judgment on the bishops who allowed this situation.

Two catechisms

Luther's reaction to the visitations was in many respects the cul-mination of everything he had done up to that point. His protest had begun with a new understanding of the way to salvation. It continued with the search for a debate or a public hearing in order to reach the truth of the matter. Faced with rejection, he had carried the debate on in print while he translated the Bible into the language of the people. At the same time he had sought to accomplish changes in actual practice in such a way that the weak might be instructed rather than offended.

Now he published his catechisms and wrote, "I therefore beg of you for God's sake, my beloved brethren who are pastors and teachers, that you take the duties of your office seriously, that you have pity on the people who are entrusted to your care, and that you help me teach the catechism to the people, especially those who are young."[6]

Never had Luther been more serious about his objective. For him, ignorance of basic Christian doctrine meant very nearly that one was not a Christian. When he announced that he was writing a catechism, he could have said he was writing it for the *rustici,* or country folk. Instead, he declared that it was for the *pagani,* or pagans.

As Erasmus had done with his book for the laity years earlier, Luther also chose the Greek word *enchiridion* (or "small dagger") as another term for *The Small Catechism.* Both of them intended that their books be readily at hand in moments of spiritual danger. But that is where every similarity between the two authors ended. Erasmus sought to inculcate enlightened spirituality that would be marked by love of God and of one's neighbor. He wished to help Christians fulfill the great commandment. Other catechisms had given instructions on how prop-erly to say the rosary, confess one's sins, or go to Mass. By contrast, Luther wrote a book containing brief explanations of the doctrinal content of the Ten Commandments, the Apostles' Creed, and the Lord's Prayer. To these he appended equally brief expositions of Baptism and the Lord's Supper, the most useful way to confess one's sins, and prayers for morning, evening, and mealtimes. He concluded with brief passages from the Scriptures that described how Christians should live with one another.

Except for this last section, Luther's *Small Catechism* contains little about how a Christian should behave or what a Christian's emotional state should be. Instead, he repeatedly emphasized the doctrine of the grace of God in Christ. He even concluded the section on the Ten Commandments with the declaration that "Therefore we are to love and trust him, and gladly do what he commands," because the commandments themselves were evidence of God's grace, even if Christians could not keep them.

Perhaps the strongest statement of Luther's Evangelical theology came in his explanation to the Third Article of the Apostles' Creed: "I believe that by my own reason or strength I cannot believe in Jesus Christ, my Lord, or come to him. But the Holy Spirit has called me through the gospel, enlightened me with his gifts, and sanctified and kept me in true faith. . . ." He reemphasized the doctrine that salvation came by grace and not by works when he came to the fifth petition of the Lord's Prayer: "And we pray that he would give us everything by grace, for we sin every day and deserve nothing but punishment." Lest it be forgotten, he then underlined the idea once more when he came to the end of the prayer: "*Amen* means 'Yes, it shall be so.' We say *Amen* because we are certain that such petitions are pleasing to our Father in heaven and are heard by him. For he himself has commanded us to pray in this way and has promised to hear us."[7]

The Small Catechism was a book of doctrine. In it Luther sought to teach Christians how to regard their life of faith as well as how to live it. For Luther, prayers themselves served as constant reminders of God's graciousness in Christ. For evening prayer he recommended the following:

> I give you thanks, heavenly Father, that you have protected me this day through your dear son, Jesus Christ. I ask you to forgive all my sin and the wrong that I have done. Graciously protect me during the coming night. Into your hands I commend my body and soul and all that is mine. Let your holy angels have charge of me, that the wicked one may have no power over me. Amen.

Title pages of the Small Catechism *and the* Large Catechism.

He concluded with one piece of practical advice: "Then quickly lie down and sleep in peace."[8]

In order to carry out this teaching mission Luther wrote more than just material suitable for children and the uneducated. He also wrote his *Large Catechism,* which he intended for the instruction of pastors and heads of households. There he treated each of the sections in greater detail. Taken together, these two works showed both the range of Luther's genius and its objective. During the same period, he reluctantly undertook a reform of the worship service. He emphasized congregational singing not only to encourage lay participation, but also, by adding music to words, to teach true doctrine to ordinary people. Although he was a professor who delighted in having a doctorate and flaunted it in the faces of his enemies, he remained a pastor whose chief concern was for the spiritual well-being of his flock. His flock had simply become larger than it had been in 1517.

Later in life, when Luther reviewed what he had accomplished, he was particularly proud of what he had done for the laity. "In the first place, I have hounded the papists into their books, especially into the Scriptures. . . . Secondly, I put an end to the hullabaloo and carnival of corrupt indulgence sales, which no council had been able to touch. In the third place, I have almost blockaded the pilgrimages and the heathen altars."[9] By contrast, he thought that most of his books should be burned. *The Small Catechism* was one of the few exceptions. The life of ordinary Christians, among whom he counted himself, absorbed him.

High politics

By means of his catechisms, hymns, and new liturgy—as well as by his other actions—Luther was taking responsibility for the future of the Evangelical movement. Meanwhile, both he and the reform movement had become a political fact of life within the empire. High politics therefore also began to consume more and more of Luther's energies. Initially, the most pressing of these political issues involved the Sacramentarian Controversy. The princes who defended Luther (Philip of Hesse in particular) looked at the struggle with the Swiss and the South Germans rather differently than Luther did. They, too, deplored doctrinal disagreement. But they also saw that political disunity (and therefore weakness) in the face of a determined emperor was one result of it.

They had good reason to be concerned. The Edict of Worms, which declared Luther and all his followers outlaws, was still a legal fact in the empire. Charles V was demanding ever more insistently that it be enforced, even against princes. Under this pressure, the alliance between the defenders of Luther and the defenders of Rome that had still existed at the Diet of Speyer in 1526 was now falling apart. The duke of Bavaria had even conducted a visitation of his own in 1526, but its purpose was to root out priests who were sympathetic to Luther. In March 1529, under the authority of Charles V, Archduke Ferdinand called for another meeting of the estates of the empire at Speyer. With Vienna under siege, the Diet was to discuss both the Turkish threat and the religious controversy together. Ferdinand declared that the fact that the Turks were advancing up the Danube had much to do with God's anger over the existence of heretics within the empire. Both the Turks and Luther ought to be dealt with summarily.

On April 1, Landgrave Philip of Hesse and Elector John of Saxony replied with a memorandum to all the other princes and city councilmen on whom they thought they could count. They denounced Archduke

Ferdinand's proposal as a threat to the gospel. Luther himself replied in the middle of the month with a book, *Concerning War against the Turks*, in which he denied that such a war could be considered a holy crusade. If Ferdinand wished divine help, then he ought to drive the pope's minions out of Germany. There were two important persons in the empire: "One is named Mr. Christian and the other Emperor Charles." Contrary to all tradition, Luther then declared that the emperor "is not the head of Christendom, neither is he the defender of the gospel or of the faith." Whatever the emperor did with his sword was "a bodily, worldly affair."[10]

Although he was acting on behalf of his brother Charles V, Archduke Ferdinand did not exactly have his way in 1529 at the second Diet of Speyer. But neither did the supporters of Luther. The vast majority of those present agreed with Ferdinand, at least in principle. But six of the territorial princes, with the support of a number of representatives from the cities, sent up a "protest" in which they declared that the action of their colleagues breached the agreement they had all made at Speyer in 1526, according to which each would be responsible for religious matters in his own territories. Such a protest had legal standing as an appeal to precedent and effectively stymied Ferdinand. These "protesting estates" (hence, "Protestants") further insisted that "in matters pertaining to the glory of God and the salvation of our souls, everyone must himself give an answer to God."[11] Even without reading Luther's latest book, which appeared too late for this Diet anyway, these politicians were just as adamant as he was.

At this moment they had even more to lose than did Luther himself. Philip of Hesse and Elector John had some allies, but precious few. Against them stood all the other princes, cities, and prelates. In addition, they were painfully aware that Charles V was perfectly capable of bringing Spanish troops with him when he returned to Germany. Philip and John faced the one imperative that any politician faces in such a situation. They had to find more friends and neutralize some of their enemies. It was imperative that they immediately make plans for a political and military alliance of the Evangelical estates.

The Marburg Colloquy

Philip of Hesse took the lead on the one issue that he and his allies must have found most baffling. The Sacramentarian Controversy, a struggle over Jesus' four little words, "This is my body," both reduced the number of helpful friends and made actual enemies. But when Luther first heard about the plans for an alliance, he opposed it in a letter to Elector John. In the first place, he wrote, the project evidenced too little trust in God. On the model of Isaiah, such alliances should be rejected. Moreover, Luther regarded Philip of Hesse as a "young and restless prince" who was not to be trusted. Above all, the southern cities, in particular Strasbourg (under the spiritual leadership of Bucer and Capito), could not be included in any list of friends, because "they work against God and the sacrament." [12]

Philip of Hesse, a slight, smooth-skinned, and dark-complexioned young man, faced a serious obstacle in the now slightly rotund, older reformer. The young ruler nonetheless persisted. What he had seen of political gatherings suggested that a meeting of people who were basically of the same mind could always produce some sort of agreement, if only it proved to be to everyone's advantage. Until the last moment, he shrewdly concealed his intention to negotiate even with the man Luther viewed as the chief viper of them all: Zwingli from Zurich.

For his part, Luther finally declared that he was willing to attend such a meeting, but he made it clear that he was coming only in deference to the wishes of Elector John and because, "God willing, I will not have it that our opponents may boast that they were more inclined toward peace and unity than I was." Even so, he called it a matter "that is perhaps dangerous for us," and added, "I cannot provide benefits for Satan no matter how handsomely he may deck himself out." [13] Luther did not even want to be associated with "the Sacramentarians," as he called them.

Marburg is a small town in a large forest due north of Frankfurt am Main. It is far west and a little south of Wittenberg, and is much easier to reach from the south. Bucer, Hedio, Zwingli, and Oecolampadius could simply float down the Rhine River, go up the Main to Frankfurt, and then travel overland, while for Luther and his party the entire trip was by wagon. In spite of the difficulties and their doubts, in early October 1529 most of the best-known Evangelical theologians from Saxony, south Germany, and even Switzerland gathered in Marburg to discuss their differences, and, in Philip's mind, to work out the theological basis for a political alliance.

"It is God who commands"

Philip of Hesse was neither the first nor the last politician to be disappointed by people of principle. The Marburg Colloquy, as it came to be called, was a failure from the young prince's point of view. He had been able to cajole or trick the chief theologians into attending. But from the very beginning, Luther and his supporters were forcefully unwilling to compromise. Philip's chancellor opened the proceedings by declaring that "everyone on both sides should present his arguments in a spirit of moderation."[14] Luther began by accusing his opponents of several venerable heresies that had nothing to do with the Lord's Supper.

Philip of Hesse (by Hans Brosamer).

Luther was a seasoned debater. When both Oecolampadius and Zwingli objected strenuously to this opening gambit, he quickly retreated by saying, "Very well, so be it." He said that he was compelled to make clear that he was not a party to any such heretical ideas, and he was sure that they would understand. He quickly characterized his opponents' argument: "You seek to prove that a body cannot be in two places at the same time." Then he said, "I will not listen to proofs . . . based on arguments derived from geometry." Luther took the position that would occupy the remainder of the discussions: "God is beyond all mathematics, and the words of God are to be revered and followed in awe. It is God who commands, 'Take, eat, this is my body.' I therefore demand compelling proof from the Scriptures to the contrary."[15]

Zwingli, Oecolampadius, and the south Germans were never able to wriggle out of the terms Luther set for the debate in this opening statement. He had placed the burden of proof on them. They had to prove that John 6:63, "The flesh is of no avail," applied to the Words of Institution, "This is my body." To underline his point, Luther took a piece of chalk and wrote on the table that separated the contenders, *hoc est corpus meum*. Then, as if the words "This is my body" were the elements themselves sitting on the altar, he covered them with a fine cloth.

Oecolampadius tried to argue the point. The Scriptures were full of metaphors, he replied. There was no reason to deny metaphor in this place if Luther accepted it in other passages, such as "I am the vine." Surely, Jesus did not mean that he was part of a plant! But Luther's reply was both shrewd and to the point. "I do not deny figurative speech [in the Scriptures], but you must prove that this is what we have here. It is not enough to say that these words . . . could be interpreted in this way. You must prove that they *must* be interpreted in this figurative sense."[16] This neither Oecolampadius nor Zwingli could do.

The castle at Marburg.

Later, Zwingli joined the discussion. He saw what Luther had done and tried to turn the tables on him by challenging Luther to prove that *hoc est corpus meum* applied to John 6:63. But Luther would not allow it. At one point Zwingli declared,

It is for you to prove that the passage in John 6[:63] speaks of a physical eating.

Luther: You express yourself about as poorly and carry the argument forward about as well as does a walking stick standing in the corner.

Zwingli: No, no, no! This is the passage that will break your neck!

Luther: Don't be so sure of yourself. Necks don't break so easily here. Remember you are in Germany and not in Switzerland.

Zwingli apologized for his remarks, which he passed off as a Swiss colloquialism. Landgrave Philip broke in and said, "Doctor Luther, do not take undue offense at this expression." [17]

The room where the Marburg Colloquy was held.

They all adjourned for lunch, and the first day was half finished. But the debate continued in much the same fashion. The parties did forego further personal attacks. But Luther clearly dominated the discussion, and he did so in a spirit of perfect intransigence. At the very end, Strasbourg's most important politician, Jacob Sturm, broke in and said that he wished to return to the questions about old heresies that Luther had raised at the beginning of the meeting. These, he said, "could be understood to the disadvantage of the city of Strasbourg." He would have Bucer rise and present their teachings on all matters except the Lord's Supper.

Bucer did so and then asked Luther whether the Strasbourg theologians were teaching any errors. Luther was unmoved. "I am neither your lord nor your judge," he replied. "What you teach in Strasbourg is no concern of mine. . . . As I have said before, for this reason we commend you to the judgment of God. Teach as you wish to be judged before God."[18] Luther would give no one any satisfaction whatsoever.

A version of concord

At this moment the host stepped in. Three days had passed and the Marburg Colloquy had seen nothing but disagreement. The struggle was so severe that on several occasions Luther begged one of his colleagues to stand in for him because he was tired. But now Landgrave Philip, in response to the request from Sturm, asked Luther to draw up articles of faith to which the others might reply. If Luther would not respond positively to their declaration of faith, perhaps the landgrave could arrange things so they could affirm Luther's teachings.

Luther reported to Katie that he dutifully composed 15 statements that summarized the Wittenbergers' teachings. They covered everything from creation through the Trinity and the incarnation, to original sin, salvation, the nature of the church, and the sacraments. For Luther, this was a simple task. Not two months earlier, he had written just such a "testament," as it was called, in the town of Schwabach. He had done so at the request of Elector John, who wished, in the aftermath of Speyer, to have a succinct statement of Luther's teachings. To Luther's surprise, everyone at Marburg agreed to each article except the one on the Lord's Supper. He wrote to Katie that although he and his colleagues could not acknowledge the opposition as "brothers and members [of Christ], we freely wished them well." To a fellow pastor, he reported, "we still gave them the hand of peace and love so that for the present we may set aside controversial books and words." The next morning Luther preached to the assembled theologians and politicians. He had agreed to a version of concord.[19]

THIRTEEN

Damnable Rome

*T*he backbiting, name-calling, and angry accusations between Luther and his opponents in the Sacramentarian Controversy did stop, at least for the time being. But the problem of a political alliance to defend the Evangelical movement against its enemies persisted. Perhaps the Swiss and south Germans could not be included in such an alliance. But was there to be one, and would Luther cooperate in what the princes regarded as politically prudent preparations?

Luther had become even more of a public figure than before. He was no longer simply a celebrity and the leader of a loose band of reformers. Now he was taking responsibility for a clearly defined, public movement in support of the gospel as he understood it. But this new phase of his life had also been part of the fabric of the young Luther. Ten years earlier he had written, "The most important thing of all is to tell what is true and what is not true."[1] These words and the convictions that lay behind them were now forcing new obligations on him.

Luther would not cooperate with the princes. In reply to Chancellor Brück, the chief advisor to Elector John, he wrote that any alliance implied armed resistance, and such resistance or even the threat of it would inevitably end in a general bloodbath. To Luther's mind, the prince ought not act even in defense of the faith of others, because "we all must believe or not believe at our own individual risk." Three weeks later a delegation from the protesting estates visited the emperor, then residing in Spain, for the purpose of discussing aid against the

Turks. Charles V threw them into prison. Yet Luther still insisted that Elector John not resist the emperor with force. To fight would be a "properly disruptive and disloyal act."[2]

Elector John was not to be refused. On January 27, 1530, he wrote Luther again on the question of resistance. He had received two other memoranda of advice. Lazarus Spengler, the city secretary in Nuremberg, insisted that resistance was never justified, even in defense of the gospel. Martyrdom was preferable. With evident relief, John also reported the views of one of Luther's closest colleagues. Bugenhagen, who was better acquainted with German history than were the others, argued that armed resistance was justified on the grounds that rulers had an obligation to protect their subjects. Elector John asked Luther to discuss the matter with his colleagues Bugenhagen, Melanchthon, and Jonas, and then, after careful reconsideration, to give his advice within three weeks in a formal memorandum.

Passive resistance

The elector had not liked Luther's original advice, nor did he like the prospect of martyrdom. Therefore he went out of his way to have his political advisors instruct Luther on the peculiarities of the German constitution. He wanted Luther to understand that the emperor did not have the same status with respect to the princes as the princes had with respect to their subjects. In particular, Luther was reminded that at his coronation Charles V had taken an oath to respect the freedoms of the individual princes and not to use force against them.

Luther apparently did not much care for having to rethink the whole issue, and he delayed responding until March 6, in spite of the elector's deadline. He granted the force of "the lawyers' " arguments about imperial or "temporal" law. But he pointed to the scriptural injunction to be loyal to the authorities, among whom he counted the emperor. He was not impressed by the legal maxim, "one may resist force with force," because to his mind it applied only to equals and not to inferiors and superiors. The elector of Saxony had no more right to resist the emperor than the mayor of a small Saxon town had to resist the elector. To be sure, the princes ought to refuse to cooperate with any attempt to suppress the gospel by force, even if it came from the emperor. But if they took up arms, they would be putting themselves in the place of the emperor. Civil war would result, and soon it would degenerate into "a war of all against all." Such an outcome would be so dreadful that "a prince should rather lose three principalities, yea, rather suffer death three times" than contribute to it.[3]

Elector John must have been deeply chagrined when he read Luther's reconsideration of the matter of armed resistance. Luther was, in fact, invincibly ignorant about the intricacies of the German constitution. In Germany at that time, a town mayor in Saxony was indeed an official of the prince. But the elector of Saxony was by no means an official of the emperor. After all, John's predecessor, Elector Frederick the Wise, had helped elect Charles V.

Luther, however, was being true to form. As in his dealings with "the false brethren" at Marburg, he refused to yield even to an ally in the face of what he took to be clear statements from the Scriptures. He might have been in need of instruction about the German constitution, but lacking that, he made good on his pledge in the *Open Letter on the Harsh Book against the Peasants* of 1525: "When I have time and occasion to do so, I shall attack the princes and lords too, for in my office as teacher a prince is the same to me as a peasant."[4] This refusal to cooperate with armed resistance did not amount to a published attack, although Luther would later launch many of those. It was, however, precisely the sort of passive resistance that Luther promised and advocated.

The political realities of the moment made Luther's refusal to budge on the question of resistance all the more remarkable. He and his colleagues and the elector and his advisors had good reason to believe that the emperor might try to suppress the Evangelical movement with force. On March 11, perhaps at the same moment he received Luther's unwelcome opinion on resistance, Elector John received a summons to yet another diet, this one to be convened at Augsburg on April 8, 1530. Charles V had defeated the combined forces of France and the pope in Italy, had been crowned Holy Roman Emperor, was holding Pope Clement VII securely under house arrest, and was now returning to Germany. He was determined to put an end to religious division in the empire, and he appeared to be in a position to do so.

The Coburg

Within two days after replying to Charles V's summons, Elector John sent out a summons of his own, this one to Luther, Jonas, Bugenhagen, and Melanchthon. They were to write a clear statement of their faith, but above all they were to draw up a list of each item in which they differed with Rome on practical matters such as the character of worship services, the organization of the church, the nature of the clergy, monasticism, and the like. Luther and his colleagues complied, and toward the end of March, they sent Elector John a full confession of faith. Then, on April 3, the entire group packed their bags and left for Torgau and the elector's residence.

The Coburg, where Luther stayed during the Diet of Augsburg.

Torgau was only the first stop. The next day Elector John and his entourage, including Luther and three other theologians, started for Augsburg. Thirteen days later (princes traveled more slowly than did individual theologians), the group reached the elector's southernmost castle, the Coburg. There they deposited Luther, who, according to the Edict of Worms, was still an outlaw and without a safe conduct. Luther was on ice once again, with little to do but read, think, and write.

The Coburg is situated near the geographical center of undivided Germany, far to the southwest of the Thuringian Forest, due south of Erfurt, and several days' ride north of Augsburg. Now Luther was even farther from his friends than he had been at the Wartburg nine years earlier. He tried very hard to put a cheerful construction on his situation. Once again he referred to himself as living in "the kingdom of the birds," and described his location as "excellently designed for scholarship." He would work first on the Psalms, then on the prophetic books of the Old Testament, and finally on a translation of Aesop's *Fables*. To his friends he wrote of the birds: "All make the same music in unison, yet with a pleasant difference between the voices of the elders and the youngsters. . . . We sit here with great pleasure in this Diet as idle spectators."[5]

Actually Luther hated it. He did make a good beginning on each of his announced projects, and he published several other shorter works, besides writing a constant stream of letters—mostly demanding to know what was happening in Augsburg. By mid-May, when he had been at the Coburg less than one of the five months that stretched before him, he was complaining to Melanchthon of general weakness, dizziness, and roaring in his ears. On June 5 he learned that his father had died a week earlier. Luther had known since February that Hans was failing, and had written the old man a consoling letter in which he urged him to lean on "that certain, true helper, Jesus Christ, the one who has gobbled up death and sin for our sakes." Some time after his father's death, Luther pronounced himself reassured, because Hans "lived until now, when he could see the light of the truth." But when he received the news of his father's death, he was so overcome that "he snatched his Psalter, went into the cellar, and sobbed so deeply that he had a headache the next day."[6] Much of Luther's second stay in a castle was a wretched experience.

In spite of these intense, personal sufferings and his announced scholarly projects, Luther directed his attention to Augsburg. Before mid-May he had written a pamphlet, *To the Clergy Assembled at Augsburg*. It amounted to one of his most potent assaults ever on the Church of Rome. The prelates at the Diet should be careful to discuss matters judiciously, he wrote, because there was enough popular unrest to unleash a revolt far worse than the Peasants' War. If such a thing were to happen, Luther warned, "Let your blood be on your own head." A few days later he received from Elector John a copy of an early draft of a confession of faith written by Melanchthon. Not long after, Luther's own *Schwabach Articles* (which were the basis for Melanchthon's confession) were published, to howls of horror from his Roman opponents. Luther turned sarcastic and urged all to have pity on "the pious, good Emperor Charles who is sitting like an innocent little lamb among so many wild boars and dogs, yea devils."[7]

The longer the Diet of Augsburg dragged on and the longer Luther was forced to cool his heels at the Coburg, the more ready for a fight he became. On June 25, Melanchthon's *Augsburg Confession* was submitted to the emperor. The protesting princes had it read in German to Charles V and the assembled estates of the Holy Roman Empire. Then they declared that they would stand by it to the very end.

The Diet of Augsburg.

As presented, the *Augsburg Confession* consisted of two parts. In the first part Melanchthon, briefly and as gently as possible, stated the doctrines to which he and Luther positively subscribed. He began by pointing out that, like Rome, they adhered to the three ecumenical creeds and rejected all the venerable heresies that those creeds rejected. Then he covered the critical topics of faith, works, grace, righteousness, and the sacraments. Only in the second section did he list the items that were in dispute. At the same time he declared, both in a preamble and in a conclusion, that the Evangelical estates would be happy to negotiate with their opponents on the basis of the Scriptures and, if possible, to come to unity and oneness of faith. When he read the first draft, Luther declared that "it pleases me very much and I do not know how I could improve on or alter it . . . for I cannot tread so softly and lightly."[8]

A little more than a month later, Luther received the final version, together with a letter in which Melanchthon expressed his fears for the future. Luther could scarcely bear such faintheartedness. He wrote, "From my heart, I despise the fears . . . that so trouble you. That they so govern your heart comes not from the great danger [that confronts us] but from our great lack of faith." They had confessed their faith and they could do no more. "For my part, I am not unsettled . . . about our cause; in fact, I am much more hopeful than before."[9]

Luther had misgivings about Melanchthon's cover letter and some of the subsequent maneuverings at Augsburg. But the confession that Melanchthon wrote, and to which the princes subscribed, delighted him and made him more feisty than ever. When he heard that his old antagonist, Archbishop Albert of Mainz, was recommending renewed negotiations with the protesting estates, Luther actually entertained the idea that Albert might be ready to convert. On the same day, July 6, he wrote words reminiscent of those with which he had marked his father's death: "I am tremendously pleased to have lived to this moment when Christ has been publicly proclaimed by his staunch confessors in such a great assembly by means of this truly most beautiful confession!"[10] The Coburg had become not such a bad place after all.

Attempts at compromise

Thunderclouds soon appeared. On July 12, Eck gave the emperor his *Confutation of the Augsburg Confession*. On August 3, Charles V presented Eck's work to the assembled politicians and demanded that every one of them, including those who had signed Melanchthon's *Augsburg Confession*, submit to it. When Luther read the *Confutation*, he asked, "It was enough that we declared the grounds of faith and offered peace; how can we hope to convert them to the truth?"[11] There was no hope. On August 6, Landgrave Philip of Hesse left Augsburg without even informing the emperor. Sensing what was to occur, he had already begun to discuss a military alliance that would include even the Swiss cantons of Zurich and Bern.

The question of unified resistance was the order of the day, and it quickly consumed Luther as well. On the one hand, he remained absolutely obdurate. He continued to turn aside every suggestion of compromise on matters of doctrine. But the Strasbourg theologians, and

Bucer in particular, were determined. The Lutheran princes did not allow them to sign the *Augsburg Confession* on the grounds of past disagreements over the Lord's Supper. Together with representatives of three smaller cities, they had submitted their own statement of faith, the so-called *Confessio Tetrapolitana*. But the four cities found little political comfort as they huddled together in a sca dominated by the ships and gunboats of the princes and the emperor. As a consequence, Strasbourg's politicians ordered Bucer to begin looking for a way to minimize his differences with Luther. They themselves had already begun the process by tricking Zwingli into sending sharply worded articles of his own, the *Ratio Fidei*, and then circulating them in Augsburg. When Melanchthon saw them, he declared, "a person would swear that he has completely lost his mind." By comparison, Bucer and Capito appeared to be conservative.[12]

From the Coburg, Luther remained highly dubious about Bucer's new approaches. To Melanchthon he wrote on September 11, "I am not responding at all to Martin Bucer," whose initiatives Luther regarded as an attempt by Satan to undermine the clarity and force of the *Augsburg Confession*. He would not budge even when he received a visit from Bucer two weeks later. Bucer left shaking his head. To his colleagues he wrote, "There will be no peace in the church unless we are willing to endure much from this man."[13]

The question of resistance

Meanwhile, the results of the Diet of Augsburg made political and military preparedness all the more important. When Charles V refused even to receive Melanchthon's *Apology to the Augsburg Confession,* Melanchthon and the delegation from Wittenberg left. Luther's continued refusal to countenance resistance was increasingly embarrassing to Elector John and Landgrave Philip. They were determined to bring him around.

Philip of Hesse took the lead. On October 21 he tried once again to instruct Luther about the true constitutional standing of the princes over against the emperor. His central point was that "different circumstances prevail with respect to German princes than with respect to those of other times." In particular, he insisted, the New Testament injunction that Christians be loyal to the authorities did not apply to 16th-century German princes, because Charles V was not Caesar. "Foreign princes do not have the same freedom . . . as do we Germans." To be sure, they had taken an oath to the emperor at his coronation. But they had also taken one to the empire, and the emperor had taken one to protect them in their liberties. According to the imperial constitution, the emperor could not take from them by force "so much as one gulden." If he did act against them militarily, "then he has turned himself into a private citizen and is no longer truly the emperor but a disturber of the peace."[14] In this circumstance, the princes would have to act for the sake of the empire.

Luther replied from Torgau, where he, Jonas, and Melanchthon had been summoned by Elector John to discuss once more the subject of resistance. He wrote that he was already at work on a book about the proceedings at Augsburg in which he would declare that no prince was obligated to cooperate with the emperor in an unjust, illegal war against the true faith. Such acts would be "blasphemous, murderous, and satanic."[15] For the rest, Luther referred Philip to his earlier opinions.

These views were not good enough for the princes. Luther's exposé of the dealings at Augsburg would help, but the main question was active resistance, not refusal to cooperate with the emperor in a war against the Protestants. Elector John therefore sat Luther and his colleagues down with his own and Landgrave Philip's lawyers for a serious discussion of the princes' liberties and obligations according to the German constitution. When they had finished, Luther, Melanchthon, and Jonas finally gave in.

According to the written memorandum to which they agreed, resistance—even armed resistance—was legitimate for a Christian prince, but only because the German constitution allowed princes to take up arms against an emperor who disregarded the law of the land. "For when we previously taught positively never to resist the established authority, we did not know that such a right was granted by the laws of that very authority, which we have at all times diligently instructed people to obey." Luther and his colleagues made it clear that they were not, as theologians, conceding anything to the lawyers of Philip and John. Rather, they declared that, "Because the gospel does not confound matters of temporal law . . . it seems proper that one should make preparations to resist with force just as quickly as it may be possible to do so."[16]

Luther was not thereby sanctioning religious war, as he made clear in a letter to Linck, his old friend in Nuremberg. Rather, both the constitutional and political situation, made it legitimate (and not un-Christian) for the princes prudently to prepare to defend themselves, should war be forced on them. Yet Luther was still uneasy about what he had done. He sensed that he (and his great public authority) were being used by others for their own purposes.

This uneasiness can be seen in letters of reassurance he wrote to other friends months later. They had been disturbed by Luther's apparent sanctioning of disobedience, and they well remembered the harsh position he had taken against the peasants only five years earlier. Luther simply replied that "we have left such matters to the competence of the lawyers. When they find that in such a case imperial law allows resistance . . . then we cannot suspend temporal law" in favor of the gospel.[17] All authority was divinely established, including the peculiarities of the German constitution. In planning to resist an imminent attack on themselves, the princes were acting as princes and not, in the first instance, in defense of the gospel, which needed no defense.

At the same time Luther completed and saw through the press two works that the princes did in fact use as propaganda when war erupted not long after his death. The first was a *Commentary on the Alleged Imperial Edict* of Augsburg. His real target was Eck's *Confutation of the Augsburg Confession,* and most of his argumentation was theological rather than political. Nonetheless, to Luther's mind the defenders of Rome had now proven themselves to be instruments of Satan. "I, however, Dr. Martin, have been called and compelled to the office of doctor . . . and I am sworn and bound to my most beloved Holy Scriptures to preach and teach them truly and loudly. . . . In this regard it has also happened with respect to [the papacy] that everything will go ever worse for it and that those who are with me cannot any longer even pray for it."[18] The die had been cast.

In the second of these works, Luther treated Rome and all its defenders to exactly the judgment he thought they merited. The *Warning to His Beloved Germans* was one of the harshest polemical works ever to come from Luther's pen. The adherents of Rome were "murderers and bloodthirsty dogs" who "intend to wage war and commit murder." If they acted on their intentions, true Christians should remember that "it is not rebellion to act against them and to defend oneself." Unspeakable horrors would result. Civil war was likely and with it a general bloodbath. Luther had little doubt that he himself would likely die in such an explosion. But he added, "then I will take an immense crowd of bishops, priests, and monks with me so that people may say that Dr. Martin went to the grave as part of a magnificent procession." Here Luther's sense of irony turned harsh and uncompromising. Lest anyone mistake his meaning, he added that the defenders of Rome "have made a terrible mistake [at Augsburg], because my life will be their hangman and my death their Satan!"[19]

The leaders of the protesting estates met in the town of Schmalkalden before the year 1530 was over. By early 1531, they settled on an alliance that would defend their faith with arms if necessary. When war did come after Luther's death, they used his words to justify their actions. For both Protestants and Catholics, the Schmalkald Wars, innumerable local conflicts thereafter, and finally the Thirty Years' War (1618–1648) were terribly difficult. By the end of these horrors, Luther had been in the grave for more than a century and much of Germany had been devastated by troops from nearly every European nation.

Impending disaster

Whatever the purposes for which Luther's words were used, there can be little doubt that his judgment of what would happen was correct. In addition, his assessment of the situation well predated his reluctant agreement at Torgau that resistance, even armed resistance, was allowable.

As early as August 1530, three months before the meeting at Torgau, Luther was becoming gloomy about the future of his beloved Germany. He declared that any compromise with Rome "amounts to resisting the Holy Spirit." About a month later, he wrote Jonas, "My request is this: break off negotiations with them and come home. They have our confession and they have [heard] the gospel. If they want to abide it, then they may do so. If they do not want to do so, then they may go where they belong. If a war comes out of all this, then so be it. We have prayed and done enough."[20]

For Luther, the great divide did not come when the politicians pressed him to consent to resistance at Torgau in late October 1530. Rather, this decision, as well as the exact language he used to describe Rome, grew from the refusal of his opponents—from Tetzel to Cajetan and Eck—even to consider the Evangelical message. The Diet of Augsburg, Melanchthon's *Augsburg Confession*, and its flat rejection by the emperor and the representatives of Rome comprised no more than the last act in this tragedy. To Luther's mind, these events proved that Rome and its defenders were utterly and hopelessly reprobate. True Christians were no longer even to pray for the pope.

FOURTEEN

To Build the Church

During the 1530s, Luther became more than an immensely influential public figure. To many, such as the students who began copying down his every word at the dinner table, he became something of an oracle, a repository of divine wisdom whose every comment, no matter what the occasion, had to be preserved. In 1523 he suddenly declared in the midst of a sermon, "For the sake of Christ I beg all who are down there committing my sermons to paper or memory not to print them until they have my own draft, or until I have myself had them printed here in Wittenberg."[1] But by 1531 he could not even eat without hearing the scratch of pen on paper.

In spite of such adulation, Luther remained determined to carry on his own work to the extent that his health and other circumstances would allow. To fulfill this objective, he dedicated himself to a perfectly prosaic task. He decided that he personally had to undertake the practical reforms of the church that his teachings demanded. The old goal of helping all to become *theodidacti,* people taught by God, remained. But now Luther changed his methods. As age and illness slowly crept up on him, he devoted his energies more and more to ecclesiastical affairs, broadly conceived, and specifically to his students and followers. For them and for heads of families he wrote *The Large Catechism* to help in teaching the faith. They would become the new leaders of a reformed church that would preserve the faith after his own death.

Personal concerns

In March 1531, Luther wrote, "I am seriously declining in strength, especially in the head. It hinders me from writing, reading, or speaking much, and I am living like a sick man." In November he begged Bugenhagen to return from the north, where he had been helping carry out reform, "because I am overwhelmed with work and often sick." At about the same time he reported that one of the elector's chief officials had invited him to go on a hunt, "so that physical exercise might drive away the roaring and weakness in my head." The hunt apparently did not help. Beginning in mid-April 1532, he gave up preaching in public for eight weeks, because every time he mounted the pulpit, an onset of dizziness made it almost impossible for him to continue. Then in July a running sore opened on one leg. He suffered from that sore, and from his doctors' attempts to cure it, for the rest of his life.

Yet Luther's personal situation during these years included more than the gloom of illness and advancing age. In January 1532 he became so ill from hypertension and a weak heart that he called his friends to his side. But he had a rather different message for them from what they might have expected. He told them he was convinced that he was not about to die. Zwingli and Oecolampadius had recently been taken, he remarked, and they were enough for the papists. The previous November, his son Martin had been born. "The Lord has given me a Martin from my Katie," he wrote, "and we are all prospering."[2]

The family prospered in other ways as well. On February 4, 1532, Elector John gave Luther and his family the Augustinian Cloister in Wittenberg, together with its lands. Two months later, Luther himself purchased an immense garden, complete with fruit trees and fishing rights, for the handsome sum of 900 gulden. He gave it to Katie. Because it was called "The Sow Market," he began to refer to her as "Madame Sow Marketer." Thanks in part to this purchase, Katie Luther was left a fairly well-to-do woman when the reformer died.

The Anabaptists

These personal pains and domestic joys nonetheless provided only the backdrop for this last stage of his career. Luther struck the keynote for these years with a letter, *On Infiltrating and Clandestine Preachers,* which was published in early January 1532. There he warned the faithful against those who were then called Anabaptists. They were for the most part lay men and women who earnestly desired to create a church of true believers. In order to guarantee the church's purity, they practiced believers' baptism, which they limited to adults on the grounds that children could not knowingly confess their faith. Standing opposed to infant baptism in a world in which everyone had been baptized as an infant, they often urged true believers to be rebaptized as a sign of their membership in the true church. Moreover, they insisted that this true church knew no territorial or political boundaries. It consisted purely, simply, and finally of the faithful.

Luther's letter called on all those in authority to be on the watch for these apparently simple people. They had taken the idea of the priesthood of all believers and turned it into license for people to preach whatever they wished. Now everyone claimed the office of preacher, but, Luther insisted, no one could have the office without authorization and a calling, and the infiltrating preachers had neither. Their preaching, he declared, was properly the work of Satan. He added that these people could be recognized by their works. "The serpents glide unnoticed," he argued, and they claimed private revelations, while the Holy Spirit "flew down from heaven publicly" so people could see it, as at Jesus' baptism and at Pentecost. Whoever listened to one of these preachers needed to recognize that they were listening "to a man possessed." The gospel and the sacraments, on the other hand, were preached and administered by regularly called and ordained pastors.[3]

As in other instances, Luther here appeared in his later years to be abandoning the principle of the free preaching of the gospel for which he apparently had stood during the dramatic encounter at Worms. But Luther's point was that these people were *not* preaching the gospel, and therefore he had to oppose them. He had said the same thing at least as far back as his controversy with Erasmus. He therefore treated the Anabaptists no differently from his opponents on the Roman side or those from Zurich and Basel. When he heard of Zwingli's death on the battlefield in Switzerland, he commented, "I sorrow for Zwingli, because I have little hope for him" in the afterlife. When Oecolampadius died suddenly just months later, Luther remarked that it could only have come to pass through "the fiery arrows and darts of the devil."[4] In his office as *doctor* or teacher, Luther condemned all who taught contrary to the gospel as he understood it, and he played no favorites in doing so. To him they were all instruments of Satan, including Zwingli, Oecolampadius, and the Anabaptists. He viewed the Anabaptists in particular as destroyers of the church precisely because they would allow no sinners to be part of it.

Reforming education

Beginning in the 1530s and continuing until his death, Luther became ever more insistent on building the church in order to ensure the survival of his vision of the gospel. This new emphasis was particularly evident in two treatises he wrote on education. The first one, *To the Councilmen of All Cities of Germany*, was composed in 1524, not long after his return to Wittenberg, and just before the outbreak of the Peasants' War. This essay is still regarded as the original rationale for public primary and secondary schools wherever they are found. The arguments Luther generated in favor of public education for both boys and girls still lie at the base of all discussions of tax-supported education.

"Even though only a single boy could thereby be trained to become a real Christian," he wrote, "we ought properly to give a hundred gulden to this cause for every gulden we would give to fight the Turk, even if he were breathing down our necks." By contrast with spending for defense, he added, "A city's best and greatest welfare, safety, and strength consist rather in its having many able, learned, wise, honorable, and well-educated citizens." From his childhood he recalled the dictum that "It is a worse sin to leave a youth uneducated than it is to deflower a virgin."[5] Public education had the benefits both of religious training and the enrichment of civic life in the here and now.

From the Coburg, Luther wrote on this subject again in 1530. The twofold values he had found in public education persisted in his *Sermon on Keeping Children in School,* but the emphasis changed. Now he was writing after seeing the results both of the visitations and the assembly at Augsburg. In 1524 he had given equal weight to the temporal and spiritual benefits of universal education. But in 1530 he strongly emphasized the necessity of creating an educated clergy. He insisted that every boy should go to school, "even those of lesser ability . . . for we need not only highly learned doctors and masters of Holy Scripture, but also ordinary pastors who will teach the gospel and the catechism to the young and the ignorant and who will baptize and administer the sacrament." Even those who did not become pastors through this process would be useful, he argued, because they would form a "ready reserve" of potential pastors in case of emergency.[6]

The need for organization

The catechisms and the *Sermon on Keeping Children in School* were just the beginning of Luther's mission to build the church. From then on, he redoubled his efforts. On the one hand, he and his colleagues at Wittenberg and elsewhere gave ever greater attention to the construction and management of what was rapidly becoming a distinct church. On the other, he personally took an ever more direct hand in the training, placement, and supervision of new pastors. Among them were those who sat at his table and copied down every word that fell from his lips.

The problem of how to build and manage the church came to Luther's attention as early as 1521, though he was reluctant to press forward. For the first time, he became aware that many others were ready to turn his theological convictions (as they understood them) into institutions. Carlstadt's haste, the outside agitators from Zwickau, and Melanchthon's indecisiveness had combined with other factors to create the Wittenberg troubles in which Luther himself had finally intervened on his return from the Wartburg. That successful intervention had turned entirely on his own charisma and public moral authority. Now, a decade later, the situation was different. Luther knew that his personal authority would not last forever. "I know I don't have long to live," he remarked once at table, "and my head is like a knife that has had its steel honed entirely off, so that nothing is left but iron. The iron won't cut anymore and neither will my head. I hope and pray that God will give me a good and blessed final moment."[7] Something else was necessary if his understanding of the gospel was to endure.

This "something" was organization, and Luther was not the only person to sense the need for it. The visitations had been a first step. From them, Luther had discovered the depths of religious ignorance that prevailed among the common people. But the civil authorities had discovered something else. They found priests who had deserted their parishes and people with no one to baptize, marry, and bury them. They found that families who had donated property to the church were reclaiming it and turning it to their own uses. They found monasteries empty, with weeds growing up in the fields or the local peasants expropriating the land. In short, they found chaos, something that no prince, city council, or bureaucrat could long tolerate.

Implementing reform

Prince after prince and town after town decided to act. This time they acted not only together, as at diets of the empire, but also individually, within their own jurisdictions. They passed what they called *Kirchenordnungen* (church ordinances) or *Reformationsordnungen* (reform ordinances), in which they sought to reorder the affairs of the church in a way that would be faithful to what they understood of Luther's teachings. Strictly speaking, these actions violated imperial law, and they remained illegal until the Peace of Augsburg of 1555, almost a decade after Luther's death. But the princes and city councilmen enacted them anyway because they thought it necessary to do so. And Luther himself advised them to proceed.

In many respects the pattern that the town of Göttingen in central Germany followed was typical of the process that began to play itself out. The reform movement came to Göttingen—then one of the most important cities in lower Saxony—in the fall of 1529, and it featured the usual outbursts of public unrest. To correct the situation, the duchy of Brunswick and Landgrave Philip of Hesse each lent Göttingen a trusted preacher whose task it was to restore order while carrying forward the reform movement. This they did, and then they drafted a church order that was read in all the parishes on Palm Sunday 1530. At the same time they assisted in the calling of a pastor, one Johann Sütel, who would serve the town permanently. He reworked the draft of the church order and then sent it to Luther for his comments.

Luther read the document, made a few changes, and returned it with a preface that he addressed to Sütel, the town government, and the citizens. The whole was then translated into the local dialect and sent back to Wittenberg to be published, because Göttingen did not yet have its own printing press.

The preface clearly revealed the concerns that guided Luther during these years. On the one hand, he congratulated the Göttingers on their care to maintain good order in accord with the command of Paul. Luther had a high regard for procedures that would guarantee, insofar as possible, that qualified and faithful pastors would be called to serve the church.

At the same time Luther went well beyond the task that was immediately at hand. He added that the central issue, no matter how the church was organized, was that the gospel be preached, for it "is not only God's ordinance but also God's power." Moreover, the Göttingers should not now place their trust in the excellent church order they had just adopted. "Even if you are utterly correct [in what you have done]," he added, "God will not endure your boasting and trusting in laws; you must also humbly pray for God's help . . . against the devil . . . who makes war against everything that is right and proper." Precisely because the Göttingers had adopted such a fine church order, they would have to expect ever greater attacks from Satan, "who also wants to be a prince in Göttingen."[8]

Honoring the gospel

Luther had indeed become intensely interested in carrying out the practical reform of the church. Nonetheless, he had no doubts about the ability of human institutions to go bad. The only defense was the preaching of the gospel and prayer for help against the prince of the world.

At just this moment, the town of Zwickau was giving Luther renewed reason not to trust human arrangements. This town was one of the earliest outside Wittenberg to cleave to the Evangelical movement. But it was also an extraordinarily unruly place. In the early 1520s it had given birth to the "Zwickau Prophets," and now the city fathers were dismissing a preacher who had been one of Luther's strong supporters in a number of controversies. On March 4, 1531, Luther wrote them that they had no right to treat a pastor like a common servant, because "you are not the lord of the church."

Luther was furious, but this time he by no means got his way. To a personal friend, who happened to be the Zwickau city secretary, he described the councilors as "beasts," but at about the same time he received a letter in which Elector John told him not to intervene. Luther grumbled that they "want, all the same, to be Evangelicals, but with little honor to the gospel." In June, he relented and wrote the Zwickauers and their pastors a short letter in which he urged everyone to be "patiently quiet and not to get into a fight with anyone over anything."

But two months later he was called to Torgau, where he was forced to listen, in the elector's presence, to complaints from the mayor of Zwickau that he was trying to have everything his way. In response Luther later declared, "I will never again have anything to do with the people at Zwickau, and I will carry my hate for them with me to the grave."[9]

Luther thus experienced his full share of disappointments in trying to create a new church. Moreover, he may very well have allowed his loyalty to one pastor in Zwickau and his unpleasant memories about the town from the days of Carlstadt and Müntzer to get the better of his judgment. Nonetheless, even in the midst of this messy local entanglement, his actions indicate that his desire for good order, however important it might be, could never override his allegiance to the preaching of the gospel.

As in so many other areas of his life, here, too, Luther was acting out of conviction. Like many people—including the Anabaptists—he might have preferred a church of true believers. In his preface to the *German Mass* of 1526, he described a congregation in which people would gather voluntarily to hear the Word, admonish one another, pray, collect alms for the poor, and banish the impenitent from their midst. "But," he added, "I neither can nor desire to begin such a congregation or assembly or to make rules for it. For I do not have the people or persons for it—not enough in all of Saxony!"[10] (to found even one such church). In the 1530s, after the visitations and the events at Augsburg, church order became ever more important to Luther. But by comparison with preaching the gospel to sinners, church constitutions were truly indifferent matters to him. It was simply a fact that the church had to be organized.

Luther the professor

By and large Luther left the business of actually composing the new church orders and seeing them established to younger colleagues such as Melanchthon and Bugenhagen, for whom extensive travel was less difficult. In addition, the political facts of the situation in Germany dictated that Luther could not participate directly in most of this work. He was still an outlaw.

Consequently, Luther's chief contribution to creating the new church lay in his role as a professor. Here he helped to train an entire generation of pastors, who in turn became the new church's clerical leadership. He had begun this work even before 1530 by recommending like-minded pastors and supporting them in their work. But it was only in the 1530s that he and his colleagues consciously began to train new pastors and systematically to examine, ordain, and place them.

Luther was convinced from the outset that the universities would play a key role in this effort. In 1518, on his way back from the Heidelberg Disputation, he had declared that reforming the church was a hopeless undertaking unless the universities were reformed first. He himself then led this effort by completely reordering the course of study at his own university. Aristotle's logic was virtually banished from the theological curriculum, and direct study of the Bible, the church Fathers, and the ancient languages was put in its place. Melanchthon himself had been called to Wittenberg in 1518 to assist in this reform. The reforms went so far that in 1523 even the disputations were ended, on the grounds that they were too reminiscent of the scholastic theology against which Luther was struggling.

The university was very much Luther's home, and it was only natural that he should turn to it to develop pastors for the new church. He himself was an extremely popular teacher, and not only because of his wide reputation. As one student commented, "He always had the material for his lectures well in hand . . . so that they never contained anything that was not sharp and to the point." [11]

Yet both Luther's university and education in general had suffered during the stormy 1520s. In this sense, Erasmus had been perfectly justified in his fear that Luther's movement would harm the revival of learning. Wittenberg's own enrollment plummeted after the Diet of Worms, and people such as Müntzer and the Zwickau Prophets bluntly rejected study as a qualification for preaching the Word of God. Carlstadt's decision in 1524 to give up his academic position in order to become "the new layman" symbolized what was happening all over Germany. To the Anabaptists, someone like Luther was learned "according to the letter" but not "according to the Spirit."

Teaching the truth

By contrast, Luther was convinced that proper education was essential. In 1530 he commented, "If I could leave the office of preacher and my other duties, or were forced to do so, there is no other office

I would rather have than that of schoolmaster or teacher of boys. For I know that next to the office of preaching, this is the best, the greatest, and the most useful there is. In fact, I am not absolutely certain which of the two is the better." Consequently, he turned his attention once again to the university. After the Plague had left Wittenberg, and in the midst of negotiations on the subject of armed resistance, he began a series of lectures on Paul's letter to the Galatians. For him, this one letter contained the most clear teaching imaginable on the central issue of justification. "Whoever is in error about Christian righteousness," he declared, "must go back to active righteousness, that is, he must trip over . . . trusting in the works of the law" And with that, "the entirety of Christian teaching is lost." [12]

These lectures, which required three years to complete, were quickly reworked by Melanchthon and his students and then published as Luther's *Great Commentary on Galatians* (to distinguish them from the ones he had given as a young professor). The letter to the Galatians was "my Katie von Bora," Luther remarked, as evidence of how very much Paul's teaching meant to him. But there was far more to these lectures than his own personal faith. Rather, as the work of Melanchthon and his students revealed, they were a self-conscious effort to convey the truth of the gospel to as many people as possible in as short a time as possible. In just this spirit, Luther once insisted that the words of Paul applied directly to his teaching: "It is no longer I who live, but Christ who lives in me" (Gal. 2:20).

This work of teaching the truth was now Luther's most important objective. In a series of new reforms of the university between 1533 and 1536, even the disputations were reinstituted. They were a means first of being able to confer the doctorate (and therefore to train new professors), and second to test students on their grasp of Evangelical religion. As a final step, at Luther's behest the elector decreed in 1535 that anyone who wished to become a pastor but had no bishop to ordain him should present himself to the Wittenberg theological faculty for examination and ordination.

Luther was clear about what he hoped to create through all this effort: "First, a good preacher should be able to teach well, correctly, and in an orderly fashion. Second, he should have a good head on his shoulders. Third, he should be eloquent. Fourth, he should have a good voice. Fifth, he should have a good memory. Sixth, he should know when to stop. Seventh, he should be constant and diligent about his

Luther confronting the Church of Rome with the Scriptures while Melanchthon stands poised with a pen.

affairs. Eighth, he should invest body and life, possessions and honor in it. Ninth, he should be willing to let everyone vex and hack away at him." [13] According to 16th-century educators, six of these nine characteristics could be taught. Just as his own mind had been changed by his work at a university, so too Luther was now trying to change the minds of his students.

First and foremost, Luther would have his students know true doctrine. At the same time, he maintained a lively interest in them as persons. He knew that they would leave Wittenberg to serve out their lives in an unfriendly world. He once remarked, "The world demands six qualities of a preacher: 1. that he have a good speaking voice; 2. that he be learned; 3. that he be eloquent; 4. that he have a handsome exterior . . .; 5. that he take no money, but give money to preach; 6. that he say what they like to hear." Of the students themselves he observed, "that many gladly hear the alarm that the Plague is coming. Some of them have developed sores from their schoolbags, some have caught a severe cough from their books, some have scabs from their pens, others have caught gout from their paper. Many have found that their ink has become moldy. Others have consumed their mothers' letters and become heartsick and homesick for their hometowns."[14]

Luther knew the weaknesses of students. Yet he persisted. He taught them, examined them, found them their first posts, and told them when they should take new ones. On occasion, he even helped arrange their marriages. Above all, he was available when they were in trouble. He advised his own son, Paul, not to become a preacher, on the grounds that he did not have the stamina for it. He suggested that he pursue an easy profession, like that of a medical doctor. Another student was constantly morose and even suicidal. Luther advised him not to spend all his time alone with his books, but to seek out the company of good friends, and to sing and dance. Satan, he advised, delights in the solitude of Christians.

The same solicitude that Luther showed for his students he now showed for the mundane practicalities of daily church life. He insisted that above all the gospel was to be proclaimed and the sacraments administered in order to turn ordinary Christians into *theodidacti*. But Luther was not the sort of person to take the throne and issue orders. He plunged into the organizing details himself.

Cartoon contrasting Protestant and Catholic services.

PART FIVE

The Mature Luther

FIFTEEN

Negotiator for the Faith

*I*n spite of the difficulties, Luther took pleasure in his work with his university, his students, and his new pastors. Yet his role in the wider affairs of the reform movement repeatedly distracted him from these local activities. The Evangelical movement became a new church in a piecemeal fashion, through the conversion of one person and then another, the training of one pastor and then another, the establishment of one church and then another. But at the same time it was now an international movement that forced all manner of people to take cognizance of it. They, in turn, forced Luther to act out his convictions on this larger stage.

Political counsel

In the early 1530s, negotiations between the Protestant princes and the emperor provided the most pressing distractions. In these Luther showed himself a consistent advocate of peace, though not quite at any price. At the very least, the establishment of the Schmalkald League had persuaded Emperor Charles to retreat somewhat from the stand he had taken at Augsburg, which was that everyone must submit to Rome. Consequently, at Schweinfurt in May 1532, negotiations began on the conditions for establishing religious peace. The emperor's situation was clear to all. He needed the help of the Protestants against the Turks, and unless something was done he was not going to get it.

Elector John, Landgrave Philip, and the other protesting estates asked Luther for his advice on this matter, just as they had on the question of armed resistance. Once again, Luther proved that he was not much of a politician. The princes had taken the position that they would not help the emperor unless he agreed that anyone who subscribed to the *Augsburg Confession* would be tolerated within the empire. Luther advised that they abandon this condition on the grounds that if they did not, "the entire peace negotiations may come unraveled."[1] Earlier they had stood up for the gospel without having any guarantees. They ought to do the same now.

In their own political wisdom, the princes virtually ignored Luther's advice. In late June they did ask him once again for his views on the peace treaty they were about to sign. They received much the same response. "If we wish to nail everything down neatly and securely through our own efforts and do not also trust God to act powerfully in it, then clearly nothing good will come of it."[2] These words were reminiscent of those Luther had written in his preface to the Göttingen church order. But the princes had in fact wrung concessions from Charles V that had solid political value. If they provided financial help for the war against the Turks, they would enjoy absolute religious freedom until the meeting of a free council of the church. Moreover, all lawsuits against them in the imperial court would be dismissed. The treaty was signed on August 3, 1532, and with it the danger of religious war in Germany disappeared—at least for the moment.

Luther's genuine abhorrence of purely political arrangements became evident in what, in worldly terms, can only be called naive advice. But he also displayed the same attitude in other ways. Above all, it could be seen in Luther's relations with specific princes. The most prominent of these was his old adversary, Duke George of Saxony. From the very beginning of the reform movement, there could be no doubt of Duke George's genuine adherence to the faith of the Church of Rome. He was therefore scandalized when he read Luther's *Warning to His Beloved Germans.* No illiterate himself, he published a book against it.

Duke George's *Against Luther's Warning* consisted of a simple, straightforward argument. Luther was inciting people to riot and insurrection against the established authorities. Regardless of the matters of doctrine that were at stake, Luther's book "seeks nothing other than to make us Germans disloyal to the emperor and insubordinate to all authority." Here Duke George ignored Luther's insistence that he was not fomenting war, but predicting it if the emperor and his supporters

1554

Duke George of Saxony (by Cranach).

did not relent. To the duke, this difference was no more than a fine point, and was precisely the sort of thing that could be expected from someone who left out works of love and said that faith alone justified sinners. Thus Luther's teachings were at heart revolutionary, as could be seen in his writings, "where one finds little by way of love, peaceableness, gentleness, patience . . . and nothing but cursing, scolding, abuse, slander, shameless tales, and lewd sayings. . . ."[3] At last, hoped Duke George, those who protected Luther would see him for the traitor and heretic he was.

Reply to Duke George

Against Luther's Warning appeared in April 1531, so Luther had time to write a response to be distributed at the forthcoming Frankfurt book fair. He had little choice but to write. An ancient scriptural teaching was at stake here—"You shall know them by their fruits"—and Duke George had driven his point home forcefully. This was also an issue that reformers all over Germany were repeatedly forced to face. Again and again their opponents charged them with disrupting the established order. Moreover, everyone remembered the Peasants' War and knew how quickly domestic peace could disappear.

Luther signaled his intentions in the title he chose for his reply, *Against the Assassin at Dresden*. Just as in the aftermath of the Peasants' War, he would retract nothing. In a point-for-point refutation, he declared that it was not the Protestants but their opponents who intended war. The recent edict of the Diet of Augsburg adequately proved that point. Moreover, everyone who knew anything about the Peasants' War knew that he, Dr. Martin Luther, stood squarely against insurrection. On the other hand, there was nothing wrong if the Catholic princes feared Protestant arms. In fact they "should be tortured by anxiety and fear that rebellion would occur," because such anxiety was the proper fate of those who opposed the Word of God.

One argument remained from Duke George's treatise. How could Luther justify the coarse condemnations that filled his own polemical works and still claim to be a man of peace? Luther's answer repeated a theme that he had been sounding ever more loudly. He hoped that people would "say of me from this moment forward how full I am of evil words, abuse, and cursing for the papists." The defenders of Rome had proven by their actions that "they are impenitent" and that "they are determined to do no good whatsoever and indeed nothing but evil to such an extent that there is no hope" for them. Because the "papal asses" were utterly reprobate, he planned "from this day forward until I am in the grave to busy myself with cursing and rebuking these miscreants."

Luther's decision that his Catholic opponents were beyond redemption had far-reaching consequences. Earlier, he had declared that he and his supporters could no longer pray for them. Now he added that true prayer carried with it curses on the papacy:

> For I cannot pray without therefore being forced to curse. If I say, "Holy be thy name," then I must add, "Cursed, damned, and disgraced must be the papists' name and that of all who slander thy name." If I say, "Thy kingdom come," then I must add, "Cursed, damned, and destroyed must be the papacy together with all the kingdoms on earth that oppose thy kingdom." If I say, "Thy will be done," then I must add, "All the thoughts and plots of the papists and all who work against thy will and counsel must be cursed, damned, and brought to nothing." In truth I, and with me all who believe in Christ, pray this way daily and without fail, both out loud and in the heart, and I am certain that we will be heard. . . .[1]

For Luther, if the Scriptures were true as he read them, then those who taught otherwise were as evil as the Turks, and no pious person could wish them well. Such people were truly and fundamentally accursed, just like Cain or the Sadducees.

These were harsh words, but they were in no way an emotional outburst from a sick, old man. Rather, like most public actions, they grew from a combination of internal convictions and external developments. If Luther had not been so convinced that Christians lived solely in a state of grace, or if Rome and the emperor had not been so intransigent, then Luther's blunt condemnations would be curious. But given Luther's convictions and the situation of the time, there was very little about them that was peculiar.

Whether Luther's most recent books served a good political purpose was, however, another matter. His *Warning* was highly useful to Protestant princes, such as Elector John or Landgrave Philip, who very much wanted the emperor to know how determined they were. But

Luther's *Against the Assassin at Dresden* appeared during the negotiations for a peace treaty, and it could do little more than exacerbate
matters. Moreover, Luther's target was not only a prince, but a relative
of his own Elector John.

Once again Duke George complained that he had been publicly
slandered. In this case, Elector John listened. Through his chancellor,
Dr. Gregor Brück, he asked Luther to restrain himself "insofar as
conscience and the truth allow . . . so that peace and the treaty may
not be disturbed or blocked." Luther agreed, but only so long as Duke
George would do the same. Without taking a breath he added that
"Duke George has gotten himself mixed up with me" and "left notable
knots and clogs."[5] With regrets, Luther temporarily left the field.

Elector John Frederick

Before long, conditions unexpectedly changed again. In mid-August
1532, Luther and Melanchthon were called to Elector John's deathbed.
On August 18, Luther preached the funeral sermon through his own
tears. "Therefore, Satan," he declared to the mourners, "take both
my righteousness and my sins with you, and gobble up the dung from
them, which is rightfully yours. They do not trouble me at all, for
Jesus Christ has died [too]."[6]

Elector John's successor, John Frederick, was a different prince from
his father. In the first place, he was young, only 29 years of age.

*The electors of Saxony during Luther's career: Frederick the Wise, John the Steadfast,
and John Frederick the Magnanimous (by Cranach).*

Second, he had been raised from childhood as a follower of Luther, whom he regarded as his spiritual father. Three days after the funeral, he came to Wittenberg, heard Luther preach, and invited the reformer and his colleagues to dinner. He visited Wittenberg far more frequently than had his predecessors, and he repeatedly called Luther to Torgau for consultations. "We have been blessed with a prince who has many fine gifts," Luther commented after he had gotten to know him. The young man had only one fault. "If I were to drink as much as the elector, I'd drown. If he drank as much as I, he'd die of thirst."[7]

One consequence of the new elector's enthusiasm for the Evangelical movement was that he tended to encourage Luther regardless of the public controversy, even when he tangled with powerful figures such as Duke George. In the fall of 1532 the zealous duke ordered close surveillance of the population to seek out all who were not going to confession, performing penance, attending Mass, and communing with bread alone. This act put Luther's followers in a difficult position, and in October several of them asked him what they should do. The reformer urged them to hold firm.

The simmering controversy burst into the open in the spring of 1533, after Duke George ordered the Leipzig city council to record the names of all his subjects who did not adhere strictly to the Catholic faith, and then to force them to sell their possessions and leave the territory. Once again, one of the Leipzigers asked Luther what they should do. In a pastoral letter, Luther likened Duke George's actions to murder and declared that they should not cooperate. When the duke learned what Luther had written, he complained in the customary way to his new relative on the throne of Electoral Saxony, John Frederick. But this time he received a rather different reply. Through Chancellor Brück, the elector declared that Luther had every right, indeed every obligation, to comfort those who suffered persecution. He added that he dearly hoped that Duke George, now old and surely near the grave, would see the truth before it was too late, give up the ways of Saul, and become another Paul.

Duke George found his kinsman's letter neither edifying nor well-intentioned. Another exchange followed, and then Elector John Frederick sent Luther copies of the correspondence. In the cover letter he declared that of course he could not tolerate Luther's inciting the Leipzigers to rebellion, but he was certain that Luther would "know

how through your writings to justify and give answer for yourself. . . ."
In July 1533, Luther delightedly replied with a little book in which he
compared Duke George to "Pilate, Herod, Judas, and people like them,
who condemned and put to death Christ and his apostles on account
of God's Word."[8]

Torgau, the principal residence of the electors of Saxony.

The exchanges quickly became a public war of print. In the midst
of it the elector wrote Duke George that he was determined "to persist
to the grave in the conviction that Luther is the one whom God has
selected as a special man to preach his holy Word clearly, purely, and
faithfully."[9] With the fervent support of his own prince, Luther was
becoming not just the teacher and organizer of the new church, but
also its principal public defender. His life was now so governed by the
public and the events he had set in motion that he could scarcely remain
silent, no matter what the issue. He could even be used. Viewed as
an oracle by many of his students and closest colleagues, he now also
became a statesman of the faith to a world of public affairs that he
scarcely understood.

Two concrete issues in the mid-1530s led Luther irreversibly onto this path. Each involved him in negotiations with people whom he considered his deepest enemies. In 1535 he found himself consulted by a papal emissary on the exact character of the much longed-for general council of the church. And only a year later he negotiated at great length with the south Germans, notably Bucer and Capito, on the nature of the Lord's Supper. The one encounter proved to be an utter failure, the other at least a qualified success.

The mission of Vergerio

The question of a future council had been at issue at least since Luther's interview with Cardinal Cajetan in 1518. At that time, Luther had waffled on whether he would appeal to a council, and if so, where and under whose auspices it might be held. During the Leipzig Debate with Eck in 1519, he had declared that even councils might and did err—as in the case of Hus at Constance a century earlier. After the dramatic moment at Worms in 1521, the German princes themselves had appealed to a free, Christian council—by which they meant one that met on German soil and was not dominated by the pope. The issue continued to plague those who made policy, and in particular those who sought to do so on behalf of Rome. Someone was always raising questions about the forthcoming council, if only as a delaying tactic. Charles V himself, in reaching a temporary peace with the Protestants in 1531, declared that their arrangements would be in force only until the council that he thought would be called for the following year.

After that, however, the hope for a council had vanished. But in 1535 it was suddenly very much alive again. A papal ambassador, Pietro Paolo Vergerio, arrived in Germany in February. Pope Paul III, the successor to Clement VII, had commissioned him to visit each of Germany's most important politicians and generate support for a general council of the church, albeit one that would not meet in Germany and that would not limit its agenda to issues that Germans thought pressing.

Vergerio had an unenviable task. He was to tell his hosts that their wishes would not be paramount at the forthcoming council, and at the same time say nothing about what would be discussed. He was nonetheless an ambitious, smooth, and learned young Venetian, who had enjoyed the favor of Clement VII, Paul III's hated predecessor. Vergerio was willing to undertake even the seemingly impossible if it meant continued papal favor.

In late August 1535, Duke George informed Elector John Frederick about Vergerio's mission and the possibility of a council. The elector could hardly refuse to discuss the matter. The peace between himself and the emperor turned explicitly on a future council. So he asked Luther for advice. Luther replied that people had been talking about a council for more than two years, and the ambassador ought to be able to say clearly what was being planned. Because Vergerio could not say anything very concrete, Luther doubted that the curia was serious about the council.

John Frederick had no desire even to receive Vergerio. But he was at last trapped into meeting with him in Prague while en route to an assembly of the Protestant estates. Caught in late November, he listened to a long Latin oration in which Vergerio protested that the pope had the highest intentions. When Spalatin had at last translated its substance into German, the elector ordered him to reply that there was no sense in talking about any council that would not be meeting on German soil. Vergerio announced that present plans were to gather at the ducal palace in Mantua. With that, the elector walked out of the room.

What John Frederick did not know was that Luther had already virtually given away the keys to the castle. Earlier in the same month, Vergerio had boldly visited Luther himself.[10] The reformer had learned that the ambassador and his party of 20 were coming just one day before their expected arrival. But Luther was up to it. He called his barber in well before the sun was up, and had his usual weekly bath, shave, and hair trim—something he commonly reserved as a preparation for preaching. He then called for his best clothing and, being such a favorite of many Protestant princes, he had it: a dark jacket with sleeves that billowed of satin, a coat lined with fox fur, the tight stockings of a nobleman, and so many fine rings on his fingers that even his Italian visitor was impressed. He topped it off with a large gold pendant, which even his barber thought was gaudy. Luther then called Bugenhagen to ride with him in a coach for the 10-minute walk to the gates of Wittenberg.

Luther was prepared for serious business. Above all, he wanted the report to get back to Rome that he was both young and in very good physical condition. Vergerio was immediately seated at a handsome banquet, if only to prove that even Wittenbergers knew how to greet important guests. But suddenly the atmosphere changed. Luther implied that he was well aware of what a dissolute life Pope Paul III had led as a young man.

Point and counterpoint continued, sometimes pleasantly and sometimes with a dash of acid. Vergerio suggested that Luther could receive favor at Rome, and Luther replied that for Christians to coexist with Rome was like day mixing with night. But the two did agree on one critical matter. Vergerio hoped for Luther's blessing on the council, and, in a backhanded way, he got it. "You," Luther declared, "are wretched men led astray by your godless teachings and you are the ones who need a council."[11] He would be there to confess his teachings.

Vergerio used these exact words in a second, more private audience with Elector John Frederick, who was now forced to listen more carefully. But Luther had been right from the beginning. Within a few months the planned council was again postponed. But in the years that followed, Luther's words to Vergerio continued to cause some difficulty, because the Protestant princes wanted nothing to do with a council that was not meeting under the terms they had set. Luther would have more negotiating to do on this subject, continuing to the very end of his life.

Attempts at concord

Relations with the south Germans were a matter much closer to Luther's heart. He was also able to prepare far more thoroughly for these negotiations. Although his suspicions remained, the unpleasant interview with Bucer at the Coburg was quickly forgotten. By late March 1531 Luther was able to declare that he had "good hopes" with respect to Bucer's person,[12] which was far more than he was able to say of Zwingli and Oecolampadius when they died a few months later. Two years passed, and a squabble over who had said what to the pastors at Frankfurt about the Lord's Supper interrupted these good feelings. But in the end, even this interlude only drove Bucer to renewed efforts for concord. Yet throughout these years Luther intervened whenever he thought that this or that group of pastors revealed "Zwinglian" tendencies.

In September 1534, the wall dividing the two sides at last began to weaken. After talking with Luther on the 16th, Melanchthon put himself forward to Landgrave Philip of Hesse as a possible negotiator with Bucer. As the basis for their discussions they would use the formula that Bucer had been showing pastors all over southern Germany. Later that month, Philip urged the work of concord on Luther and declared that, for his part, he would spare no effort or cost to see an end to the disunity that was such a plague to the Evangelical princes. Luther declared that he was now willing to negotiate. It was agreed that Melanchthon should meet with Bucer.

The meeting occurred in December 1534, even though Luther's misgivings had returned. "The more I reconsider the matter," he wrote, "the less favorable I am toward this hopeless union." For Melanchthon's benefit, he added yet another description of what happened in the Lord's Supper. "The body of Christ is distributed, eaten, and chewed with the teeth," he wrote. But when Melanchthon and Bucer met on December 27, Melanchthon subscribed to Bucer's new formula and brought a copy with him back to Wittenberg on January 9, 1535. When Elector John Frederick then asked Luther for his views on the matter, Luther declared that he had nothing in particular against the formula. But he added that so much had transpired between the two parties that it was better not to proceed until "there are calm waters on both sides." [13]

Luther remained full of suspicions. In particular, he likely wanted to see if the Strasbourg theologians would involve themselves in another affair like the one that had occurred in Frankfurt am Main, when they supported a pastor who was teaching Zwingli's understanding of the Lord's Supper. But he was also full of hope, and soon hope overcame suspicion. In July he wrote the pastors and city councilors in Augsburg that he was "heartily delighted" with the efforts for unity and declared that he would do all he could "to strengthen and maintain it." When the Strasbourg theologians learned of this letter, they too were delighted, and made certain that all their associates knew it. Even better news came in October, just before Vergerio's sudden visit. Luther sent a general letter to the major south German cities; there he declared that he favored a meeting of the respective theologians, "so that we can become intimately acquainted, one side and the other." [14]

Face-to-face negotiations

Unpredictably, Luther also showed himself willing to overlook, at least for the moment, one misstep on the part of the Strasbourg pastors. In February Bucer and Capito participated in writing a confession for the Baslers in which they minimized the physical presence of Christ in the bread and the wine. Perhaps unaware of what had transpired, Luther still invited them and other south German theologians to a meeting at Eisenach on May 14. There they could discuss whatever differences remained.

In the interim, Luther's suspicions had returned. When the southerners arrived at Eisenach, there was no Luther. Days passed, and he had still not arrived. They traveled further east and there received a message from Luther in which the reformer pleaded yet another outbreak of illness and asked them to meet him not far beyond Leipzig. Bucer preempted these delays. He replied that the entire party would come to Wittenberg.

When they arrived, they learned that for unexplained reasons Luther would not meet with them. But then early the next morning they were suddenly called into his presence. Equally suddenly, the meeting was adjourned until mid-afternoon. Finally Bucer had a chance to explain at length all he had done in the last years for the sake of concord. Luther still appeared to be filled with suspicion. He replied by declaring that Bucer and Capito had to condemn Zwingli's teachings explicitly and declare their belief in the real presence without regard to the communicants' faith or lack of faith. After listening to a few words in response, Luther said that he felt faint and had to leave so that he could rest.

Skilled debater that he was, Luther had exposed the sorest point between them. With great care, Bucer and Capito had covered over the issue of what a person without faith received in the Lord's Supper. Did the real presence of Christ's body and blood depend on the communicant's disposition? To an unbeliever, were the elements merely bread and wine? How was Paul's declaration that whoever ate and drank in an "unworthy manner" brought "judgment on himself" to be understood? True to his reading of the gospel, Luther held that one who believed the words of Christ's institution was a Christian. In this passage, therefore, the unfaithful and the unworthy were identical, and they received Christ's body and blood, although they did so to their judgment. By the same token, for Bucer and Capito it remained un-thinkable that bread and wine could—in and of themselves, with only the Words of Institution and without faith—be the body and blood of Christ.

Luther's last demand crushed the delegation from south Germany. They could freely deny that they had ever taught as Zwingli had done, or at least like the Zwingli of the *Ratio Fidei* that had been circulated at the Diet of Augsburg. But granting that infidels could eat the body of Christ with their teeth and drink his blood with their tongues was another matter. What the south Germans did not know was that Luther himself was unable to sleep that night.

The next afternoon, Bucer replied. He and his colleagues had never taught that the bread and the wine were mere symbols of Christ's body and blood. To the extent that Zwingli had done so, he was in error. As to the second demand, Bucer declared that all who came to the Lord's Supper were among the unworthy, and that all (even those without a living faith) were offered the body and blood of Christ in the Supper.

Luther asked if each of the south Germans was in agreement with Bucer's confession. When they said they were, he turned to his col-leagues from Wittenberg and asked if they were satisfied. They talked a little, but nodded their agreement. Luther asked Bucer, Capito, and the others once again if they truly believed what Bucer had said. They said they did. Abruptly, Luther radiated joy and kindliness. He declared that they were all in concord and brothers in Christ.

Bucer and Capito wept. Luther had gone an uncharacteristic extra step. He had passed over the question of what the unworthy *received* in the Lord's Supper and the problem of the precise relationship between "faith" and "worthiness." For the sake of unity, he had contented himself with what Bucer offered.

SIXTEEN

Defender of the Faith

*T*he Strasbourg theologians took their delight back home with them. Bucer and Capito soon announced to Luther that the city's politicians and all its pastors were in full accord with their agreement. Before long Capito, the diplomat of the group, set to work to seal the renewed friendship. He sent Katie effusive letters of thanks and even a gift of a golden ring. Plans were laid to have a press in Strasbourg publish a new edition of Luther's works. Capito even suggested that Luther send one of his sons to study with himself and Bucer. In turn, they would send one of their young theologians to study at Wittenberg. In time the Wittenberg Concord proved to be an immense success. It bound together the religious futures of Saxony and the Upper Rhineland.

The Antinomian Controversy

Luther's agreement with the Strasbourg pastors did not mean that he had compromised on a matter of faith so much as overlooked a potential source of disagreement. During the same years he tried to avoid yet another controversy by using the same technique. A bitter struggle had developed with his former student, John Agricola, the same man who had opposed the visitations a decade earlier. Now, in the late 1530s, Agricola began to argue that good works had so little place in the life of Christians that parishioners should not even be exhorted to perform them. In particular, the law should not be preached to believers as law. Rather, all apostolic admonitions were properly part of the gospel. Law itself—the law that condemned—belonged in the courthouse but not in the chancel.

To Luther's mind, Agricola had thus misconstrued the two parts of *On the Freedom of a Christian*, the declarations that "A Christian is a perfectly free lord of all, subject to none," and, "A Christian is a perfectly dutiful servant of all, subject to all."[1] Luther repeatedly reminded him that the law was to be preached to Christians (just as good works were to be expected of them), even if fulfilling the law could not affect their standing in the presence of God. But above all, he repeatedly urged Agricola to keep his reservations and criticisms to himself.

Luther's admonitions were not successful. Agricola began to question Melanchthon's teachings, and when these attacks became public, Luther could endure no more. In July and again in September 1537, he preached against Agricola's disregard for the law, but without naming his target. In December he set forth a group of academic theses against the same ideas, once again without naming Agricola. Finally, in August 1538, he published a new edition of *The Great Commentary on Galatians*, which he had revised in order to use as a vehicle to critique Agricola's teachings. At last he declared in print that Agricola and his followers, whom he now labeled 'Antinomians,' had "waited for my death, after which they could make of me what they would."[2] Never again would the reformer have any dealings with Agricola, even though he was then rector of the school in the town of Luther's own birth.

Taken together, the Wittenberg Concord and the Antinomian Controversy (as it later came to be called) provide a clue to understanding Luther during his last years. Although less than a decade long, this period was marked by extremely harsh polemics. Turks, Jews, papists, fellow Germans, and hostile rulers were Luther's targets, and he treated them all with equal violence. Moreover, in each instance he knew full well what he was doing. He even commented, "I was born to go to war and give battle to sects and devils. That is why my books are stormy and warlike. I must root out the stumps and bushes and hack away the thorns and brambles. I am the great lumberjack who must clear the land and level it."[3]

Even so, Luther was not now looking for trouble any more than he had been 20 years earlier during the events that led to the Diet of Worms. Both then and now, those whom Luther attacked did far more than deviate in some implied or inconsequential way from his teachings. Rather, by their deeds and words they flatly contradicted the truth as Luther saw it. To his mind, these people were enemies of the gospel and therefore instruments of Satan.

The Schmalkald Articles

The papacy and the emperor naturally occupied much more of Luther's attention than others did, because of their political power and forceful opposition to the Reformation. Less than a year after the Wittenberg Concord had been signed, Luther and his colleagues were called to Schmalkalden, where the Protestant princes were once again meeting. Once more Luther was to write a summary of his teachings, but this time he was to do so in response to the call for a church council. It was to meet in Mantua, as Vergerio had announced. Luther's task was to help the princes prepare for the council by paying particular attention to those articles and practices that could not be compromised under any circumstances.

Luther set to work immediately. For him the core of the matter was the Second Article in each of the ecumenical creeds, faith in Christ. "On this article rests all that we teach and practice against the pope, the devil, and the world."[4] Then, in the body of the *Schmalkald Articles*, as they came to be called, he treated specific issues, such as the Mass, clerical celibacy, good works, monasticism, and the like, much in the manner of the *Augsburg Confession* or the earlier *Schwabach Articles*. Luther was pleased to have the opportunity to stick to the heart of the matter and not be drawn off into side issues. The *Schmalkald Articles* were Luther's last will and testament, a statement that the princes could take with them to a council even if Luther himself had died in the meantime.

The reformer almost did die in Schmalkalden. In fact he could not even write all of the *Schmalkald Articles*. The January trip had proved to be a leisurely meandering through the mountains into Hesse. When the party arrived, even the clouds rolled away and left the crisp, clear sunlight of a winter day. But a few days later a kidney stone dropped into Luther's bladder and completely blocked it. The many physicians who were present to attend the great princes were of no help. First they forced Luther to consume great quantities of liquids in the hope that sheer pressure might force the stone out. Then they fed him a mixture of horse manure and garlic, apparently with the intent to create gastric distress sufficient to do what the liquids had failed to accomplish.

Soon friends and supporters began to gather, fearing that the end was near. When Elector John Frederick entered Luther's room, he declared, "Our dear Lord God will have mercy on us for his name's sake and he will extend your life, dear Doctor." Luther insisted on returning to Saxony. He was loaded into a carriage, and another followed. The procession stopped 10 miles down the road. Luther urinated that night, nearly a gallon and a half in total. "In this way," he wrote, "joy makes me measure this liquid, so vile to others and so precious to me."[5]

Luther had many thoughts during these difficult days, among them regret at the prospect of leaving friends and family behind. But as he told Bugenhagen in what they both regarded as Luther's final confession, the reformer's chief concerns went far beyond his personal situation. He prayed for those who would now have to preserve the gospel. "Command them in my name," he told Bugenhagen, "that they should act with confidence in God for the course of the gospel in whatever way the Holy Spirit might suggest." He had no particular marching orders for Elector John Frederick or Landgrave Philip, no details that he wished them to attend to immediately. He had given his testament. Now he wished the princes to be true to it.

The gospel and its defense meant everything to Luther. He reported that he was proud of one thing in his life: "I know that I did right to storm the papacy with the Word of God."[6] After returning to Wittenberg, he slowly came back to health. Within a month he had published two treatises against Rome. One was a letter from *Beelzebub to the Holy Papist Church,* in which Satan instructed Paul III on how he was to conduct the business of the council. Later the same month the pope postponed the council until November. Luther republished this bull with a commentary in which he asked his readers to question just how serious the pope was about reforming the church. Then in June, Paul III published yet another bull in which he declared that all who made special donations and dedicated masses and prayers against the Turks would receive even greater indulgences than before. Luther republished this bull as well, but with marginal notes in which he bluntly stated that Pope Paul's message came from "the Antichrist." A month passed and he published yet another treatise against Rome. For Luther, defending the gospel and attacking the papacy had become one and the same thing.

"Against the Jews"

During these months of recovery, Luther suddenly found himself embroiled in yet another controversy. This time it concerned the Jews. Many people believe that his reputation was permanently tarnished by the attitude he took toward them. As was so commonly the case, this controversy originated with a problem that was thrust on Luther. In August 1536, Elector John Frederick issued a decree in which he banished all Jews from his territories and forbade Jews to pass through them.

By itself there was nothing unusual about this decree, however reprehensible it may be to a generation that remembers the Holocaust. The elector was doing no more than following political custom of the time. In fact, by comparison with more powerful and well-known rulers, many German princes were behind the times. In addition to commissioning Columbus's first voyage, Ferdinand and Isabella of Spain had banished Jews from their territories in 1492, more than forty years earlier. The 15th and 16th centuries in Europe featured a wave of banishments whose effect was to move an immense Jewish population far to the east, to Poland and Russia. Scholars still speculate about the attitudes and convictions that led to this outburst of anti-Jewish sentiment. One thing is certain: such views were widespread. Shakespeare's Shylock with his pound of flesh in *The Merchant of Venice* was an all-too-common caricature.

Luther might easily have restricted his writings about the Jews to an essay of 1523, *That Jesus Christ Was Born a Jew,* in which he urged compassion and hoped for their conversion now that the gospel had been restored to its rightful place. But an accident of history intervened. As with the Sacramentarian Controversy, the accident came from Strasbourg. In April 1537, Capito, still one of Europe's most eminent Hebrew scholars, learned of Elector John Frederick's decree. He had had many dealings with Jewish scholars, and he wrote Luther and urged him to intervene with the elector on behalf of Josel Rosheim, one of their leaders. It was this specific request that brought the whole matter to Luther's attention.

On June 11, Luther responded to Rosheim directly. He saw the entire issue through the same spectacles as he saw relations with Rome, the Sacramentarians, the Anabaptists, or the Turks. He would not intervene, he informed Rosheim, "because you and your people have so shamefully abused everything I have done." They had not converted to Christianity even though the gospel had been clearly preached for nearly two decades. Christians, he wrote, regarded as the true God "this damned, crucified Jew," while the Jews regarded him as "a heathen" and even "after his death pray for a Lord."[7] To Luther's mind, the Jews exhibited hardened hearts, and he would do nothing for them.

There was no anti-Semitism in this response. Moreover, Luther never became an anti-Semite in the modern, racial sense of the term. In March 1538 he published a *Letter against the Sabbatarians* in which he declared that the Jews could not be the people of God because they were still waiting for the Messiah to come. Luther was anti-Jewish in the sense that he opposed anyone who taught contrary to his doctrine. But, as with so many of his other opponents, he could never let the issue go. Instead, five years later he published yet another treatise, *Against the Jews and Their Lies,* then wrote an addendum to it, and finally yet one more little book on the same subject. In the process, he moved from tacitly accepting the elector's policies to actively advocating the banishment of the Jews. At the very least, their synagogues and books were to be burned, and they were to be forced to leave the cities, give up their commercial activities, and work as day laborers on the land. Like papists, Sacramentarians, and Anabaptists, Luther regarded Jews as a poisonous yeast in the Christian loaf. The pity remains that he simply repeated the prejudices of his age in proposing specific policies for them.

These last writings came from Luther's pen just after he had learned, erroneously, that certain Jews were trying to convert Christians and had even performed circumcisions on some of them. Such stories abounded in Europe at the time, but they explain no more than Luther's decision to write against the Jews at this particular moment. During the last decade of his life, Luther vehemently assaulted any opposition to the gospel, whether it came from Jews or anyone else. On November 20, 1538, he learned from Landgrave Philip that Bucer had recommended dealing gently with Anabaptists that he found in his territories. Luther replied that they, like the Jews, should be given a chance to convert and then, if they did not, they should be banished. They were all part of the same wild yeast, which, if allowed to grow, would surely poison the true church.

The question of a council

At the same time, circumstances conspired to put Luther into an awkward position. Charles V and his designated successor, Archduke Ferdinand, were becoming increasingly desperate for help in stopping the triumphant march of the Muslim Turks up the Danube River. They argued that this movement imperiled not just their own crown lands in Austria but the entire empire. In this they were probably right, for the Danube stretched west all the way across Germany to the eastern slope of the Black Forest.

The Protestant princes were equally determined to provide no financial or military assistance unless their religious position within the empire were secure. They knew that from the Edict of Worms in 1521 through the Diet of Augsburg in 1530 Charles had consistently pressed for measures against Luther and his followers. Nor did they trust the emperor. They knew full well that he might take an army that had been collected for the purpose of fighting the Turks and turn it against them. Charles V did just that not long after Luther's death and thereby scored

Caricature of a monk (by Erhard Schön).   *The seven-headed Luther.*

an initial victory in the Schmalkald Wars. The position taken by the likes of Elector John Frederick and Landgrave Philip was therefore also a prudent one.

Another issue likewise became ever more pressing after Luther's meeting with Vergerio. Would the Protestants attend a church council? Luther had pledged that, if invited under the right circumstances, he would attend. For their part, many of the Protestant princes had, at least initially, justified their refusal to act against Luther and his followers on the grounds that the religious dispute had not yet been adjudicated by a free council of the church.

With the pontificate of Paul III, circumstances changed. In spite of all the delays, Pope Paul III was genuinely convinced of the necessity of a council. This pope was by no means above enriching his own family and friends at the expense of those who were neither, but he was also tough and shrewd in dealing with the Protestants. And he had called their hand. In March 1537 he even received a report from a special reform commission which was composed of some of the most eminent prelates in the church, including a future pope. It declared that the chief cause of all the church's current miseries lay in the subversion of a spiritual office, the papacy, into a temporal one and called for bold actions to reunite the church into one body. The document itself was supposedly preparatory to a council that would accomplish this longed-for work. If there truly was to be a council of the church that would render definitive judgments on all the issues (and it increasingly began to look as if there would be), then how could the Protestant princes refuse to join a combined effort against the heathen Turks?

Luther had said he would participate, but would the princes and their theologians agree? Or would they insist on so many conditions regarding a council that they could declare it invalid, and then in good conscience continue to demand religious guarantees from the emperor before supporting any war against the Turks?

The situation was immensely complex. But politicians like Elector John Frederick and Landgrave Philip had thought the matter through with great care. They believed that talk of a council was only a trap. They would not attend and they would not sanction the attendance of any of their theologians. The conflict that might have developed between Luther and his protectors on this issue never surfaced, however, because they were not invited when the Council of Trent at last did meet. When the Council of Trent finally held its first session, shortly before Luther's death, it did so without the presence of any Protestant princes or theologians.

Every announcement and postponement of a council simply provided more opportunities for Luther to doubt the sincerity of the "whore of Babylon," as he now called the papacy. It also suited the princes' purposes and confirmed them in their suspicions about papal and imperial intentions.

The Regensburg Colloquy

Defenders of Rome, and in particular those who found themselves battling it out with the Protestants in the trenches of Germany, were especially depressed by the on-again, off-again council. None were more distraught than Charles V and Archduke Ferdinand. No matter what they did, they could get no help from Rome in putting an end to the religious disunity that so imperiled their own struggle with the Turks. They therefore decided to act on their own. They would sponsor colloquies between Roman and Protestant theologians in Germany. These meetings would not exactly constitute a council, but at least they would not occur in Italy under papal domination and they might produce enough agreement to elicit some help from the Protestant princes. Even Pope Paul III cooperated with this effort by sending a delegation of official observers to each of the colloquies which were held in 1540–1541 at Hagenau, near Strasbourg, then at Worms, and then again during the Imperial Diet of 1541 in Regensburg.

Luther attended none of these meetings. Perhaps for this very reason, the negotiators at Regensburg came very close to agreement. After the earlier failures, Bucer and Capito agreed with their Roman counterparts on such critical issues as human nature before the fall of Adam, the freedom of the will, the source of sin, and the nature of original sin. They agreed to disagree on the questions of authority, the power of excommunication, and the sacraments. Cardinal Contarini, who had chaired the reform commission three years earlier, even came to an understanding with Melanchthon on the core question of justification by faith. If this issue could be resolved, Emperor Charles and Archduke Ferdinand might yet rescue the situation.

Melanchthon carried the document back to Wittenberg and Luther flatly rejected its article on justification. Contarini carried it back to Rome and found himself accused of heresy on the basis of the same article. The object of all this displeasure came to be known as the doctrine of "double justification." According to this view, only the grace of God in the merits of Christ justified sinners and saved them through faith. But on the other hand, this very faith had to be a living faith that showed itself in works of love for one's neighbor. In essence, Contarini and Melanchthon had found a formula that resolved the differences between St. Paul and the St. James whose letter Luther had called "an epistle of straw."

Rome saw in this article no defense of indulgences or of the necessity for sacramental piety in general. In fact, the decrees of the Council of Trent several years later declared that both faith and works were necessary for salvation and that works included all the traditional labors of piety to which Luther and his followers so strongly objected. For his part, Luther was deeply suspicious of giving quick agreement to clever wording. This was the same attitude he had shown in the initial negotiations with Bucer in the Sacramentarian Controversy. The idea that faith had to show itself in works that others could judge was only a source of further suspicion. Christians might again be encouraged to look to their works, rather than to Christ alone, for assurance of their salvation. For Luther such an idea was anathema. Both Rome and Wittenberg had blocked the plans of Charles V and Archduke (now King) Ferdinand once again. Great effort had once more produced little except increased suspicion on all sides.

Luther remained as thoroughly consistent during his later years as he had been while a young professor. Regardless of the level of friendship or the dangerous consequences of disunity, he would not compromise on essential matters of faith. Attempts by his opponents to compromise served only to reinforce his confidence in his own position. In September 1538 he wrote a friend, "Were there no other proof that we are the ones who have been called and elected to the kingdom of God and have the true word of God, this one fact would suffice: we are attacked by so many sects that constantly disagree with one another. . . ."[8] Luther now included the pope among their number.

The Turkish threat

It is in fact impossible to overstate the reformer's allegiance to doctrine. He held firmly to what he believed was the truth, even in the midst of the delicate balance of considerations involved with the calling of a council, the Turkish threat, and the need for religious guarantees from the emperor. He was so committed to his understanding of the Christian faith that he was willing to give away the Protestant princes' only bargaining chip.

Unlike so many others, Luther was unable to play politics even on the question of aiding a war against the Turks. "His Most Christian Majesty," King Francis I of France, allied himself with the Turks in order to weaken Emperor Charles, while Elector John Frederick, Landgrave Philip, and their allies withheld support until their demands were met. Luther's personal advantage and that of his followers also lay with an emperor who was so distracted on every side that he could not act. Yet in late May 1538 Luther recommended that the Protestant princes go to Charles' assistance and do so unconditionally, "for necessity has no law. Where there is a need, there is an end to what law, alliance, or treaty says. The need supercedes everything." Everyone knew the atrocities that the Turks had committed against Christians under their authority. In this situation "we must dare good and evil with our brothers, and like comrades . . . endure the bitter with the sweet. God will be able to find his own, even in death."[9] In late February 1539 he wrote *An Admonition to All Pastors* in which he declared that the threats both from the Turks and from the pope were God's punishment on the Evangelicals for their evil lives and neglect of Word and sacrament. Luther did not play favorites in defending the faith.

In 1541, negotiations between Charles and the Protestant princes at last evolved to the point where the princes agreed to levy a special tax to provide aid against the Turks. Luther happily did his part. In March 1542 he wrote the elector, "If I were not too old and weak, I would prefer personally to be part of the army."[10] Just two months earlier, he had composed his own will, so he was able to include a detailed description of all his holdings, down to five cows, nine calves, three goats, and ten pigs. By this time, Luther was in fact a fairly well-to-do man. The previous December, Elector John Frederick had awarded him the sum of 1000 gulden, with five percent interest to be paid to

Luther annually and the principal to be distributed among his heirs at his death. Having received Luther's statement of good faith on the Turkish threat, the elector now declared that he personally would pay Luther's tax.

The many emerging sects, the advance of the Turks up the Danube, and the hostility of emperor and pope even led Luther to contemplate whether God's special judgment was not finally coming down on his beloved Germany. In September 1541 he wrote—as his contribution to the common defense—*An Admonition to Prayer against the Turks.* In this work he declared that Germany had brought the Turkish threat on itself because Germans were "fully replete with all manner of sin against God."[11] Above all, the defenders of Rome needed to turn from their evil ways. Evangelical pastors then needed to admonish their parishioners to confess their sins and begin to live life aright. The soldiers themselves had to be constant in prayer, in hearing the Word, and in receiving the Lord's Supper. To prepare for disaster, children were to be especially diligent in learning the catechism, so that the true faith might be preserved even in captivity, as in the time of Daniel. For Luther the Turkish threat was not so much a political and military matter as it was an episode in the history of salvation. It was therefore to be countered not so much with political and military means as with repentance.

SEVENTEEN

The Last Years

*I*t is a wonder that Luther was able to keep his wits about him, to say nothing about being consistent from word to deed and moment to moment. Issues of immense importance for the present and the future constantly poured in on him. To them were added the day-to-day burdens of lecturing, preaching, conducting the affairs of the church, and his own daily life. Much of his work he accomplished by means of correspondence. He wrote fully a third of his total extant letters during these later years, and that third amounts to four fat, quarto volumes. He commonly began these letters by apologizing for being so tardy or for answering three incoming letters with only one of his own. Nor was he above complaining to his colleagues from time to time. "It is enough," he said once at table. "I have worked myself to death. For one person, I have done enough. I'll go lie down in the sand and sleep now. It is over for me, except for just an occasional little whack at the pope."[1]

In spite of everything, however, Luther retained his sense of humor as well as his sense of purpose. On one occasion when he was apologizing for taking so long to respond to a letter, he blamed the delay on all "the business, work, age, and spiritual struggles" to which he was subject. Later he added, "I, an exhausted old man, tired out from so many labors, constantly become younger from day to day; that is, new sects always rise up against me, and renewed youth is necessary to fight against them." He was well aware that much of this renewed vigor came from one highly undesirable characteristic. "Wrath just will not let go of me. Why, sometimes I rage about a silly little thing not worth mentioning. Whoever crosses my path has to pay for it, and I won't say a kind word to anyone. Isn't that shameful? I might be entitled to other sins, material comforts for example, but I let some trifle get me all worked up!"[2] By no means were most of these things small matters, but Luther knew that it was rage itself that often kept him going.

Katie Luther

Rage, ability, and the importance of the issues at hand—these things kept Luther productive to the very end. Yet without the person of his wife Katie, the mature Luther would be incomprehensible.

There can be little doubt of Luther's genuine love and high affection for Katie. In mid-1540 he was urgently called to Weimar because Melanchthon, who was on his way to the religious colloquy at Hagenau, had suddenly fallen deathly ill. Luther was gone for about six weeks. He addressed his first letter home "to my dearly beloved Katie, Mrs. Doctor Luther, etc., to the Madame of the New Pig Market, personal." He announced that Melanchthon had recovered and that "I wish humbly to inform Your Grace that I am doing well here. I eat like a Bohemian and drink like a German, thanks be to God, amen."[3] When writing Katie, jokes were always at Luther's fingertips. But Katie may not have appreciated the first pun in this letter. In German a "new pig market"—the name of the field they had just purchased—could also refer to a brothel, which would make of Katie a "madam" indeed.

Katie was in fact taking care of business at the New Pig Market. As a result, she may not have received Luther's letters. In any event, she did not answer them. Two weeks passed and he asked her to please write to him. Almost two more weeks passed without word and he became a bit testy. "I am not sure whether this letter will find you at Wittenberg or at the Pig Market; otherwise I would like to write about more things." He hoped that when he came home, she would have "a good measure of beer" waiting for him. It is not known whether either Katie or the beer was present when he arrived. Luther could become quite testy. A little over a year later, he told her to disregard rumors of marauding Turks and then added, "Also, it seems strange to me that you write or send absolutely nothing to us even though you certainly know that we are concerned about you. . . ." He concluded by telling her to "sell and arrange what you can, and come home."[4]

The family's main room.

Katie Luther was fully as serious about her business as the defender of the faith was about his. She was also good at it, and Luther freely deferred to her. On this same expedition he gave her some advice about renovating the Black Cloister, but it is clear from the letter that the exact changes were her responsibility and not his: "I have an idea how you could have the windows in the new roof constructed, which I forgot to mention when I left," he wrote. "But I am afraid I am too late." Nothing could be clearer than that Katie was also the manager of the household's finances. In the same letter he wrote, "I am sending you . . . forty-two taler, the salary due this coming St. Michael's Day, and also forty gulden" from a loan that was due them. The field called the "New Pig Market" was hers to manage, as was another piece of real estate they owned. In 1542, when Luther made provision for the disposition of his estate, he did not make Katie the ward of his oldest son or his entire family the wards of a male executor, as would have been expected. Instead, he willed everything to her on the grounds that "a mother will be the best guardian for her own children."[5] Luther entrusted his wife with everything that was his.

Yet Katie and Martin Luther's life together also had its tensions. Even at an advanced age, Luther freely admitted that other women could turn his eye. For her part, Katie was not at all amused when her husband proved from the Scriptures, and in the presence of others, that a man might take more than one wife without violating the law of God. If Luther acted on this truth, she replied, she would return to the convent and leave him to manage the children. No one present, including the learned doctor, had any doubt that she was serious. Katie Luther was a tough woman. She consistently resisted his nearly profligate wish to give away everything they had. She also had her way in nearly all matters of household finance, much to the irritation of some of Luther's friends, who thought he should be more manly. Once she purchased a piece of land against Luther's will. "I can hold my own against neither her requests nor her tears," Luther commented.[6]

Luther accorded Katie love, honor, and, most of the time, even obedience as mistress of the household. This was her calling, but it was an immense one complete with severe trials. Their daughter, Magdalena, a previously sturdy teenager, fell suddenly into a raging fever in 1542. Katie sobbed uncontrollably for days. Luther tried to be the brave father and husband. He came to "Little Lena's" side and said, "You would like to stay here with me, your father, but are you also willing to go to that other father, or not?" Whatever her earthly father wished, she too wished, was the reply. When Magdalena breathed her last, Katie collapsed. When the carpenters brought in the coffin, Luther did the same thing he had done when he learned of his father's death. He fled. This time he shouted through the closed door, "Pound away!"[7]

Luther the pastor

The word *father* (or *Vater, pater,* or *papa*) had several meanings for people of the late Middle Ages. To be sure, they used it to call on their own earthly fathers. But they also used it in speaking with their priest when they went to confession, as the proper name of any priest they met, and for the pope himself. But as in the opening line of the Lord's Prayer, "Our Father in heaven," the connotation was always of someone with compassionate authority. A true father could forgive and direct one onto a better path.

As a pastor, Luther sought above all to console troubled consciences. His medieval predecessors had debated whether a thorough confession was worth the tortured spirit that might result from it, and they had agreed that it was. In both theory and practice, however, Luther insisted that consolation came first.

During these years he had many opportunities to practice "the care of souls," as pastoral care was commonly called. The advice that he gave was frequently enough to scandalize the pious. Once a young man confessed that he had made love with a maiden who utterly infatuated him but whom he could not marry because he was only a student. Luther advised him to marry her, but not simply because it was the honorable thing to do for her sake. Rather, he said, "If you do not marry her, you will suffer from a bad conscience and many torments. Beware, my dear fellow, of a bad conscience. You know what a worm it is. It will gnaw at you even if you marry some other very honest girl."[8]

There was good reason to protect the conscience first and foremost. It was here that Luther found Satan at work most powerfully. Faith or the absence of faith was all that counted in the end, and it was faith that Satan sought to destroy. "Paul's 'thorn in the flesh,' " he said, "refers to the tempting of our faith. He regarded it as a big skewer that would impale our soul and flesh." In spite of all his own labors, Luther confessed that "nothing has so exhausted me as sorrow, especially at night." From his own experience and that of others, he declared, "To raise one conscience up out of despair is worth more than a hundred kingdoms."

For Luther, nothing was more important than this struggle for faith. The first thing a Christian had to do was always to look at Christ, who was both Savior and cosufferer. Luther told one dying man,

God will not forsake you. He is not a tyrant who holds a good, crude blunder against you either, not even blasphemy when you are in distress, or denial of God, such as Peter committed and Paul too. Do not be disturbed by people to whom Christ is just a joke and a laughingstock, like Erasmus and his kind . . . they live on, certain of everything and untroubled by the devil. Why should he bother them? They already belong to him. You and I are the ones he would like to seize. Now how will he do that? He will continue attacking you with small things until he gets to your substance. But resist him. He who is within us is greater than he who is in the world.[9]

Luther looked the reality of human existence directly in the face, complete with all its horrors. But as in his hymns, he declared that in Christ alone the final victory was certain.

Common-sense advice

Luther also used common sense—as well as strictly theological or religious tactics—to defeat Satan. One strategy that he recommended repeatedly was to seek out the company of friends. "I," he said, "have had help from people who didn't have as much theology in their whole body as I do in one finger." When he was low, he would search out company wherever he could find it. Even his pigs would do. To a woman who feared that her husband was suicidal, he wrote, "Whatever you do, do not let the room grow lonely or still around him, for fear that he will sink into thought. It will do no harm if you make him angry. Act as if you are sorry for having done so and fuss about it, but go right ahead and do it anyway." To another depressed person he wrote, "Whenever the devil pesters you with these thoughts, at once seek out the company of men, drink more, joke and jest, or engage in some other form of merriment."[10] Just being alone could give Satan his opportunity.

As a last resort, Luther advised mocking the devil. He was convinced that pride lay behind genuine sin and that pride was Satan's chief characteristic. "No one is able to describe in words just how variously that damned majesty can transform himself. If we once recognize Satan to be Satan, then it is easy enough to destroy his pride by saying, 'Kiss my ass,' or 'Shit in your pants and hang them around your neck.' "[11]

In many respects Luther's spiritual advice came from his own experiences as a monk and a reformer. There can be no doubt that Satan was a reality for Luther, and his bouts with the devil remain legendary. Still, many of these legends amount to pious or, in some cases, vicious frauds. For example, there is no evidence (except that which was once provided annually by eager caretakers) that while he was at the Wartburg Luther threw an inkwell at the devil. The story may have originated from one of Luther's own remarks, however. But what Luther said was, "I have thrown ink at Satan." He was referring to his many books and his translation of the New Testament.

There was also no doubt in Luther's mind, or in the minds of his contemporaries, that Satan caused personal disasters here on earth. At the same time, Luther exercised common sense when he heard bizarre tales of strange events. In 1536 a pastor wrote him about the case of a young girl who made gold coins appear from unlikely places, but then quickly ate them. A priest had tried to exorcise the demon within her but without success. Luther replied that he had heard this story earlier. But now that he had heard it from a reliable source, he considered it "a sign that God is permitting Satan to imitate and portray the practice of certain princes who are everywhere robbing and devouring wealth without producing anything." He recommended prayer for the girl and public ridicule for the demon that possessed her. But he added another recommendation:

Investigate everything carefully to discover whether any deception is being practiced, especially whether the money or coins which the girl takes feel hard in the hands of others and are of the kind that can be used in the marketplace. For I have before been harassed by so many dissimulations, artifices, frauds, lies, tricks, etc., that I am necessarily reluctant to believe everything and everybody.

Luther closed with one more bit of advice: "As the proverb puts it, 'Let experience be your guide.' "[12]

Faith and conscience

Disasters and bizarre occurrences were indeed the work of Satan. But they paled to insignificance by comparison with faith or the absence of faith. Faced with an attack on faith, Luther even had little regard for common morality, at least if it was used to make believers feel guilty. He was frequently very explicit on this subject.

Sometimes it is necessary to drink a little more, play, joke, or even commit some sin in defiance and contempt of the devil in order not to give him an opportunity to make us scrupulous about small things. We will be overcome if we worry too much about falling into some sin. . . . What do you think is my reason for drinking wine undiluted, talking freely, and eating more often if it is not to torment and vex the devil who has made up his mind to torment and vex me? Would that I could commit some token sin simply for the sake of mocking the devil, so that he might understand that I acknowledge no sin and am conscious of no sin. When the devil attacks and torments us, we must completely set aside the entire Ten Commandments.[13]

Nothing, absolutely nothing was more important to Luther than faith and, with it, a free conscience.

Like so many of his other central convictions, this singleminded pastoral focus on the individual conscience also caused Luther difficulties. In late 1539, Philip of Hesse unburdened himself to Bucer. His marriage was a terribly unhappy one and Philip was having an affair with one of the ladies at court. There was nothing unusual about this situation for politicians and rulers of the time, whose marriages were rarely made with more than the tacit consent of the couple. But Philip alleged that his sin caused him so much distress that he was unable to partake of the Lord's Supper. Bucer informed Luther of the situation. After discussing the matter with Philip, Luther and Melanchthon deliberated and recommended that the landgrave marry the other woman. As the Scriptures freely attested, bigamy was not contrary to the law of God. It was far preferable to a courtly liaison, because it would protect both Philip's conscience and the woman's status.

Bigamy did, however, violate both imperial law and common morality. Partly for these reasons, Luther urged Philip to keep the matter secret. He also regarded his advice as having been given within the confessional. For this reason, too, it was to remain secret. Very soon, however, both Philip of Hesse's bigamy and Luther's cooperation with it were well-known. The landgrave could not keep quiet on either matter. As a result, his position was made so tenuous that he was forced to act in secret once again. This time, in exchange for immunity with respect to his bigamy, he agreed with Charles V to retire from the field of religious politics within the empire. For his part, Luther publicly refused to reveal exactly what he had advised Landgrave Philip. It would be better, he declared, for people to say, "Dr. Martin has been made a fool by giving way" to the landgrave.[14]

With the bigamy of Philip of Hesse, Protestant forces in the empire lost one of their strongest leaders. Only a year earlier, even political fortunes seemed to have been going Luther's way. On April 17, 1539, his old adversary Duke George of Saxony died. He was succeeded by Duke Henry, who with his wife had long been sympathetic to Luther's cause and had introduced the Reformation into their small territory. Now, acting on a bigger stage, they called Luther and three of his colleagues back to Leipzig, the scene of the debate with Eck 20 years earlier. This time Luther inaugurated Evangelical worship services in the city in which the duke resided. In early July, Luther recommended that Duke Henry abolish the Mass in his territories and conduct a visitation of all its parishes.

Rarely had Luther's relations with princes been so cordial. But he had grave doubts as to whether politicians could ever create anything better than what already existed. With respect to improving the temporal world, he once remarked, "I would not advise that any changes be made. We merely have to patch and stitch back together as best we can while we live, punish the abuses, and lay bandages and poultices over the sores." Nor did he have any doubts about the objectives of princes. "There is no office so small," he wrote, "but that it merits hanging the officeholder. Office in itself is divinely instituted and it is good, be it the office of the prince or that of his ministers. But those who occupy these offices are usually put there by the devil."[15]

In most people, such an attitude toward the affairs of this world leads to cynicism and social passivity. Here again, Luther differed. Nothing could so enrage him and move him so quickly to action as patent injustice. Wherever he saw injustice, he saw also an attack on the faith. One of the most notable of these instances came in 1541 in the person of Duke Heinrich of Braunschweig.

Against duke and pope

The duke had been in controversy with Landgrave Philip and Elector John Frederick for several years before Luther joined the fray. The issues between the two sides were partly political and partly religious, including the charge that the duke had a hand in sending arsonists to burn down Protestant churches in nearby lands. By 1541 the legal and political arguments were laced on both sides with blunt name-calling. The duke freely wrote about Philip's bigamy and John Frederick's drinking habits, while the Protestants pointedly referred to the duke's notorious sexual appetite.

Luther outdid them all in pure invective. He did carefully argue that the Protestant princes were acting in the name of the true gospel, while Duke Heinrich was defending the blasphemous papacy. But the title of Luther's book revealed his true intentions. *Against Hans Wurst* referred to a clown, one who walked about with a sausage around his neck while entertaining the crowds. In addition, the duke was not only a junior-grade devil, an arsonist, and a eunuch in a harem, but also an "archwhore." Luther's recommendation for those who disagreed with his assessment was equally blunt. He told them they could "do it in your pants and hang it around your neck and make a sausage of it for yourself, and gobble it down, you gross asses and sows!"[16] Luther's language left people on both sides gasping.

Yet Luther reserved his harshest words for those whose attack on the faith he regarded as the most direct and the most dangerous. To the very end, the papacy brought forth everything that was in him. He wrote his last such work in 1545. *Against the Papacy at Rome, Founded by the Devil* came forth in response to two concrete situations. One was a delay in the opening of the Council of Trent, which could not meet because, once again, too few participants had appeared for the first session. The other was a papal letter to Charles V in which Paul III sharply criticized the emperor for further concessions he had made to the Protestants.

The pope's shrill insistence that only he had the authority to define the true faith was too much for Luther. This time he devoted most of his book to a careful theological and historical argument against the papacy's claims. Having established this point to his satisfaction, he drew the obvious inference. The papacy was usurping the authority of Christ. Therefore it was the Antichrist incarnate.

Next came the most abusive language that Luther could muster. The pope was

> . . . the head of the damned church of the very worst knaves on earth; vicar of the devil; an enemy of God; an opponent of Christ; and a destroyer of the church of Christ; a teacher of all lies, blasphemy, and idolatries; an archthief of the church and robber of the keys—all the goods of both the church and the secular lords; a murderer of kings and inciter of all sorts of bloodshed; a brothel-keeper above all brothel-keepers and all lewdness, including what cannot be named; an antichrist; a man of sin and a child of perdition; a genuine werewolf.[17]

Just in case anyone should miss the point, Luther also commissioned Lucas Cranach to do a series of woodcuts on these subjects. They graphically conveyed Luther's meaning to those who could not read.

During his final years, Luther defended the faith in every way he could. For him, true defense included a powerful offense. It was during these years that he became convinced there was no hope for his opponents. Their words and their deeds revealed that their hearts were hardened. So while he tried to guard the consciences of his followers, he at last recommended that they cease their prayers even for Emperor Charles V and King Ferdinand. Luther's mind was set, and with it the minds of his followers.

EIGHTEEN

"We Are All Beggars"

The counts of Mansfeld were a notoriously factious lot. Their constant struggles with one another derived in part from the fact that they had so little to fight over. Three brothers shared rule over a territory that was so small it got its name from the idea that a man could ride around it in one day. Had it not been for the fact that Luther's brothers, sisters and their husbands, and their families on both sides lived in the county of Mansfeld, the counts might well have spent their entire lives in petty squabbles.

The first to come to Luther's attention in the 1540s was Albrecht, the eldest of the three brothers. His territory featured mines and commerce as well as the usual peasant farms, and the senior count was determined to make the most of his potential fortune. He insisted on laying such a heavy burden of taxation on miners and merchants that both they and his own brothers began to complain. At the same time, he was loathe to pay what his brothers regarded as his full share of the costs for schools, marriage courts, and public welfare, even though each of the counts had profited handsomely from seizing church property that was supposed to be turned to these ends. So the three fell to squabbling among one another. They very nearly came to armed conflict.

A reformer's warnings

Luther could scarcely ignore this shabby little struggle. Like his father, Hans, the family members who still lived there were miners and had interlocking interests with the local merchants. They were therefore among Count Albrecht's targets, and in May 1540 Luther wrote him to protest tax policies that he had heard were confiscatory. Less than two years later, Luther learned from the two brothers that the situation had not improved. So he wrote and urged them to impress on Count Albrecht that he had to treat his subjects fairly.

Luther may also have urged one of the local preachers to speak up on the question of how rulers ought to treat their subjects. In 1544, Albrecht accused his own court pastor of sedition on the grounds that he dared to preach against him. On September 19, Luther warned the count that "It is not seditious for the pastor of a church to condemn the morals of the authorities, even if he should be in error about the matter."[1] Every preacher, he declared, must preach against the vices of the upper classes. For them not to do so would be to neglect their duty. Even princes needed to listen and repent.

Offer to mediate

Little by little, the trials of the counts of Mansfeld ensnared a willing Luther through just such complaints and casual encounters. By October 1545 he had become sufficiently troubled by the situation to force an unwilling Melanchthon into making a detour to the county's principal town while they were on their way home from another mission. There, in Eisleben, the place of his birth, Luther investigated the charges and countercharges of which he had been learning from afar. Only Count Albrecht and his immediate family were available. The other two counts were supporting Elector John Frederick's war against Duke Heinrich of Braunschweig, whom Luther had called Hans Wurst. Unable to resolve matters on this surprise visit, Luther left behind him a letter to the two younger brothers. He offered to mediate the dispute. In particular, he urged them to think again about the mine over which they had seized political control from their brother and which was owned by Luther's own brother-in-law.

Luther's behavior in this matter was typical of the man, even in his last years. The struggles of the counts of Mansfeld were indeed his personal business, if only because they intimately involved his own extended family. He freely took up the cause of a brother and his relatives whose futures were threatened by this unstable political situation. Above all, Luther now feared that the two younger counts might seize his brother-in-law's mine and smelter just as they had seized the right to tax it.

On the other hand, even while intervening for his own family, Luther asked no special favors. Nor did he make any spiritual threats, as was the custom of the papacy when its temporal objectives were threatened. Rather, he urged the two younger counts to act graciously and even offered the practical advice that if the counts taxed his relatives out of existence they might end up the poorer for it because they would have no one left to tax. At the same time he stated that he hoped above all to restore peace in the combined territories. "Because I am a son of Mansfeld, I cannot bear such misadventures and dangerous circumstances in my beloved fatherland," he wrote.[2]

Perhaps to Luther's surprise, the younger counts of Mansfeld accepted his offer. With alacrity, Luther promised to come as quickly as he could. On December 6, 1545, he wrote, "I have no doubt that Your Graces . . . will happily see this disagreement put behind you."[3] He himself was so eager to see an end to it all that he left for Mansfeld on December 22 with his colleague Melanchthon. But Melanchthon fell ill again, and they were forced to turn back and spend Christmas in Wittenberg. The trip had to be postponed until after New Year's.

By this time Luther had turned 62. He was an old man, and he knew it. His longtime comrade, Spalatin, had died in mid-January. In March 1545 he had completed the preface to his *Latin Works*. There he reflected on his early years and related what a wondrous experience it had been when he had rightly understood the *iustitia dei,* the righteousness of God, for the first time. It was there that he declared how he felt "as if the gates of heaven had been flung open" as a result of his labors as a professor.

Luther also knew that he was ill. In June and July he had been so depressed and angry at the lack of response to the gospel that he left Wittenberg and vowed he would never return. Only the elector himself had been able to persuade him to go back to Wittenberg and do his duty. In November Luther had ended his university lectures on Genesis with the words, "Here is the beloved book of Genesis. May God give grace that others after me do better. I can do no more, for I am too weak. Pray to God for me that he will grant me a good and blessed last moment."[4] The same month he celebrated his last birthday in the company of his closest friends.

Luther had every reason to remain aloof from the squabble at Mansfeld, even if it did involve his own relatives and the inheritance his father had left them. Alternatively, he might simply have written a little tract or a letter in which he exercised his considerable polemical skills and condemned all parties to it. Instead, he became the mediator in this squalid barnyard battle, and it became his last effort.

With his sons leading the way, Luther finally left to do his work with the counts of Mansfeld on January 23. Travel in January in 16th-century Germany was normally hard. It was especially hard in 1546. Two days after he left Wittenberg, he wrote Katie from Halle that flooding in the river Saale had forced them to pause. "We were greeted by an immense Anabaptist lady [in German the word *Salle* is in the feminine gender] who threatened to rebaptize us with huge waves and great chunks of ice . . . . [To ward her off] we are taking good Torgauer beer and Rhine wine, with which we console ourselves in the meantime . . . ."[5] When the waters receded, his sons returned home and Luther went on toward Eisleben with his colleague Justus Jonas.

On the road and while in Eisleben, Luther wrote six such letters to Katie. He was in fine form. He addressed her as his "housewife of the heart," "Madame Doctor," "Mrs. Brewmaster," "Madame Pig-Marketer," and "Madame Sow-Marketer in Wittenberg," and signed them, "your old love-bird," and "the willing servant of Your Holiness." On one occasion Luther wrote that there had been a fire at their doorway and they had almost been crushed by a stone that fell out of an archway. "I am worried," he reported, "that if you do not stop worrying about us, the earth might open up and swallow us . . . ."[6]

Luther's ham-handed humor may have been little more than an attempt to take his mind off the situation in which he found himself. Just before his arrival in Eisleben, he was suddenly overcome with weakness. He blamed it on a village through which they had passed and which was populated with many Jews. He noted that after they had left the village, "a hard wind blew on my head from behind the wagon."[7] Luther knew he had offended the Jews with his writings, and he believed firmly in the effects of hard looks.

Difficult negotiations

The negotiations with the three counts proved to be even more difficult than the trip. On February 6 he wrote to complain about the lawyers that each of the counts brought with them to the negotiations.

He declared that it was the character of lawyers "to suspect poison is being served to them in each syllable" of the discussion.[8] To Luther's mind, lawyers accomplished little more than to advise Christians (who ought to know better) on how to be selfish in protecting their own rights and privileges.

To the end, Luther maintained a singleminded, religious point of view about the matter at hand. He was just as suspicious of lawyers as he was of Jews who refused to convert. When it came to matters of principle, he never could acknowledge the integrity of the other side's point of view. The last book he ever wrote was a little tract he titled *Against the Asses at Paris and Louvain.* Those theologians had condemned him once again. Luther professed amazement at their stupidity. Surely, now that the *Augsburg Confession,* Melanchthon's writings, and his own *Catechism* were available, they could have found more than a mere 32 articles to condemn. Their failure to do so proved just how weak their position was.

In spite of the lawyers, in spite of the difficulties of the journey, and even in spite of his critics at Louvain and Paris, Luther was able to clear his mind and bring the negotiations at Eisleben to a successful conclusion. That little place was a perfect nothing in the great sweep of history. But in mid-February its counts at last agreed to live with one another in peace. They even agreed to found and pay for a school for both boys and girls in the area.

As was customary once such an agreement was reached, Luther concluded the business by preaching. His text was Matt. 11:25-30, where Jesus declared that his Word confounded the world's understanding of things. True to himself, true to the situation, and true to the text, Luther urged all his hearers to turn away from worldly wisdom, which he characterized as "lies," and to turn to Christ and his Word.

Suddenly Luther was again overcome by weakness. Apologizing, he quickly ended the sermon. For the next two days he remained in his own room. By this point in his life he was almost never alone, yet no one in his party reported that he wrote or even read anything during these days. His health did not seem to worsen, at least not noticeably. No one had any idea that the end was near.

Luther's death

The only remarkable thing witnesses noticed about these days came from a scrap of paper they found in Luther's pocket. In this little note he declared that "No one can think that he has tasted the Holy Scriptures thoroughly until he has ruled over the churches with the prophets for a hundred years." Then Luther added something else: "Hoc est verum. Wir sind alle Pettler."

"This is true. We are all beggars."[9]

The end came quickly. Luther rested the day after the final papers were signed. That evening his heart began beating wildly. His friends tried to comfort him, and Count Albrecht brought some medications from his personal physician.

Later in the evening Luther felt better. He went to bed and slept well while his friends and the count waited in the next room. At 1:00 A.M. he suddenly woke up. "Oh, dear Lord God!" he shouted, "My pain is so great! Oh, dear Dr. Jonas, I am certain that I will remain here in Eisleben where I was born and baptized!"

The room in which Luther died.

The whole crowd rushed to Luther's bedside. Each tried to comfort him. But Luther kept repeating, "For God so loved the world that he gave his only son. . . ."

Jonas knew what was happening. He broke in and asked, "Do you want to die standing firm on Christ and the doctrine you have taught?" Luther's body moved, and in a loud voice he said, "Ja!"[10]

It was now almost 3:00 A.M. Luther's heart burst. The reformer died.

That very morning Luther's remains were brought to St. Andrew's, the largest church in Eisleben. There Jonas preached a sermon, and that night 10 citizens stood vigil. On February 20, the corpse, now clad in a long, white robe, was put into a hearse. With an escort of 50 horsemen, the mourners began their long trip home. That evening, when the party reached Halle, all the bells in the city began to ring. By now the cortege had become so immense that people in the sidestreets and the public market could not move in the crush.

The traditional death mask was prepared, and then the sculptors went one step further than usual. They also did a casting of his hands. By now *rigor mortis* had set in, and they had become fixed in their natural position. The fingers on his left hand were splayed out, flat, as if holding a book or piece of paper down on his desk. The thumb and index finger of the right hand were curled as if to hold a pen and to begin writing one more book.

Two days later, at about 9:00 A.M., the entire party neared Wittenberg. It was met outside the city gates by Luther's family, the clergy and professors, the city council, and a crowd of citizens. The cortege moved directly to the Castle Church, where Bugenhagen preached the funeral sermon before a crowd numbered in the thousands. Melanchthon responded for the university with a eulogy in Latin. At last Luther's body was buried, inside the Castle Church. To this day, whoever stands directly in front of the pulpit in this church is standing next to Luther's grave.

Luther's death mask.

Luther's grave and pulpit.

The man and his legacy

In his eulogy, Melanchthon declared that his dead colleague was a noble figure in the proud line of teachers and prophets that began with

Old Testament times and included the church Fathers. Luther was one of their number, according to Melanchthon, because "it is clear that the light of the gospel was recognized with greater splendor when Luther spoke" than others in recent times.[11]

Katie Luther was heartbroken. Two months after his death, she wrote her sister that everyone with any sort of heart must be mourning her dead husband. She herself could neither eat nor sleep, she was utterly disoriented, and she could not even write or dictate her letter in an orderly fashion. To her, Martin Luther was "this dear and precious man." The years that followed were bitter for Katie. The Schmalkald War broke out the same year Luther died. She was forced to flee Wittenberg and all her property was destroyed. Her own prince was imprisoned and she could depend only on King Christian III of Denmark. She did return to the city, but then had to flee again. She returned once more during the summer of 1552, only to be driven away by an outbreak of the Plague. The wagon she was riding in tipped over and threw her into a canal, and she died at Torgau on December 20, 1552.[12]

The cause of these horrors for Katie was Emperor Charles V's smashing victory over the remaining troops of the Schmalkald League in the Battle of Mühlberg. He then entered Electoral Saxony for the first and last time. He stood in front of the pulpit in the Castle Church, and some of those present urged him to have Luther's body dug up, burned, and its ashes scattered to the winds. Charles looked down and replied, "I do not make war against dead men."[13]

From word to deed

Luther's life exhibits amazing consistency. He was certainly consistent from word to deed within a maelstrom of events that would have left most people simply bewildered. He happily borrowed the intellectual tools of a great humanist like Erasmus, and then with regret condemned Erasmus's religion. He tried mightily to be loyal to Rome, and then condemned Rome utterly. He tried to create *theodidacti*, people taught by God, but then rejected even his most fervent supporters if they strayed from the Word of God as he understood it. He would not compromise on matters of faith.

Events also drove him—with equal fidelity to his innermost faith—to the actions of his later years. In his funeral oration, Melanchthon, the one who knew him best, felt obliged to note that "Some who are not scoundrels have nonetheless questioned whether Luther was not more harsh than he ought to have been. I will not discuss both sides of the issue, but rather respond as Erasmus often did, 'God gave this last age a sharp physician on account of its great sickness.' " Melanchthon granted that people are prone to sin in vehemence. But he recalled words of Plutarch and Euripides along with St. Paul to suggest that excesses from a stalwart champion of a great cause do not make the person less praiseworthy.[14]

The words and deeds of the older Luther reflected his most deeply grounded convictions just as surely as did those of the young man. Building and defending a church—and doing so in the teeth of "false brethren," ignorant peasants, grasping politicians, and bitter enemies— was just as perilous an undertaking as defying pope and emperor. Whether rightly or wrongly, Luther kept to it. It is therefore not possible to speak well of the young man and cringe at the old man. Luther was a whole man.

Notes

Except for the Preface, the references below are limited almost solely to direct quotations from Luther's works. Those who are interested in further reading should consult the bibliography. The notes have been constructed according to the following abbreviations and format:

WA	*D. Martin Luthers Werke. Kritische Gesamtausgabe.* 61 vols. Weimar, 1883–
WABr	*D. Martin Luthers Werke. Briefwechsel.* 18 vols. Weimar, 1930–
WADB	*D. Martin Luthers Werke. Deutsche Bibel.* 12 vols. Weimar, 1906–1961.
WATr	*D. Martin Luthers Werke. Tischreden.* 6 vols. Weimar, 1912–1921.
AE	*Luther's Works.* 55 vols. Jaroslav Pelikan and Helmut T. Lehmann, general editors. St. Louis: Concordia; Philadelphia: Fortress Press, 1955–1986.
Smith & Jacobs	*Luther's Correspondence and Other Contemporary Letters.* 2 vols. Preserved Smith and Charles M. Jacobs, eds. Philadelphia: Lutheran Publication Society, 1913–1918.
CR	*Corpus Reformatorum.* 99 vols. Halle, Berlin, and Leipzig, 1834–
St. L.	*Dr. Martin Luthers Sämmtliche Schriften.* 23 vols. Ed. Johann Georg Walch. St. Louis: Concordia, 1881–1910.

Where a reference is followed by another reference in parentheses, the first reference is the direct source and the second another location for the same material. Multiple references are set apart by a semicolon. Thus, WA 44, 712 (AE 8, 182); AE 8, 102 (WA 44, 72) consists of two references. In the first, the direct source is WA and in the second, AE. Translation presents problems to those who write about Luther, just as it did to Luther himself. Whenever the material quoted in the text is from a standard translation (such as AE), the translation appears first in the note with the reference to WA (the standard critical edition) in parentheses behind it. Most translations, however, are my own and are recognizable as such because the order of the references is reversed in the note. There may nonetheless be discrepancies between my translation and AE, even when AE is the direct source, because I have tried to follow Luther's example by letting him speak as much as possible in contemporary, standard, American English.

Preface

1. John M. Todd, *Luther: A Life* (New York: Crossroad, 1982), xvi.
2. Roland H. Bainton, *Here I Stand: A Life of Martin Luther* (Nashville: Abingdon, 1950).
3. The most recent general account of the literature is by Mark U. Edwards Jr., "Martin Luther," *Reformation Europe: A Guide to Research*, ed. Steven Ozment (St. Louis: Center for Reformation Research, 1982), 59-83. See also Helmar Junghans, "Aus der Ernte des Lutherjubiläums," *Lutherjahrbuch* 53 (1986): 55-138.
4. Todd, *Luther*. Daniel Olivier, *The Trial of Martin Luther* (St. Louis: Concordia, 1978) and *Luther's Faith* (St. Louis: Concordia, 1983).
5. E. Gordon Rupp, *Luther's Progress to the Diet of Worms* (New York: Harper & Row, 1964). Martin Brecht, *Martin Luther: His Road to Reformation 1483-1521* (Philadelphia: Fortress, 1985). Heinrich Boehmer, *Martin Luther, Road to Reformation* (Cleveland: World, 1967).
6. Heinrich Bornkamm, *Luther in Mid-Career, 1521-1530* (Philadelphia: Fortress, 1983). H. G. Haile, *Luther: An Experiment in Biography* (Garden City, N.Y.: Doubleday, 1980). Mark U. Edwards, *Luther's Last Battles* (Ithaca, N.Y.: Cornell, 1983).
7. Gerhard Ebeling, *Luther: An Introduction to His Thought* (Philadelphia: Fortress, 1970). Paul Althaus, *The Theology of Martin Luther* (Philadelphia: Fortress, 1966).
8. Erik H. Erikson, *Young Man Luther* (New York: Norton, 1962). John Osborne, *Luther* (New York: New American Library, 1963).
9. See Abraham Friesen, *Reformation and Utopia: The Marxist Interpretation of the Reformation and Its Antecedents* (Wiesbaden: 1974), and Thomas A. Brady Jr., "Social History," in *Reformation Europe: A Guide to Research*, ed. Steven E. Ozment (St. Louis: Center for Reformation Research, 1982), 162-181, for a more

positive reading. The most recent and carefully nuanced treatment is Brent O. Peterson, " 'Workers of the World Unite—for God's Sake!': Recent Luther Scholarship in the German Democratic Republic," in James D. Tracy, *Luther and the Modern State in Germany*, 16th-Century Studies Essays, no. 7 (Kirksville, Mo.: 16th century Publishers, 1986), pp. 77-99.

10. Fernand Braudel, *The Mediterranean and the Mediterranean World in the Age of Phillip II* (New York: Harper & Row, 1973), and Philippe Ariès, *Centuries of Childhood* (New York: Knopf, 1962). Jaroslav Pelikan, *The Christian Tradition: A History of Christian Doctrine*. Vol. 4, *Reformation of Church and Dogma* (Chicago: University of Chicago, 1984).

Chapter 1. The Son of a Peasant

1. Some scholars question the traditional date for Luther's birth. See Reinhart Staats, "Luthers Geburtsjahr 1484 und das Geburtsjahr der evangelischen Kirche 1519," *Bibliothek und Wissenschaft* 18 (1984): 61-84. This author is probably a victim of Luther's well-known love for irony. Most of the details regarding Luther's early life, as reported here, come from Boehmer, *Road to Reformation*.
2. WATr 3, 415-416.
3. WA 30², 576.
4. Cited by E. Jane Dempsey Douglass, *Justification in Late Medieval Preaching: A Study of John Geiler of Keisersberg* (Leiden: Brill, 1966), p. 142.
5. Cited by Otto Scheel, *Martin Luther* (Leipzig: 1921), vol. 1, p. 95, n. 65.
6. The following account is from Thomas N. Tentler, *Sin and Confession on the Eve of the Reformation* (Princeton, N.J.: Princeton University, 1977), esp. pp. 162ff.

Chapter 2. A Man of Sorrows

1. WATr 4, 440, but see also WATr 5, 99.
2. WATr 2, 660.
3. WA 8, 660 (AE 44, 387).
4. WA 38, 143.
5. WA 44, 712 (AE 8, 182).
6. WA 1, 558.
7. WA 6, 444 (AE 44, 180).
8. WATr 1, 47 (AE 54, 15).
9. WA 54, 185 (AE 34, 336).
10. WATr 3, 313.
11. WA 54, 179 (AE 34, 328).
12. The words of Johann Nider, a Dominican, cited by Hubert Jedin, *A History of the Council of Trent* (St. Louis: Herder, 1957), vol. 1, p. 139.
13. AE 46, 234 (WA 30³, 550).

Chapter 3. A Student of Theology

1. WATr 1, 17.
2. WA 18, 685 (AE 33, 139).
3. Cited by Douglass, *Geiler von Kaysersberg*, p. 142.
4. WA 3, 430.

5. Desiderius Erasmus, *The Praise of Folly*, trans. and with an introduction by Clarence H. Miller (New Haven: Yale University, 1979), p. 4.
6. Erasmus, *Handbook of the Militant Christian*, trans. and with an introductory essay by John P. Dolan (Notre Dame: Fides, 1962), pp. 72-73.
7. WA 45, 86.
8. WA 38, 143.

Chapter 4. The Maturing Professor

1. WATr 2, 379; WATr 5, 654-655. See also WATr 5, 98.
2. WATr 5, 98; AE 34, 103 (WA 30³, 386).
3. WA 44, 819 (AE 8, 326).
4. WATr 6, 106-107; WA 40², 15 (AE 27, 13).
5. WABr 1, 72 (AE 48, 27-28).
6. AE 54, 50 (WATr 1, 146).
7. AE 34, 338 (WA 54, 186).
8. WA 54, 185 (AE 34, 336-337).
9. WA 3, 14 (AE 10, 8).
10. WA 3, 465 (AE 10, 407).
11. WA 3, 458 (AE 10, 402). See also WA 56, 279 (AE 25, 267).
12. WA 3, 208; WA 3, 289 (AE 10, 237); WA 3, 345 (AE 10, 290); WA 3, 285.
13. WA 3, 238 (AE 10, 197); WA 3, 94 (AE 10, 99, where the translator renders *synteresis* as "conscience."); WA 3, 535 (AE 11, 17); WA 5, 163.
14. WA 56, 237 (AE 25, 222, where the translation inexplicably omits the word "not.").
15. AE 25, 261 (WA 56, 274).
16. WA 56, 275 (AE 25, 262); WA 56, 355 (AE 25, 345).
17. WA 56, 355 (AE 25, 344); WA 56, 312 (AE 25, 299); AE 25, 300 (WA 56, 313).
18. AE 25, 313 (WA 56, 325).
19. AE 25, 345 (WA 56, 356); WA 56, 362 (AE 25, 351-352); AE 25, 346 (WA 56, 357).
20. AE 25, 233 (WA 56, 246).
21. WA 56, 207 (AE 26, 191-192).
22. AE 25, 236 (WA 56, 249); AE 25, 153 (WA 36, 173); AE 25, 438 (WA 56, 446).
23. WA 56, 198 (AE 25, 286).
24. WA 56, 204 (AE 25, 188).
25. WABr 1, 37-38; WABr 1, 35 (AE 48, 12-13).
26. WA 56, 231 (AE 25, 215).
27. WA 56, 442 (AE 25, 434).
28. WA 56, 287 (AE 25, 274-275).
29. WA 56, 281 (AE 25, 268).
30. WA 56, 350 (AE 25, 339); AE 25, 267 (WA 56, 279-280).
31. AE 25, 268 (WA 56, 280-281).
32. WA 56, 283 (AE 25, 270).
33. AE 25, 260 (WA 56, 272); WA 56, 350 (AE 25, 339).
34. AE 25, 336 (WA 56, 347).
35. WA 56, 226 (AE 25, 210-211); WA 56, 219 (AE 25, 204).
36. WA 56, 400 (AE 25, 390); WA 56, 387 (AE 25, 377-378); WA 56, 272 (AE 25, 260).

37. WA 56, 3-4 (AE 25, 3).

Chapter 5. The Explosion

1. Walther Köhler, ed., *Dokumente zum Ablassenstreit von 1517*, 2nd rev. ed. (Tübingen: 1934), pp. 125, 127.
2. WA 7, 126.
3. WABr 1, 94 (AE 48, 42).
4. The theses are in AE 31, 25-33 (WA 1, 233-238). Theses 32, 26, 73, 58, 37, and 81 have been quoted. The translation of thesis 32 is my own. WABr 1, 111.
5. WATr 3, 656, but see also 1, 601.
6. The comment on Tetzel is from WA 54, 185 (AE 34, 336).
7. WA 1, 245. See also Kurt Aland, ed., *Martin Luther's 95 Theses*, trans. by P. J. Schroeder *et al.* (St. Louis: Concordia, 1967), p. 61.
8. WA 57¹, 70; 102.
9. WA 57², 110; 135 (AE 29, 119, 141).
10. The Heidelberg theses can be found in WA 1, 353-355 (AE 31, 39-42).
11. Adalbert Horowitz, ed., *Briefwechsel des Beatus Rhenanus* (Leipzig: 1886), p. 108.
12. WABr 1, 170.
13. WA 1, 525-526 (AE 48, 65-68).
14. WA 1, 631.
15. WATr 5, 34-35; AE 31, 250 (WA 1, 627). The translation of the last clause is my own.
16. WA 1, 529 (AE 31, 83).

Chapter 6. The Lines Drawn

1. WA 1, 385.
2. WABr 1, 178 (Smith and Jacobs 1, 87).
3. WABr 1, 185 (partially trans. in Smith and Jacobs 1, 97).
4. WABr 1, 188 (AE 48, 71-72).
5. WABr 1, 192; WA 1, 656-657.
6. WA 1, 662.
7. WA 1, 670.
8. WA 4, 403 (AE 11, 545).
9. WA 1, 228 (AE 31, 16).
10. WATr 2, 595.
11. WABr 1, 208.
12. WABr 1, 209 (Smith and Jacobs 1, 116).
13. WABr 1, 209-210 (partly trans. in Smith and Jacobs 1, 117).
14. This account is a conflation of WA 2, 16 (AE 31, 275); WABr 1, 214 (AE 48, 84); WABr 1, 224-225 (AE 48, 91); WABr 1, 237; WA 2, 16 (AE 31, 275).
15. WABr 1, 217 (Smith and Jacobs 1, 120).
16. WABr 1, 223 (AE 48, 89).
17. WABr 1, 224 (AE 48, 90).
18. WABr 1, 234-235.
19. WABr 1, 253 (AE 48, 94); WA 54, 181 (AE 34, 331).
20. WABr 1, 236, 238-241, 243, 245, 250.

21. WABr 1, 253 (AE 48, 94); WABr 1, 260-261 (Smith and Jacobs 1, 134); WABr 1, 264 (Smith and Jacobs 1, 137); WABr 1, 267.
22. WABr 1, 281.

Chapter 7. The Public Disputant

1. WABr 1, 268 (Smith and Jacobs 1, 138).
2. WABr 1, 262.
3. WABr 1, 308 (AE 48, 303).
4. WA 15, 38 (AE 45, 360).
5. WA 54, 185-186 (AE 34, 336-338).
6. WABr 1, 270.
7. WABr 1, 198; 2, 71.
8. WABr 1, 307-308 (Smith and Jacobs 1, 155); WA 2, 160-161 (AE 31, 318).
9. WABr 1, 351, 348.
10. WA 2, 487 (AE 27, 216); WABr 1, 354.
11. WABr 1, 359 (AE 48, 114).
12. WABr 1, 421 (AE 31, 320-321); WABr 1, 422 (AE 31, 322); WABr 1, 424 (AE 31, 325).
13. WABr 2, 42 (AE 48, 153).
14. WABr 1, 475, 478; WA 2, 387; WABr 1, 503 (Smith and Jacobs 1, 215).

Chapter 8. The Outlaw

1. Alfred Hartmann, ed., *Die Amerbach Korrespondenz* (Basel: 1942–1958), vol. 2, p. 217.
2. Karl Kaulfuss-Diesch, ed., *Das Buch der Reformation, Geschrieben von Mitlebenden*, 2nd ed. (Leipzig: 1917), pp. 168-169.
3. WABr 1, 543.
4. WA 2, 646; 723.
5. St. L. 19, 450; WA 6, 79.
6. WABr 1, 595.
7. WABr 2, 117.
8. WABr 2, 138; WA 6, 296-297.
9. WABr 2, 137.
10. WA 6, 419, 417 (AE 44, 142-145).
11. WA 6, 537, 527-529, 512, 514-515, 573 (AE 36, 72, 58-61, 39-40, 125).
12. WA 7, 42-48 (AE 31, 334-341).
13. WA 7, 49-52, 61, 70-73 (AE 31, 344-347, 360-361, 373, 376).
14. Paul Kalkoff, ed., *Die Depeschen des Nuntius Aleander vom Wormer Reichstage 1521* (Leipzig: 1886), p. 43.
15. WABr 2, 263, 249.
16. *Buch der Reformation*, pp. 238-239; WATr 5, 69.
17. WABr 2, 389, 395-396.
18. WABr 2, 300.
19. *Buch der Reformation*, pp. 243-246.

Chapter 9. The Exile

1. *Buch der Reformation*, p. 247.
2. WABr 2, 305 (AE 48, 201-202).
3. AE 48, 257 (WABr 2, 356-357).
4. WABr 2, 337 (AE 48, 225).
5. WA 7, 574-575 (AE 21, 328-329); WA 7, 593-594 (AE 21, 347-348).
6. WA 6, 181-182 (AE 32, 135); WA 8, 106-107 (AE 32, 228).
7. WA 8, 184.
8. WABr 2, 377 (AE 48, 290). See WABr 2, 385 (AE 48, 303).
9. WA 8, 483 (AE 36, 134).
10. WABr 2, 415 (AE 48, 359); AE 48, 286 (WABr 2, 374).
11. WA 8, 331, 317.
12. AE 48, 328 (WABr 2, 403).
13. WA 8, 574 (AE 48, 332); WA 8, 664 (AE 44, 393).
14. WABr 2, 431 (AE 48, 375).
15. WABr 2, 410 (AE 48, 351).
16. WA 8, 681, 685 (AE 45, 63-64, 70).
17. WABr 2, 490 (AE 49, 4); WA 10^2, 60.
18. WADB 6, 2, 8 (AE 35, 357, 360).
19. WADB 7, 6 (AE 35, 368).
20. WADB 6, 8 (AE 35, 361); WADB 7, 20 (AE 35, 377).
21. AE 35, 377 (WADB 7, 20, 22); WADB 7, 22 (AE 35, 377).
22. WADB 6, 10 (WA 35, 361-362).
23. AE 35, 361 (WADB 6, 8); WADB 6, 10 (AE 35, 362).

Chapter 10. Return to the Fray

1. WABr 2, 448 (AE 48, 387).
2. WABr 2, 452; WABr 3, 9.
3. AE 48, 391 (WABr 2, 455-456).
4. WA 10^3, 1, 4 (AE 51, 70-71).
5. WABr 2, 515; WA 10^3, liii. *Archiv für Reformationsgeschichte* 34 (1943): 149.
6. WABr 2, 435. Capito as cited by James M. Kittelson in *Wolfgang Capito from Humanist to Reformer* (Leiden, 1975), pp. 83-84.
7. Quoted by Daniel Cramer, *Das Grosse Pomerische Kirchen Chronicon* (Stettin: 1628), vol. 3, p. 43; WATr 1, 47 (AE 54, 16).
8. CR 94, 245.
9. WABr 2, 523.
10. WA 11, 355.
11. Günther Franz, ed., *Thomas Müntzer, Schriften und Briefe: Kritische Gesamtausgabe* (Gütersloh: 1968), p. 504.
12. WA 10^3, 18-19 (AE 51, 77).
13. AE 51, 72-73 (WA 10^3, 8).
14. AE 46, 54, 52, 50 (WA 18, 361, 359, 358).
15. AE 46, 75 (WA 18, 393).

Chapter 11. "False Brethren"

1. WA 2, 742-743.
2. WABr 2, 530-531, 559-562 (Smith and Jacobs 2, 125-129); WA 11, 434 (AE 36, 279).
3. CR 95, 248; WABr 3, 383.
4. WA 15, 394 (AE 40, 68).
5. WA 6, 80 (see also WABr 2, 531ff.).
6. WABr 3, 537.
7. WABr 3, 537 (AE 49, 117).
8. WABr 3, 534, 537.
9. WATr 4, 701.
10. WABr 1, 90 (AE 38, 40).
11. WA 18, 786 (AE 33, 294).
12. WABr 3, 368.
13. AE 33, 170 (WA 18, 636); WA 18, 636 (AE 33, 67).
14. AE 33, 68 (WA 18, 636); WA 18, 635 (AE 33, 65-66).
15. E. Gordon Rupp and A. N. Marlow, eds. and trans., *Luther and Erasmus: Free Will and Salvation*, vol. 17, The Library of Christian Classics (Philadelphia: Westminster, 1969), p. 37.
16. AE 33, 19 (WA 18, 603); WA 18, 603 (AE 33, 20); AE 33, 22 (WA 18, 604), italics mine.
17. AE 37, 270 (WA 26, 402); AE 37, 27 (WA 23, 85-86).
18. St. L. 20, 582.
19. WA 30³, 130 (AE 38, 44).
20. WA 23, 189 (AE 37, 92); WA 23, 193 (AE 37, 95).
21. WATr 2, 222.
22. *Deutsche Reichstagsakten, Jüngere Reihe*, 3 (Göttingen: Vandenhoek & Ruprecht, 1963): 747-748.
23. WABr 4, 89 (Smith and Jacobs 2, 374).
24. WABr 4, 277 (Smith and Jacobs 2, 420).
25. AE 43, 126 (WA 23, 354).
26. WABr 4, 226-227 (Smith and Jacobs 2, 409).
27. WA 35, 455-457 (AE 53, 284-285). Translation adapted from that by Frederick H. Hedge (1805–1890).

Chapter 12. Pastor and Teacher

1. WABr 4, 241.
2. See WA 6, 413 (AE 44, 137); WA 18, 298-299 (AE 46, 22); WA 10³, 6-7 (AE 51, 72).
3. WABr 4, 234; WABr 4, 265 (Smith and Jacobs 2, 415).
4. WABr 4, 603, 605; WABr 5, 1, 5.
5. WATr 5, 498.
6. Theodore G. Tappert, ed. and trans., *The Book of Concord* (Philadelphia: Fortress, 1959), p. 338, cited hereafter as Tappert. *(Die Bekenntnisschriften der evangelisch-lutherischen Kirche*, 6th ed. [Göttingen: 1967], pp. 501-502, cited hereafter as BK.)
7. BK, 510-512, 514-515 (Tappert, 344-345, 347-348).

8. BK, 522 (Tappert, 353).
9. WA 26, 530.
10. WA 30², 116, 130-131 (AE 46, 170, 185-186).
11. Cited from M. Reu, *The Augsburg Confession: A Collection of Sources with an Historical Introduction* (Chicago: 1930), p. 489.
12. WABr 5, 77 (AE 49, 226).
13. WABr 5, 101-102 (AE 49, 230-231).
14. Donald J. Ziegler, ed., *Great Debates of the Reformation* (New York: Random, 1969), p. 73.
15. WA 30³, 112 (AE 38, 16); WA 30³, 153 (AE 38, 75).
16. See WA 30³, 114 (AE 38, 17) and AE 38, 37.
17. See WA 30³, 123 (AE 38, 25-26) and WA 30³, 145 (AE 38, 64).
18. See WA 30³, 149-150 (AE 38, 70) and WA 30³, 155 (AE 35, 78).
19. WABr 5, 154 (AE 49, 236); WABr 5, 160.

Chapter 13. Damnable Rome

1. WABr 2, 431 (AE 48, 375).
2. WABr 5, 183 (AE 49, 250).
3. WABr 5, 258-260 (AE 49, 275-280).
4. AE 46, 75 (WA 18, 393).
5. WABr 5, 285 (AE 49, 288-289); AE 49, 293-294 (WABr 5, 291); WABr 5, 379.
6. WABr 5, 240, 379 (AE 49, 269); WATr 1, 128.
7. AE 34, 60 (WA 30', 355); WA 30², 196.
8. WABr 5, 319 (AE 49, 297-298).
9. WABr 5, 399-400 (Reu, 314).
10. AE 49, 354 (WABr 5, 442).
11. WABr 5, 578.
12. WABr 5, 475.
13. WABr 5, 617; Bucer cited by Johann Wilhelm Baum, *Capito und Butzer: Strasbourgs Reformatoren* (Elberfeld: 1859), p. 474.
14. WABr 5, 653-654.
15. WABr 5, 660 (AE 49, 435).
16. WABr 5, 662 (AE 49, 432-433).
17. WABr 6, 56.
18. WA 30', 386-387 (AE 34, 103).
19. WA 30³, 282, 279-280 (AE 47, 19, 15-16). See also WA 30³, 279, n. 4.
20. WABr 5, 593, 629.

Chapter 14. To Build the Church

1. WA 10³, 176.
2. WABr 6, 52, 231; WA 31¹, 430; WABr 6, 232.
3. AE 40, 384 (WA 30³, 518); WA 30³, 527 (AE 40, 394).
4. WATr 1, 53; WA 38, 204 (AE 38, 157).
5. AE 45, 350, 353, 356 (WA 15, 30, 31, 34).
6. AE 46, 231 (WA 30², 545-546).
7. WATr 6, 301.
8. WA 30³, 251.

9. WABr 6, 46-47, 49, 126; WA 38, 135-136.
10. AE 53, 64 (WA 19, 75).
11. WA 57, lxxvi.
12. AE 46, 253 (WA 30², 579-580); WA 40¹, 48 (AE 26, 9).
13. WATr 2, 531.
14. WATr 5, 121.

Chapter 15. Negotiator for the Faith

1. WABr 6, 308.
2. WABr 6, 326 (AE 50, 58).
3. WA 30³, 416, 419.
4. WA 30³, 470.
5. WABr 6, 154.
6. WA 36, 252 (AE 51, 241).
7. WATr 4, 414.
8. WA 38, 99.
9. WA 38, 135-136.
10. The description follows Haile, *Luther,* pp. 19-20.
11. WATr 5, 634.
12. WABr 6, 60.
13. WABr 7, 130; WA 38, 299; WA 15, 300.
14. WABr 7, 290.

Chapter 16. Defender of the Faith

1. AE 31, 344 (WA 7, 49).
2. AE 47, 109-110 (WA 50, 470).
3. WA 30², 28.
4. Tappert, p. 292 (BK, 416).
5. WATr 3, 392; WABr 8, 49.
6. WABr 8, 55-56.
7. WABr 8, 89-90.
8. AE 50, 183 (WABr 8, 292).
9. WABr 8, 235.
10. WABr 10, 20.
11. WA 51, 589 (AE 43, 221).

Chapter 17. The Last Years

1. WATr 4, 325.
2. AE 50, 182-183 (WABr 8, 291-292); WATr 5, 380.
3. AE 50, 208 (WABr 9, 168).
4. WABr 9, 205 (AE 50, 221-222); WABr 9, 518-519 (AE 50, 224-225).
5. WABr 9, 171-173 (AE 50, 215-217); AE 34, 296 (WABr 9, 573).
6. WATr 2, 290.
7. WATr 5, 189 (AE 54, 430); WATr 5, 194.
8. WATr 4, 346.
9. WATr 3, 439, 341 (AE 54, 207); WATr 2, 263; WATr 3, 507.

10. WATr 3, 506; WABr 6, 389; WABr 5, 519 (Theodore Tappert, ed. and trans., *Luther: Letters of Spiritual Counsel*, vol. 18, The Library of Christian Classics [Philadelphia: Westminster, 1955], p. 86, cited hereafter as *Letters of Spiritual Counsel*).

11. WATr 2, 306. Such language was typical of Luther and many writers of his time. Translators have traditionally been extraordinarily charitable in rendering these expressions into English.

12. WABr 7, 489-490 (*Letters of Spiritual Counsel*, pp. 44-45).

13. WABr 5, 519 (*Letters of Spiritual Counsel*, p. 86).

14. WABr 9, 149.

15. AE 13, 217, 212 (WA 51, 258, 254).

16. WA 51, 471 (AE 41, 187). See n. 11.

17. WA 54, 283-284 (AE 41, 357-358).

Chapter 18. "We Are All Beggars"

1. WABr 10, 659.

2. WABr 11, 189.

3. WABr 11, 226 (AE 50, 284).

4. WA 44, 825 (AE 8, 333).

5. WABr 11, 269 (AE 50, 286-287).

6. WABr 11, 291 (AE 50, 306).

7. WABr 11, 275-276 (AE 50, 291).

8. AE 50, 299 (WABr 11, 285).

9. WATr 5, 318 (AE 54, 476).

10. St. L. 21/2, 3385, 3387.

11. CR 11, 728.

12. Cited by Ernst Kroker, *Katharina von Bora: Martin Luthers Frau*, 2nd ed. (Zwickau: Johannes Hermann, 1925), p. 224.

13. Cited by Lewis W. Spitz, *The Protestant Reformation*, p. 121.

14. CR 11, 729-730.

Maps

p. 333   For a more complete reconstruction of Luther's travels, see the map developed by Christoph Strohm, Franz Irsigler, and Klaus Lonsdorfer printed inside the back cover of Germanisches Nationalmuseum, *Martin Luther und die Reformation in Deutschland* (Frankfurt am Main: Insel, 1983).

p. 334   Adapted and reprinted from Charles S. Anderson, *Augsburg Historical Atlas of Christianity in the Middle Ages and Reformation* (Minneapolis: Augsburg, 1967), pp. 38–39, which involves more detail and a historical overview of the period.

Introductory Bibliography

Most scholarly bibliographies attempt to provide a complete list of all relevant titles. For Martin Luther, this is an impossible task. To overcome this obstacle at least partially, the list that follows begins with bibliographies and guides to research. Titles under the other headings have been included because they are reliable, recent works (with a bias toward those published in English), and because for the most part they contain references to yet further publications. Readers with an interest in primary sources are referred to the notes.

Not all titles listed are currently in print. The most recent edition of a work is given, and publishers' names have for the most part been included only for North American imprints.

Bibliographies and Guides to Research

Aland, Kurt. *Hilfsbuch zum Lutherstudium.* 3rd rev. ed. Witten: 1970.
Archiv für Reformationsgeschichte/Archive for Reformation History. Literaturbericht/ Literature Review (published annually).
Atkinson, James. "Luther Studies." *Journal of Ecclesiastical History* 23 (1972): 69-77.
Bainton, Roland, and Gritsch, Eric W., eds. *Bibliography of the Continental Reformation: Materials Available in English.* 2nd ed. Hamden, Conn.: Shoe String, 1973.
Bietenholz, Peter G., and Deutscher, Thomas B., eds. *Contemporaries of Erasmus: A Biographical Register of the Renaissance and Reformation.* 2 vols. Toronto: University of Toronto, 1985–
Bigane, Jack, and Hagen, Kenneth. *Annotated Bibliography of Luther Studies, 1967– 1976.* St. Louis: Center for Reformation Research, 1977.
Buchwald, Georg. *Luther-Kalendarium.* Leipzig: 1929.
Comité internationale des sciences historiques. *Bibliographie de la Réforme 1450– 1648; Ouvrages parus de 1940 a 1955.* 6 vols. Leiden: 1958-1982.

Green, Lowell C. "Luther Research in English-Speaking Countries since 1971." *Lutherjahrbuch* 44 (1977): 105-126.

Junghans, Helmar. "Aus der Ernte des Lutherjubiläums 1983." *Lutherjahrbuch* 53 (1986): 55-138.

Junghans, Helmar. "Lutherbiographien zum 500. Geburtstag des Reformators 1983." *Theologische Literaturzeitung* 110 (1985): 403-442.

Klug, Eugene F. "Word and Scripture in Luther Studies since World War II." *Trinity Journal* 5 (1984): 3-46.

Lienhard, Marc. "Chronique: Quelques Publications Recentes Rélatives à Martin Luther." *Revue d'Histoire et de Philosophie Religieuses* 65 (1985): 461-480.

Lindberg, Carter. "Luther Research in America, 1945-1965." *Lutheran World* 13 (1966): 291-302.

Lutherjahrbuch (an annual publication).

Moeller, Bernd, ed. *Luther in der Neuzeit*. Gütersloh: 1983.

Ozment, Steven E., ed. *Reformation Europe: A Guide to Research*. St. Louis: Center for Reformation Research, 1982.

Pesch, Otto H. "Twenty Years of Catholic Luther Research." *Lutheran World* 13 (1966): 302-316.

Peterson, Brent O. " 'Workers of the World Unite—for God's Sake!': Recent Luther Scholarship in the German Democratic Republic." In James D. Tracy, *Luther and the Modern State in Germany*. 16th-Century Studies Essays. No. 7. Kirksville, Mo.: 16th-Century Publishers, 1986.

Robbert, George S. "A Checklist of Luther's Writings in English." *Concordia Theological Monthly* 36 (December 1965): 772-791; *Concordia Theological Monthly* 41 (April 1970): 214-220; *Concordia Journal* 4 (March 1978): 73-77.

Schottenloher, Karl. *Bibliographie zur deutschen Geschichte im Zeitalter der Glaubensspaltung, 1517-1585*. 7 vols. Leipzig: 1933–1966.

The Sixteenth-Century Journal (an annual publication).

Spitz, Lewis W. "Current Accents in Luther Study: 1960–1967." *Theological Studies* 28 (1966): 302-316.

Tjernagel, Neelak S. *The Lutheran Confessions: A Harmony and Resource Book*. Mankato, Minn.: Evangelical Lutheran Synod, 1979.

Vajta, Vilmos, ed. *Lutherforschung Heute*. Berlin: 1958.

Van Dulmen, Andrea. *Luther-Chronik: Daten zu Leben und Werk*. Munich: 1983.

General Works on the Reformation

Bainton, Roland. *The Reformation of the Sixteenth Century*. Boston: Beacon, 1952, 1985.

Chadwick, Owen. *The Reformation*. Pelican History of the Church series. New York: Penguin, 1964.

Dickens, A. G. *Reformation and Society in Sixteenth-Century Europe*. History of European Civilization Library. New York: Harcourt, Brace Jovanovich, 1966.

Elton, G. R., ed. *The New Cambridge Modern History*. Vol. 2. *The Reformation*. Cambridge: 1958.

Grimm, Harold J. *The Reformation Era: 1500–1650*. 2nd ed. New York: Macmillan, 1973.

Ozment, Steven. *The Age of Reform, 1250-1550: An Intellectual and Religious History of Late Medieval and Reformation Europe*. New Haven: Yale University, 1980.

Pauck, Wilhelm. *The Heritage of the Reformation*. Glencoe, Ill.: Free Press, 1961.

Pelikan, Jaroslav. *The Christian Tradition: A History of the Development of Doctrine*. Vol. 4. *Reformation of Church and Dogma (1300–1700)*. Chicago: University of Chicago, 1984.

Spitz, Lewis W. *The Protestant Reformation, 1517–1559*. The Rise of Modern Europe series. New York: Harper and Row, 1985.

Spitz, Lewis W. *Renaissance and Reformation*. 2 vols. St. Louis: Concordia, 1971, 1980.

Biographical Studies

Bainton, Roland H. *Here I Stand: A Life of Martin Luther*. Nashville: Abingdon, 1950, 1978.

Boehmer, Heinrich. *Road to Reformation: Martin Luther to the Year 1521*. Philadelphia: Muhlenberg, 1946.

Bornkamm, Heinrich. *Luther in Mid-Career, 1521-1530*. Philadelphia: Fortress, 1983.

Brecht, Martin. *Martin Luther: His Road to Reformation, 1483-1521*. Philadelphia: Fortress, 1985.

Edwards, Mark U. *Luther and the False Brethren*. Stanford: Stanford University, 1975.

Edwards, Mark U. *Luther's Last Battles: Politics and Polemics, 1531–1546*. Ithaca, N.Y.: Cornell University, 1983.

Erikson, Erik H. *Young Man Luther*. New York: Norton, 1962.

Gritsch, Eric W. *Martin—God's Court Jester: Luther in Retrospect*. Philadelphia: Fortress, 1983.

Haile, H. G. *Luther: An Experiment in Biography* (Garden City, N.Y.: Doubleday, 1980).

Junghans, Helmar, ed. *Leben und Werk Martin Luthers von 1526 bis 1546: Festgabe zu seinem 500. Geburtstag*. 2 vols. Berlin: 1983.

Lienhard, Marc. *Martin Luther: Un Temps, une Vie, un Message*. Geneva: 1983.

Lohse, Bernhard. *Martin Luther: Eine Einführung in sein Leben und sein Werk*. Munich: 1983.

Oberman, Heiko A. *Luther: Man Between God and the Devil*. New Haven: Yale University, 1986.

Olivier, Daniel. *The Trial of Luther*. St. Louis: Concordia, 1979.

Osborne, John. *Luther*. New York: New American Library, 1963.

Rogge, Joachim. *Martin Luther: Sein Leben, Seine Zeit*. Berlin, 1983.

Rupp, E. Gordon. *Luther's Progress to the Diet of Worms*. Chicago: Wilcox and Follet, 1951.

Schwiebert, E. G. *Luther and His Times: The Reformation from a New Perspective*. St. Louis: Concordia, 1950.

Siggins, Ian. *Luther and His Mother*. Philadelphia: Fortress, 1981.

Todd, John. *Luther: A Life*. New York: Crossroad, 1982.

Von Loewenich, Walther. *Martin Luther: The Man and His Work*. Minneapolis: Augsburg, 1986.

Luther's Context

Theology and Religious Thought

Aldridge, John William. *The Hermeneutics of Erasmus*. Richmond: John Knox, 1966.

Bainton, Roland H. *Erasmus of Christendom.* New York: Scribner, 1969.

Bentley, Jerry H. *Humanists and Holy Writ: New Testament Scholarship in the Renaissance.* Princeton: Princeton University, 1983.

Douglass, E. Jane Dempsey. *Justification in Late Medieval Preaching: A Study in John Geiler of Kaysersberg.* Leiden: 1966.

Grane, Leif. *Contra Gabrielem: Luthers Auseinandersetzung mit Gabriel Biel in der Disputatio contra Scholasticam Theologiam.* Gyldendal: 1962.

Grossmann, Maria. *Humanism in Wittenberg, 1485-1517.* Nieuwkoop: 1975.

Hägglund, Bengt. *The Background of Luther's Doctrine of Justification in Late Medieval Theology.* Philadelphia: Fortress, 1971.

Hyma, Albert. *The Brethren of the Common Life.* Grand Rapids, Mich.: Eerdmans, 1950.

Janz, Denis R. *Luther and Late Medieval Thomism: A Study in Theological Anthropology.* Atlantic Highlands, N.J.: Humanities, 1984.

Kittelson, James M., and Transue, Pamela J., eds. *Rebirth, Reform and Resilience: Universities in Transition, 1300-1700.* Columbus: Ohio State University, 1984.

Leff, Gordon. *Heresy in the Later Middle Ages: The Relation of Heterodoxy to Dissent, c. 1250-c. 1450.* 2 vols. Manchester: 1967.

Nauert, Charles. *Agrippa and the Crisis of Renaissance Thought.* Urbana, Ill: Illinois University, 1965.

Nauert, Charles. "The Clash of Humanists and Scholastics: An Approach to Pre-Reformation Controversies." *The Sixteenth-Century Journal* 4 (1973): 1-18.

Oakley, Francis. *Omnipotence, Covenant, and Order: An Excursion in the History of Ideas from Abelard to Leibnitz.* Ithaca, N.Y.: Cornell University, 1984.

Oberman, Heiko A. *The Harvest of Medieval Theology.* Durham, N.C.: Labyrinth, (1963) 1983.

Oberman, Heiko A., ed. *Forerunners of the Reformation: The Shape of Late Medieval Thought.* Philadelphia: Fortress, (1966) 1981.

Oberman, Heiko A., and Brady, Thomas A. Jr., eds. *Itinerarium Italicum.* Leiden: 1975.

Overfield, James. *Humanism and Scholasticism in Late Medieval Germany.* Princeton: Princeton University, 1984.

Ozment, Steven. *Homo Spiritualis: A Comparative Study of the Anthropology of Tauler, Gerson, and Martin Luther (1509-1516).* Leiden: 1968.

Payne, John B. *Erasmus: His Theology of the Sacraments.* Richmond, Va.: John Knox, 1970.

Pesch, Otto. *Theologie der Rechtfertigung bei Martin Luther und Thomas von Aquin.* Mainz: 1967.

Philips, Margaret Mann. *Erasmus and the Northern Renaissance.* Rev. ed. Totowa, N.J.: Rowman, 1981.

Post, R. R. *The Modern Devotion: Confrontation with Reformation and Humanism.* Leiden: 1968.

Spitz, Lewis W. *The Religious Renaissance of the German Humanists.* Cambridge: Harvard University, 1963.

Steinmetz, David C. *Misericordia Dei: The Theology of Johannes von Staupitz in Its Late Medieval Setting.* Leiden: 1968.

Tavard, George. *Holy Writ or Holy Church: The Crisis of the Protestant Reformation.* Westport, Conn.: Greenwood, (1959) 1978.

Tentler, Thomas N. *Sin and Confession on the Eve of the Reformation.* Princeton: Princeton University, 1977.

Tracy, James D. *Erasmus, the Growth of a Mind.* Geneva: 1972.

Trinkaus, Charles. *"In Our Image and Likeness": Humanity and Divinity in Italian Humanist Thought.* 2 vols. Chicago: 1970.

Trinkaus, Charles. *The Scope of Renaissance Humanism.* Ann Arbor, Mich.: University of Michigan, 1983.

Trinkaus, Charles, and Oberman, Heiko A., eds. *The Pursuit of Holiness in Late Medieval and Renaissance Religion.* Leiden: 1974.

Popular Religious Culture

Ariès, Philippe. *Centuries of Childhood: A Social History of Family Life.* New York: Random, 1965.

Ariès, Philippe. *L'homme devant la mort.* Paris: 1977.

Burke, Peter. *Popular Culture in Early Modern Europe.* New York: Harper and Row, 1978.

Chaunu, Pierre. *La mort à Paris: XVIe, XVIIe, XVIIIe siécles.* Paris: 1978.

Christian, William A. Jr. *Local Religion in Sixteenth-Century Spain.* Princeton: Princeton University, 1981.

Davis, Natalie Zemon. *Society and Culture in Early Modern France: Eight Essays.* Stanford: Stanford University, 1975.

Delumeau, Jean. *La peur en Occident: XVIe-XVIIIe siécles.* Paris: 1978.

Galpern, A. N. *The Religion of the People in Sixteenth-Century Champagne.* Historical Studies series. No. 92. Cambridge, Mass.: Harvard University, 1976.

Ginzburg, Carlo. *The Cheese and the Worms: The Cosmos of a Sixteenth-Century Miller.* New York: Penguin, 1982.

Ladurie, Emmanuel Le Roy. *Montaillou: The Promised Land of Error.* New York: Random, 1979.

Thomas, Keith. *Religion and the Decline of Magic.* New York: Macmillan, 1975.

Toussaert, Jacques. *Le sentiment réligieux en Flandre à la fin du môyen âge.* Paris: 1960.

Trexler, Richard C. *Public Life in Renaissance Florence.* New York: Academic Press, 1980.

The Church

Bernstein, Alan E. *Pierre d'Ailly and the Blanchard Affair.* Leiden: 1978.

Black, A. J. *Council and Commune: The Conciliar Movement and the 15th-Century Heritage.* Shepherdstown, W.Va.: 1979.

D'Amico, John F. *Renaissance Humanism in Papal Rome: Humanists and Churchmen on the Eve of the Reformation.* Baltimore and London: Johns Hopkins University, 1983.

Favier, Jean. *Les Finances pontificales à l'époque du Grande Schisme d'Occident.* Paris: 1966.

Hay, Denys. *The Church in Italy in the Fifteenth Century.* Cambridge: 1977.

Jacob, E. F. *Essays in the Conciliar Epoch.* 3rd ed. Manchester: 1963.

Jedin, Hubert. *A History of the Council of Trent.* Vol. 1. London: 1957.

Kaminsky, Howard. *A History of the Hussite Revolution.* Berkeley and Los Angeles: University of California, 1967.

Oakley, Francis. *The Western Church in the Later Middle Ages.* Ithaca, N.Y.: Cornell University, 1985.

O'Malley, John W. *Giles of Viterbo on Church and Reform: A Study in Renaissance Thought.* Leiden: 1968.

O'Malley, John W. *Praise and Blame in Renaissance Rome: Rhetoric, Doctrine and Reform in the Sacred Orators of the Papal Court, ca. 1450–1521.* Durham, N.C.: Duke University, 1979.

Rapp, Francis. *L'Église et la vie religieuse en Occident à la fin du Môyen Âge.* Paris: 1971.

Tierney, Brian. *Foundations of the Conciliar Theory.* Cambridge: 1955.

Tierney, Brian. *Origins of Papal Infallibility: 1150-1350.* Leiden: 1972.

Society and Politics

Baron, Hans. "Religion and Politics in the German Imperial Cities during the Reformation." *English Historical Review* 52 (1937): 514-633.

Benecke, Gerhard. *Society and Politics in Germany, 1500-1750.* London: 1974.

Blickle, Peter. *The Revolution of 1525: The German Peasants' War from a New Perspective.* Baltimore: Johns Hopkins University, 1982.

Brady, Thomas A. Jr. *Turning Swiss: Cities and Empire, 1450–1550.* Cambridge Studies in Early Modern History. Cambridge: 1985.

Brandi, Karl. *The Emperor Charles V: The Growth and Destiny of a Man and of a World Empire.* Atlantic Highlands, N.J.: Humanities, (1939) 1968.

Braudel, Fernand. *The Mediterranean and the Mediterranean World in the Age of Philip II.* 2 vols. 2nd rev. ed. New York: Harper and Row, 1976.

Brendler, G. *Das Täuferreich zu Münster 1534/35.* Berlin: 1966.

Carsten, F. L. *Princes and Parliaments in Germany from the Fifteenth to the Eighteenth Century.* Oxford: 1959.

Cipolla, Carlo M., ed. *Fontana Economic History of Europe.* Vol. 2. *The Sixteenth and Seventeenth Centuries.* New York: Barnes and Noble, 1977.

Clasen, C. P. *Anabaptism: A Social History, 1525-1618.* Ithaca, N.Y.: Cornell University, 1972.

Cohn, Henry J. *Government in Early Modern Europe, 1520-1560.* London: 1971.

Cohn, Norman. *The Pursuit of the Millennium.* 3rd ed. London: Oxford, 1970.

Fabian, Ekkehart. *Die Entstehung des Schmalkaldischen Bundes und seiner Verfassung 1524/29–1531/35.* 2nd ed. Tübingen: 1962.

Fischer-Galati, Stephen A. *Ottoman Imperialism and German Protestantism, 1521–1555.* New York: Octagon, (1959) 1972.

Franz, Günther. *Der deutsche Bauernkrieg.* 11th ed. Darmstadt: 1977.

Friesen, Abraham. *Reformation and Utopia: The Marxist Interpretation of the Reformation and Its Antecedents.* Wiesbaden: 1974.

Koenigsberger, H. G. *Estates and Revolutions: Essays in Early Modern European History.* Ithaca, N.Y.: Cornell University, 1971.

Koenigsberger, H. G. *The Habsburgs and Europe, 1516–1660.* Ithaca, N.Y.: Cornell University, 1971.

Lau, Franz. "Der Bauernkrieg und das angebliche Ende der lutherischen Reformation als spontane Volksbewegung." *Lutherjahrbuch* 26 (1959): 119-134.

Miskimin, Harry A. *The Economy of Later Renaissance Europe: 1460–1600.* Cambridge: 1977.

Rich, E. E., and Wilson, C. H., eds. *The Cambridge Economic History of Europe.* Vol. 4. *The Economy of Expanding Europe in the Sixteenth and Seventeenth Centuries.* Cambridge: 1967.

Scribner, R. W. "Is There a Social History of the Reformation?" *Social History* 4 (1976): 483-505.

Strauss, Gerald, ed. *Manifestations of Discontent in Germany on the Eve of the Reformation: A Collection of Documents.* Bloomington, Ind.: Indiana University, 1971.

Von Greyerz, Kaspar, ed. *Religion and Society in Early Modern Europe: 1500–1800.* London: Allen Unwin, 1984.

Wallerstein, Immanuel. *The Modern World System: Capitalist Agriculture and the Origins of the European World Economy in the Sixteenth Century.* New York: Academic, 1974.

Wohlfeil, Rainer. *Reformation oder frühburgerliche Revolution?* Munich: 1972.

Luther's Theology

General Works

Althaus, Paul. *The Theology of Martin Luther.* Philadelphia: Fortress, 1966.

Bornkamm, Heinrich. *Luther's World of Thought.* St. Louis: Concordia, 1958.

Ebeling, Gerhard. *Luther: An Introduction to His Thought.* Philadelphia: Fortress, 1970.

Elert, Werner. *The Structure of Lutheranism: The Theology and Philosophy of Life of Lutheranism, 16th and 17th Centuries.* Vol. 1. St. Louis: Concordia, 1962, 1974.

Forde, Gerhard O. *Where God Meets Man: Luther's Down-to-Earth Approach to the Gospel.* Minneapolis: Augsburg, 1972.

Holl, Karl. *The Cultural Significance of the Reformation.* New York: World, 1959.

Loeschen, John R. *Wrestling with Luther: An Introduction to the Study of His Thought.* St. Louis: Concordia, 1976.

Olivier, Daniel. *Luther's Faith: The Cause of the Gospel in the Church.* St. Louis: Concordia, 1982.

Pesch, Otto Hermann. *Hinführung zu Luther.* Mainz: 1982.

Pinomaa, Lennart. *Faith Victorious.* Philadelphia: Fortress, 1963.

Rupp, E. G. *The Righteousness of God: Luther Studies.* 3rd ed. London: 1968.

Von Loewenich, Walther. *Luther's Theology of the Cross.* Minneapolis: Augsburg, 1976.

Watson, Philip S. *Let God Be God: An Interpretation of the Theology of Martin Luther.* Philadelphia: Fortress, 1966.

Particular Topics

Aarts, Jan. *Die Lehre Martin Luthers über das Amt in der Kirche: Eine genetisch-systematische Untersuchung seiner Schriften von 1512 bis 1525.* Helsinki: 1972.

Althaus, Paul. *The Ethics of Martin Luther.* Philadelphia: Fortress, 1972.

Asendorf, Ulrich. *Eschatologie bei Luther.* Göttingen: 1967.

Aulen, Gustaf. *Christus Victor.* New York: Macmillan, 1969.

Baylor, Michael J. *Action and Person: Conscience in Late Scholasticism and the Young Luther.* Leiden: 1977.

Bizer, Ernst. *Fides ex Auditu: Eine Untersuchung über die Entdeckung der Gerechtigkeit Gottes durch Martin Luther.* Neukirchen: 1961.

Bluhm, Heinz. *Martin Luther: Creative Translator.* St. Louis: Concordia, 1965.

Bornkamm, Heinrich. *Luther and the Old Testament.* Philadelphia: Fortress, 1969.

Bornkamm, Heinrich. *Luther's Doctrine of the Two Kingdoms.* Philadelphia: Fortress, 1966.

Bring, Ragnar. *Luthers Anschauung von der Bibel.* Berlin: 1951.

Brosseder, Johannes. *Luthers Stellung zu den Juden im Spiegel seiner Interpreten: Interpretation und Rezeption von Luthers Schriften und Äusserungen zum Judentum im 19. und 20. Jahrhundert vor allem in deutschsprachigen Raum.* Munich: 1972.

Carlson, Edgar M. *The Reinterpretation of Luther.* Philadelphia: Muhlenberg, 1948.

Cranz, F. Edward. *An Essay on the Development of Luther's Thought on Justice, Law, and Society.* Cambridge: Harvard University, 1959.

Dillenberger, John. *God Hidden and God Revealed: The Interpretation of Luther's Deus Absconditus.* Philadelphia: Muhlenberg, 1953.

Ebeling, Gerhard. *Evangelische Evangelienauslegung: Eine Untersuchung zu Luthers Hermeneutik.* Darmstadt: 1962.

Forell, George Wolfgang. *Faith Active in Love: An Investigation of the Principles Underlying Luther's Social Ethics.* Minneapolis: Augsburg, 1954.

Gerrish, Brian. *Grace and Reason: A Study in the Theology of Martin Luther.* Oxford: 1962.

Grane, Leif. *Modus loquendi Theologicus: Luthers Kampf um die Erneuerung der Theologie.* Leiden: 1975.

Grane, Leif, and Lohse, Bernhard, eds. *Luther und die Theologie der Gegenwart: Referate und Berichte des Fünften Internationalen Kongresses für Lutherforschung.* Göttingen: 1980.

Haendler, Gert. *Luther on Ministerial Office and Congregational Function.* Philadelphia: Fortress, 1981.

Hagen, Kenneth. *A Theology of Testament in the Young Luther: The Lectures on Hebrews.* Leiden: 1974.

Harran, Marilyn J. *Luther on Conversion: The Early Years.* Ithaca, N.Y.: Cornell University, 1983.

Harran, Marilyn J., ed. *Luther and Learning.* Selinsgrove, Penn.: Susquehanna University, 1985.

Headley, John M. *Luther's View of Church History.* Northford, Conn.: Elliot's Books, 1963.

Hendrix, Scott. *Ecclesia in Via: Ecclesiological Developments in the Medieval Psalms Exegesis and the Dictata super Psalterium (1513–1515) of Martin Luther.* Leiden: 1974.

Hendrix, Scott. *Luther and the Papacy: Stages in a Reformation Conflict.* Philadelphia: Fortress, 1981.

Henning, Gerhard. *Cajetan und Luther: Ein historischer Beitrag zur Begegnung von Thomismus und Reformation.* Stuttgart: 1966.

Hoffman, Bengt R. *Luther and the Mystics.* Minneapolis: Augsburg, 1976.

Hoffmann, Manfred, ed. *Martin Luther and the Modern Mind: Freedom, Conscience, Toleration, Rights.* New York and Toronto: Edwin Wellen, 1985.

Junghans, Helmar. *Der junge Luther und die Humanisten.* Weimar: 1984.

Klug, Eugene F. *From Luther to Chemnitz on Scripture and the Word.* Kampen: 1971; Ft. Wayne, Ind.: Concordia Theological Seminary, 1981.

Kooiman, Willem J. *Luther and the Bible.* Philadelphia: Muhlenberg, 1961.

Lau, Franz. *Luthers Lehre von den beiden Reichen*. Berlin: 1953.

Lieberg, Hellmut. *Amt und Ordination bei Luther und Melanchthon*. Göttingen: 1962.

Lienhard, Marc. *Luther: Witness to Jesus Christ: Stages and Themes of the Reformer's Christology*. Minneapolis: Augsburg, 1982.

Lohse, Bernhard. *Mönchtum und Reformation: Luthers Auseinandersetzung mit dem Mönchsideal des Mittelalters*. Göttingen: 1963.

Lohse, Bernhard. *Ratio und Fides: Eine Untersuchung über die Ratio in der Theologie Luthers*. Göttingen: 1958.

Lutherjahrbuch: Martin Luther 1483-1983, Werk und Wirkung: Referate und Berichte des Sechsten Internationalen Kongresses für Lutherforschung. Göttingen: 1985.

Maurer, Wilhelm. "Die Zeit der Reformation." *Kirche und Synagoge: Handbuch zur Geschichte von Christen und Juden*. Karl Heinrich Rengstorf and Siegfried von Kartzfleisch, eds. Vol. 1. Stuttgart: 1968. Pp. 363-452.

McGrath, Alister E. *Luther's Theology of the Cross: Martin Luther on Justification, 1509-1519*. New York and London: Basil Blackwell, 1985.

Müller, Gerhard. *Die Rechtfertigungslehre: Geschichte und Probleme*. Gütersloh: 1977.

Nettl, Paul. *Luther and Music*. Philadelphia: Muhlenberg, 1948.

Nicol, Martin. *Meditation bei Luther*. Göttingen: 1984.

Oberman, Heiko A., ed. *Luther and the Dawn of the Modern Era: Papers for the Fourth International Congress for Luther Studies*. Leiden: 1974.

Oberman, Heiko A. *The Roots of Antisemitism: In the Age of the Renaissance and Reformation*. Philadelphia: Fortress, 1983.

Pelikan, Jaroslav. *Obedient Rebels: Catholic Substance and Protestant Principle in Luther's Reformation*. New York: Harper and Row, 1964.

Pelikan, Jaroslav. *Spirit vs. Structure: Luther and the Institutions of the Church*. New York: Harper and Row, 1968.

Peters, Edward. "Luther and the Principle: 'Outside of the Use, There Is No Sacrament.' " *Concordia Theological Monthly* 42 (1971): 543-552.

Prenter, Regin. *Spiritus Creator*. Philadelphia: Muhlenberg, 1953.

Preus, James S. *From Shadow to Promise: Old Testament Interpretation from Augustine to the Young Luther*. Cambridge: Harvard University, 1969.

Saarnivara, Uuras. *Luther Discovers the Gospel: New Light on Luther's Way from Medieval Catholicism to Evangelical Faith*. St. Louis: Concordia, 1951.

Schoenberger, Cynthia Grant. "Luther on Resistance to Authority." *Journal of the History of Ideas* 40 (1979): 3-20.

Schwarz, Reinhard. *Fides, Spes und Charitas beim jungen Luther*. Berlin: 1962.

Siggins, Ian. *Martin Luther's Doctrine of Christ*. New Haven: Yale University, 1970.

Stein, Wolfgang. *Das kirchliche Amt bei Luther*. Wiesbaden: 1974.

Steinmetz, David C. *Luther and Staupitz: An Essay in the Intellectual Origins of the Protestant Reformation*. Durham, N.C.: Duke, 1980.

Steinmetz, David C. "Luther and Late Medieval Augustinians: Another Look." *Concordia Theological Monthly* 44 (1973): 363-452.

Stock, Ursula. *Die Bedeutung der Sakramente in Luthers Sermonen von 1519*. Leiden: 1982.

Thompson, Cargill W. D. J. *Studies in the Reformation: Luther to Hooker*. London: 1980.

Vajta, Vilmos. *Luther and Melanchthon in the History and Theology of the Reformation.* Philadelphia: Muhlenberg, 1961.

Von Loewenich, Walther. *Luther als Ausleger der Synoptiker.* Munich: 1954.

Wingren, Gustav. *Luther on Vocation.* Philadelphia: Muhlenberg, 1959.

Zur Muhlen, Karl-Heinz. *Nos extra Nos: Luthers Theologie zwischen Mystik und Scholastik.* Leiden: 1972.

Luther's Contemporaries

Bainton, Roland H. *David Joris.* Leipzig: 1937.

Baker, J. Wayne. *Heinrich Bullinger and the Covenant: The Other Reformed Tradition.* Athens, Ohio: Ohio University, 1980.

Bender, Harold S. *Conrad Grebel ca. 1498-1526: The Founder of the Swiss Brethren, Sometimes Called Anabaptists.* Studies in Anabaptist and Mennonite History. No. 6. Scottsdale, Pa.: Herald Press, 1950. (= Ann Arbor, Mich.: Books On Demand).

Bergsten, Torsten. *Balthasar Hubmaier: Seine Stellung zur Reformation und Taufertum.* Kassel: 1961.

Bizer, Ernst. *Theologie der Verheissung: Studien zur theologischen Entwicklung des jungen Melanchthons 1519-1524.* Neukirchen: 1964.

Bornkamm, Heinrich. *Martin Bucers Bedeutung für die europaische Reformationsgeschichte.* Gütersloh: 1952.

Brunner, Peter. *Nikolaus von Amsdorf als Bischof von Naumburg.* Gütersloh: 1961.

Clebsch, William A. *England's Earliest Protestants, 1520-1535.* Yale Publications in Religion. No. 11. New Haven: Yale University, 1964.

Courvoisier, Jacques. *Zwingli: A Reformed Theologian.* Richmond: John Knox, 1963.

Deppermann, Klaus. *Melchior Hoffman: Soziale Unruhen und Apokalyptischen Visionen im Zeitalter der Reformation.* Göttingen: 1979.

Eells, Hastings. *Martin Bucer.* New Haven: Yale University, 1931.

Elliger, Walter. *Thomas Müntzer: Leben und Werk.* Göttingen: 1975.

Fraenkel, Peter. *Testimonia Patrum: The Function of the Patristic Argument in the Theology of Melanchthon.* Geneva: 1961.

Gäbler, Ulrich. *Huldrych Zwingli: Eine Einführung in sein Leben und sein Werk.* Munich: 1983.

Garside, Charles Jr. *Zwingli and the Arts.* New York: Da Capo, 1966.

Gerrish, Brian A. *Reformers in Profile.* Philadelphia: Fortress, 1967.

Goertz, Hans-Jürgen. *Profiles of Radical Reformers: Biographical Sketches from Thomas Müntzer to Paracelsus.* Scottsdale, Penn: Herald Press, 1982.

Greschat, Martin. *Melanchthon neben Luther: Studien zur Gestalt der Rechtfertigungslehre zwischen 1528 und 1537.* Witten: 1965.

Grimm, Harold J. *Lazarus Spengler: A Lay Reader of the Reformation.* Columbus: Ohio State University, 1978.

Gritsch, Eric W. *Reformer without a Church: The Life and Thought of Thomas Müntzer, 1488?-1525.* Philadelphia: Fortress, 1967.

Haendler, Klaus. *Wort und Glaube bei Melanchthon.* Gütersloh: 1968.

Holborn, Hajo. *Ulrich von Hutten and the German Reformation.* New Haven: Yale University, 1937.

Holzberg, Niklas. *Willibald Pirckheimer: Griechischer Humanismus in Deutschland.* Munich: 1981.

Kisch, Guido. *Melanchthons Rechts- und Soziallehre.* Berlin: 1967.

Kittelson, James M. *Wolfgang Capito from Humanist to Reformer.* Leiden: 1975.
Klassen, Walter. *Michael Gaismair: Revolutionary and Reformer.* Leiden: 1978.
Köhler, Walther. *Zwingli und Luther: Ihr Streit über das Abendmahl nach seinen politischen und religiösen Beziehungen.* 2 vols. Leipzig: 1924-1953.
Kolb, Robert. *Nicholas von Amsdorf.* Nieuwkoop: 1978.
Lehman, Martin. *Justus Jonas, Loyal Reformer.* Minneapolis: Augsburg, 1963.
Maier, Paul L. *Caspar Schwenckfeld on the Person and Work of Christ.* Assen: 1954.
Manschreck, Clyde L. *Melanchthon: the Quiet Reformer.* Westport, Conn.: Greenwood, (1958) 1970.
Maurer, Wilhelm. *Der junge Melanchthon.* 2 vols. Göttingen: 1967-1969.
Meijering, E. P. *Melanchthon and Patristic Thought: The Doctrines of Christ and Grace, the Trinity and the Creation.* Leiden: 1983.
Näf, Werner. *Vadian und seine Stadt St. Gallen.* 2 vols. St. Gallen: 1944-1957.
Neuser, Wilhelm. *Der Ansatz der Theologie Phillip Melanchthons.* Neukirchen: 1957.
Neuser, Wilhelm. *Die Abendmahlslehre Melanchthons in ihrer geschichtlichen Entwicklung (1519-1530).* Neukirchen: 1968.
Potter, G. R. *Ulrich Zwingli.* London: 1977.
Rich, Arthur. *Die Anfänge der Theologie Huldrych Zwinglis.* Zurich: 1949.
Rilliet, Jean Horace. *Zwingli: Third Man of the Reformation.* Philadelphia: Fortress, 1964.
Rupp, E. Gordon. *Patterns of Reformation.* Philadelphia: Fortress, 1969.
Schutte, Anne Jacobson. *Pier Paolo Vergerio: The Making of an Italian Reformer.* Geneva: 1977.
Seebass, Gottfried. *Das reformatorische Werk des Andreas Osiander.* Nuremberg: 1967.
Sick, Hansjorg. *Melanchthon als Ausleger des Alten Testaments.* Tübingen: 1954.
Sider, Ronald J. *Andreas Bodenstein von Karlstadt: The Development of His Thought.* Leiden: 1974.
Sporl, Adolf. *Melanchthon zwischen Humanismus und Reformation.* Munich: 1959.
Spitz, Lewis W. "Humanism in the Reformation." *Renaissance Essays in Honor of Hans Baron.* Ed. Anthony Molho and John A. Tedeschi. Firenze: 1971.
Staehelin, Ernst. *Das theologische Lebenswerk des Johannes Oekolampadius.* Leipzig: 1939.
Stephens, W. P. *The Holy Spirit in the Theology of Martin Bucer.* Cambridge: Harvard University, 1970.
Van der Poll, Jan. *Martin Bucers Liturgical Ideas.* Assen: 1954.
Walton, Robert C. *Zwingli's Theocracy.* Toronto: University of Toronto, 1967.

The Reform Movement

Abray, Lorna Jane. *The People's Reformation: Magistrates, Clergy, and Commons in Strasbourg, 1500–1598.* Ithaca, N.Y: Cornell University, 1985.
Andersson, Christiane, and Talbot, Charles, eds. *From a Mighty Fortress: Prints, Drawings, and Books in the Age of Luther.* Detroit: Detroit Institute of Arts, 1983.
Batori, Irmgard, ed. *Städtische Gesellschaft und Reformation.* Stuttgart: 1980.
Birnbaum, Norman J. "The Zwinglian Reformation in Zurich." *Past and Present* 15 (1959): 27-47.
Bizer, Ernst. *Studien zur Geschichte des Abendmahlsstreits in 16. Jahrhundert.* Gütersloh: 1940.

Brady, Thomas A. Jr. *Ruling Class, Regime and Reformation at Strasbourg, 1520–1555.* Leiden: 1978.

Brecht, Martin. *Südwestdeutsche Reformationsgeschichte: Zur Einführung der Reformation im Herzogtum Württemberg.* Stuttgart: 1984.

Brooks, Peter Newman, ed. *Reformation Principles and Practice.* London: 1980.

Buck, Lawrence, and Zophy, Jonathan, eds. *The Social History of the Reformation.* Columbus: Ohio State University, 1972.

Chrisman, Miriam. *Strasbourg and the Reform.* New Haven, Conn.: Yale University, 1967.

Christensen, Carl C. *Art and the Reformation in Germany.* Studies in the Reformation. Vol. 2. Columbus: Ohio State University, 1981.

Clasen, Claus-Peter. *Anabaptism, a Social History, 1525–1618: Switzerland, Austria, Moravia, South and Central Germany.* Ithaca, N.Y.: Cornell University, 1972.

Daniel, David P. "Highlights of the Lutheran Reformation in Slovakia." *Concordia Theological Quarterly* 42 (1978): 21-34.

Delumeau, J. *Naissance et affirmation de la Réforme.* Paris: 1965.

Dickens, A. G. *Martin Luther and the German Nation.* London: 1974.

Hsia, R. Po-chia. *Society and Religion in Münster, 1535-1618.* Yale Historical Publications. No. 131. New Haven: Yale University, 1984.

Kittelson, James M. "Humanism and the Reformation in Germany." *Central European History* 9 (1976): 303-322.

Moeller, Bernd. *Imperial Cities and the Reformation: Three Essays.* Durham, N.C.: Labyrinth, (1972) 1982.

Ozment, Steven E. *The Reformation in the Cities: The Appeal of Protestantism to Sixteenth-Century Germany and Switzerland.* New Haven: Yale University, 1975.

Preus, J. S. *Carlstadt's Ordinaciones and Luther's Liberty: A Study of the Wittenberg Movement, 1521–1522.* Cambridge: Harvard University, 1974.

Oyer, John S. *Lutheran Reformers against Anabaptists: Luther, Melanchthon and Menius, and the Anabaptists of Central Germany.* The Hague: 1964.

Rapp, Francis. *Réformes et Réformation à Strasbourg: Église et Societé dans la Diocèse (1450-1525).* Paris: 1975.

Rublack, Hans-Christoph. *Die Einführung der Reformation in Konstanz.* Gütersloh: 1971.

Rublack, Hans-Christoph. *Eine bürgerliche Reformation: Nördlingen.* Gütersloh: 1982.

Schmidt, Heinrich Richard. *Reichstädte, Reich, und Reformation: Korporative Religionspolitik, 1521-1529/30.* Wiesbaden: 1986.

Schultze, Alfred. *Stadtgemeinde und Reformation.* Tübingen: 1918.

Scribner, R. W. *For the Sake of Simple Folk: Popular Propaganda for the German Reformation.* Cambridge Studies in Oral and Literate Culture. No. 2. Cambridge: 1981.

Sessions, Kyle C., and Bebb, Philip N., eds. *Pietas et Societas: New Trends in Reformation Social History.* Kirksville, Mo.: Sixteenth-Century Publishers, 1985.

Stayer, James. *Anabaptists and the Sword.* 2nd rev. ed. Lawrence, Kan.: Coronado, 1976.

Von Greyerz, Kaspar. *The Late City Reformation in Germany: The Case of Colmar, 1522-1628.* Wiesbaden: 1980.

Wettges, Wolfram. *Reformation und Propaganda: Studien zur Kommunikation des Aufruhrs in süddeutschen Reichstädten.* Stuttgart: 1978.

Williams, George H. *The Radical Reformation.* Philadelphia: Westminster, 1962.

The New Church

Allbeck, Willard Dow. *Studies in the Lutheran Confessions.* Philadelphia: Muhlenberg, 1952.

Bergendoff, Conrad. *The Church of the Lutheran Reformation.* St. Louis: Concordia, 1967.

Brecht, Martin. *Kirchenordnung und Kirchenzucht in Württemberg vom 16. bis 18. Jahrhundert.* Stuttgart: 1967.

Burgess, Joseph, ed. *The Role of the Augsburg Confession: Catholic and Lutheran Views.* Philadelphia: Fortress, 1980.

Estes, James Martin. *Christian Magistrate and State Church: The Reforming Career of Johannes Brenz.* Toronto: University of Toronto, 1982.

Fagerberg, Holsten. *A New Look at the Lutheran Confession.* St. Louis: Concordia, 1972, 1981.

Gerrish, Brian. *The Old Protestantism and the New: Essays on the Reformation Heritage.* Chicago: University of Chicago, 1983.

Grane, Leif. *The Augsburg Confession: A Commentary.* Minneapolis: Augsburg, 1987.

Hareide, Bjarne. *Die Konfirmation in der Reformationszeit: Eine Untersuchung der Lutherischen Konfirmation in Deutschland, 1520–1585.* Göttingen: 1971.

Karant-Nunn, Susan. *Luther's Pastors: The Reformation in the Ernestine Countryside. Transactions of the American Philosophical Society,* 69, 8. Philadelphia: 1979.

Kittelson, James M. "Luther on Education for Ordination." *Lutheran Theological Seminary Bulletin* 65 (1985): 27-40.

Kittelson, James M. "Luther's Impact upon the Universities—and the Reverse." *Concordia Theological Quarterly* 48 (1984): 23-38.

Kittelson, James M. "Successes and Failures in the German Reformation: The Report from Strasbourg." *Archive for Reformation History* 73 (1982): 153-175.

Maurer, Wilhelm. *Historischer Kommentar zur Confessio Augustana.* 2 vols. Gütersloh: 1976-1978.

Ozment, Steven E. *When Fathers Ruled: Family Life in Reformation Europe.* Cambridge: Harvard University, 1983.

Roth, Friedrich. *Augsburgs Reformationsgeschichte.* 4 vols. Munich: 1901-1911.

Safley, Thomas Max. *Let No Man Put Asunder: The Control of Marriage in the German Southwest: 1550–1600.* Studies and Essays. Vol. 2. Kirksville, Mo.: 16th-Century Journal Publishers, 1984.

Sasse, Hermann. *This Is My Body: Luther's Contention for the Real Presence.* Minneapolis: Augsburg, 1959.

Scaer, David P., and Preus, Robert D., eds. *Luther's Catechisms—450 Years: Essays Commemorating the Small and Large Catechisms of Dr. Martin Luther.* Ft. Wayne, Ind.: Concordia Theological Seminary, 1979.

Schlink, Edmund. *Theology of the Lutheran Confessions.* Philadelphia: Fortress, 1961.

Strauss, Gerald. *Luther's House of Learning: Indoctrination of the Young in the German Reformation*. Baltimore: Johns Hopkins University, 1978. (= Ann Arbor: Books on Demand.)

Veit, Patrice. *Das Kirchenlied in der Reformation Martin Luthers: Eine Thematische und Semantische Untersuchung*. Wiesbaden: 1986.

Wolgast, Eike. *Die Wittenberger Theologie und die Politik der evangelischen Stände: Studien zu Luthers Gutachten in politischen Fragen*. Gütersloh: 1977.

Index of Names

Agricola, John, 214-215, 269-270
Albert (of Hohenzollern) (archbishop of Mainz), 104-105, 107-108, 136, 172, 203, 234
Albrecht (of Mansfeld) (count), 116, 292-293, 297
Aleander, Jerome, 150, 154, 158
Amsdorf, Nicolaus, 201
Aquinas, Thomas, 131, 136
Aristotle, 46, 67, 107
Augustine, 86, 107

Biel, Gabriel, 67, 69-74
Brück, Gregor, 228, 260-261
Bucer, Martin, 112, 187, 197-200, 206-207, 234-235, 263, 265-269, 277
Bugenhagen, John, 186, 200, 230-231, 241, 247, 272, 298

Cajetan (cardinal), 117-118, 121-129, 131-132, 142, 149, 160
Capito, Wolfgang, 136, 172, 183, 187, 197-200, 206-207, 263, 267-269, 277
Carlstadt, Andreas, 115, 119, 124, 137-140, 169, 179-180, 184, 186, 188-189, 196-198, 200-201, 203, 248

Charles V (Charles I of Spain, holy Roman emperor), 58, 133, 139, 152, 157-163, 220, 228-230, 234, 255-256, 275, 277 279, 288, 291, 299
Christian II (king of Denmark), 208-209
Clement VII (pope), 263
Contarini (cardinal), 277-278
Cranach, Lucas, 164, 173, 290

Eck, John (of Ingolstadt), 111, 115-116, 131-132, 135, 137-141, 145-146, 149-150, 154-155, 168, 234
Egidio (of Viterbo), 61
Emser, Jerome, 167-168
Erasmus, Desiderius (of Rotterdam), 37, 48, 67-68, 76-78, 112, 136, 150, 154, 203-206, 217, 248, 299-300

Ferdinand (archduke of Austria and king of Germany), 220-221, 277-278, 291
Frederick the Wise (elector of Saxony), 85, 105, 110, 116-118, 121, 123-130, 132-133, 146, 149-152, 154, 157-159, 166, 169, 180-182, 191, 203-204, 230
Froben, Johann, 146
Fugger, Jakob, 104-105, 122

Geldennupf, Wiegand, 39
George (duke of Saxony), 139, 147, 164, 173, 181, 209-210, 256-260, 288

Heinrich (duke of Braunschweig), 289-290, 293
Henry (duke of Saxony), 288-289
Hessus, Eobanus, 159
Hus, Jan (including Hussites, Bohemian Brethren), 118, 140-142, 147, 189, 196, 200
Hutten, Ulrich von, 149, 159

John (elector of Saxony), 203, 210, 214-215, 221-222, 228-232, 236, 241, 259-260
John Frederick (elector of Saxony), 260-261, 264-266, 272-273, 279-280, 293
Jonas, Justus, 230-231, 238, 297
Julius II (pope), 60

Lang, John, 62
Latomus, James, 167
Leo X (pope), 104-105, 108, 114, 125, 135, 154-155
Linck, Wenceslaus, 116, 121-122, 135-136, 171, 237
Lombard, Peter, 67
Luder, Hans, 31-36, 39, 49-51, 54-55, 171-172, 232
Luder, Margaretta, 33-34
Luder, "young" Hans, 35
Luther, Hans (Luther's son), 209
Luther, Katharina (von Bora), 201-203, 210, 226, 241, 249, 282-284, 295, 299
Luther, Martin (Luther's son), 241
Luther, Paul (Luther's son), 251

Melanchthon, Philip, 110, 125, 131, 137, 142, 169, 171-172, 180, 184-186, 203, 210-211, 230-239, 247-249, 266, 277-278, 293-294, 296, 298-300
Miltitz, Karl von, 132-133, 154-155

Mosellanus, Peter, 110, 139, 145
Müntzer, Thomas, 189-191, 248

Oecolampadius, Johannes, 146, 187, 200, 206-207, 222-224, 241-242

Paul III (pope), 263, 265, 272, 276
Peutinger, Conrad, 121, 136
Philip, (landgrave of Hesse), 215, 220-226, 235-236, 259, 266, 274-276, 288
Pirckheimer, Willibald, 136-137, 158
Prierias, Sylvester, 117-119, 122, 126, 136

Rab, Hermann, 116-117
Reuchlin, Johannes, 110, 131, 136
Rhegius, Urbanus, 187
Rosheim, Josel, 273-274
Rubeanus, Crotus, 146, 159

Schalbe, 40
Scheurl, Christoph, 116, 136, 145
Sickingen, Franz von, 154
Spalatin, Georg, 117, 121, 124, 127, 130-131, 137-138, 147, 152, 159, 163, 165, 171-173, 175, 182, 209, 294
Spengler, Lazarus, 136, 146, 158
Speratus, Paul, 196
Staupitz, Johann von, 57-58, 62, 83-85, 113, 121, 124-125, 130, 190

Tauler, Johannes, 74-78
Tetzel, Johann, 102-108, 111, 115-117, 119, 123, 169
Trebonius, John, 39

Vergerio, Pietro Paolo, 263-265, 271, 276

William (prince of Anhalt), 41
Wycliffe, John, 196

Zwingli, Ulrich, 187, 197-200, 206-207, 222-227, 241-243, 267-268

Index of Subjects

Anabaptists, 241-243, 248
Anfechtungen, 55-57, 84, 97-98, 111, 165, 168-169, 173, 210-212, 284-285, 287-288
Antinomian Controversy, 269-270
Anxiety. *See Anfechtungen*
Augsburg, city and Diet of, 121, 125, 128, 142, 160, 230-239, 247, 255

Baptism, 147, 153, 180, 242-243
Black Cloister (Erfurt), 51-53, 57, 66
Brethren of the Common Life, 37

Castle Church, 63, 298
Church, authority of the, 117-121, 123-124, 132, 137-138, 140-142, 149-152, 242-243, 290
Church orders. *See Kirchenordnungen*
Coburg (castle), 231-235
Confession, 41-43, 146-147, 153, 168
Conscience. *See Anfechtungen*
Constance, Council of, 140, 263
Council (of the church), 263-265, 275-277

Decalog. *See* law
Doubts. *See Anfechtungen*

Eisenach, 38-39

Eisleben, 32
Erfurt, city and University of, 43-51, 64-67, 79-80, 139
Eucharist, 67, 147-149, 153-155, 169-171, 179, 189, 195-201, 206-208, 221-227, 265-268

Göttingen, 245-246

Heidelberg, city of and Disputation, 110-114, 125, 248
Human beings, nature of, 71-72, 97, 167
Humanism, 77-78, 136, 145-146
Humanists. *See* humanism
Humility, 90-91, 93-94, 166

Indulgences, 101-109, 119, 124, 128, 132, 136, 278
Iustitia dei, 70-74, 87-98, 111-112, 134-135, 156, 176, 249, 294

Jews, 273-275

Kirchenordnungen, 245-246

Law, works of the, 93, 111-112, 134, 176-177, 182-183, 269-270

Leipzig, city of and Debate, 131-132, 135, 138-142, 145, 173
Lord's Supper. See Eucharist

Magdeburg, 37-38
Mansfeld, 32-33, 39, 50
Mass. See Eucharist
Mercy of God. See misericordia dei
Misericordia dei, 70, 134
Möhra, 31, 163
Mysticism, 75-76

Nicea, Council of, 137
Nominalist theology. See via moderna
Nuremberg, 112, 136

Penance. See repentance

Regensburg, Colloquy of, 277
Repentance, 70-71, 96, 113-114
Righteousness of God. See iustitia dei

Sacraments, efficacy of the, 73-74

Schools, 243-244, 248-249
Scriptures, authority and content of the, 115-116, 123-124, 128, 136-138, 149, 167, 175-178
Spark of goodness. See synteresis
Speyer, diets of, 220-221
Strasbourg, 34, 197-199
Synteresis, 72-73, 91-93

Tentatio tristitiae. See Anfechtungen
Trent, Council of, 277-278
Turk, Turks, 135, 157, 220-221, 256, 272, 277-280

Via moderna, 67-74
Visitations, 214-217, 244-245, 247

Wartburg (castle), 163-178, 181
Will, freedom of the, 92-94, 111-112, 204-206
Worms, Diet and Colloquy of, 157-163, 167

Zwickau and Zwickau Prophets, 179, 188-189, 246-248

Index of Luther's Principal Works Cited*

Address to the Christian Nobility, 150-152, 215
Admonition against Sedition, 173-175, 188
Admonition to All Pastors, 279
Admonition to Peace, 191
Admonition to Prayer against the Turks, 280
Against the Assassin at Dresden, 258 260
Against the Asses at Paris and Louvain, 296
Against Hans Wurst, 289-290
Against the Heavenly Prophets, 195, 200, 207
Against the Idol at Halle, 172
Against the Jews and Their Lies, 274
Against the Murderous and Thieving Hordes of Peasants, 191-192
Against the Papacy at Rome, Founded by the Devil, 290-291

On the Babylonian Captivity of the Church, 152-155
Beelzebub to the Holy Papist Church, 272
On the Bondage of the Will, 205-206

To the Clergy Assembled at Augsburg, 232
Commentary on the Alleged Imperial Edict, 237
Concering War against the Turks, 221
On Confession: Whether the Pope Has the Power to Require It, 168
To the Councilmen of All Cities of Germany, 243

"Disputation against Scholastic Theology," 107, 121

---

*Citations from Luther's correspondence and the *Table Talk* are not included.

Explanation of Certain Articles on the Holy Sacrament, 200

On the Freedom of a Christian, 155-157, 168
Fourteen Consolations, 146-147

Galatians, Lectures on, 109
German Mass, 247
Göttingen Church Order, 245-246,
Great Commentary on Galatians, 249, 270

Hebrews, Lectures on, 109

On Infiltrating and Clandestine Preachers, 241-243
Invocavit Sermons, 182-183

That Jesus Christ Was Born a Jew, 273

Large Catechism, 219, 240
Letter against the Sabbatarians, 274-275
Letter to the Christians in Strasbourg, 199

On Monastic Vows, 171-172

The 95 Theses, 106, 125, 136, 140

Open Letter on the Harsh Book against the Peasants, 192, 230

On the Papacy at Rome, 149-150
Preface to the Latin Works, 294
Preface to the New Testament, 175-176
Preface to Romans, 176-177
Psalms, First Lectures on *(Dictata super Psalterium)*, 120, 152
Psalms, Second Lectures on *(Operationes in Psalmos)*, 131, 133-134

Resolutions Concerning the 95 Theses, 113

Sermon on the Body of Christ, 196
Sermon on Keeping Children in School, 243-244, 248-249
Schwabach Articles, 232
Small Catechism, 216-220

On Temporal Authority, 188

Warning to His Beloved Germans, 237-238, 256, 259
Whether One May Flee from Death, 210

rtin Luther's Travels 1483–1546

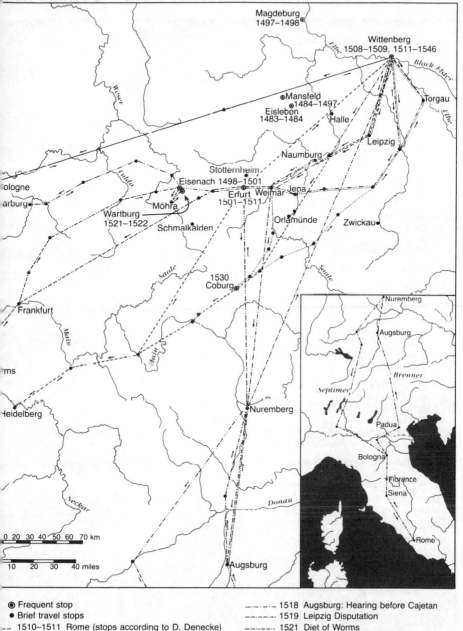

Magdeburg 1497–1498

Wittenberg 1508–1509, 1511–1546

Torgau

Mansfeld 1484–1497
Eisleben 1483–1484
Halle

Leipzig

Naumburg

Stotternheim

Eisenach 1498–1501
Möhra
Erfurt 1501–1511
Weimar
Jena

Wartburg 1521–1522
Schmalkalden

Orlamünde

Zwickau

1530 Coburg

Frankfurt

Nuremberg

Augsburg

Brenner

Septimer

Padua

Bologna

Florence
Siena

Donau

Rome

Heidelberg

Neckar

rms

ologne
arburg

Cologne

Weser
Fulda
Saale
Main
Main
Saale
Black Elster
Elbe
Elbe

0 20 30 40 50 60 70 km

10   20   30   40 miles

⊚ Frequent stop
● Brief travel stops
‒‒ 1510–1511 Rome (stops according to D. Denecke)
— 1512 Cologne
‒‒‒ 1518 Heidelberg Disputation

‒‒‒‒ 1518 Augsburg: Hearing before Cajetan
‒‒‒‒ 1519 Leipzig Disputation
‒‒‒‒ 1521 Diet of Worms
‒‒‒‒ 1529 Marburg Colloquy
············ 1530 Trip to Coburg during Diet of Augsburg

333

The Europe of Charles V (c. 1519)

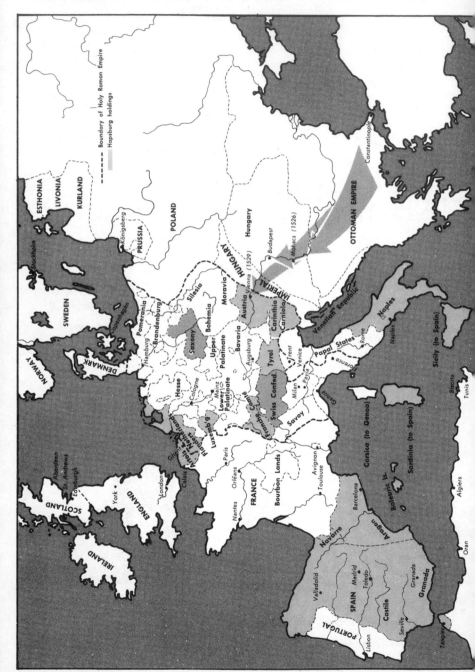